Motoring in Mitteleuropa

Exploring castles and châteaux

Philip Cole

First published in the United Kingdom in 2024 by
The Cloister House Press

ISBN 978-1-913460-84-6

Dedication

This book is dedicated to my travelling companions for putting up with me and to my wife for allowing me to go.

Contents

Introduction

⎯⎯⟫⬦⟪⎯⎯

This is not a guidebook. It is essentially extracts from my travel journals, relating to trips made to Mitteleuropa with friends from my home in Luxembourg where I worked for the European Parliament. If you want a good modern guide book, try the relevant Rough Guides and Lonely Planet Guides. They are useful and reliable, although they don't always contain information on places where *I* want to go. I have mentioned hotels and restaurants that appear in those and other guides.

Nor does it pretend to be a work of great literature: it's not Leigh Fermor, for example. And I am not Pevsner, so don't expect references to soffits, squinches or architraves.

There is quite a lot of historical information, normally indented, often barely digestible. Feel free to skip it. The trips largely but not exclusively involve visits to castles and châteaux.

To assist you: Czech and Slovak *hrad* = castle; Czech *zamek* and Slovak *zamok* = château; Czech.and Slovak *pokladna* = ticket office. There are some linguistic jokes (possibly hidden).

Guidebooks 'translated' into English by non-native speakers are, of course, fair game for a laugh. Translating out of one's mother tongue is unethical.

Where is Mitteleuropa? Anywhere in Europe where German is, or has been in living memory, widely spoken. Quite a few places in Mitteleuropa look as though they would be at home in Anthony Hope's 'Ruritania'. As for the 'motoring', I enjoy driving but have no great interest in cars and can't tell one from another. Sorry.

The friends mentioned are Henry, Jonathan and Ivor (possibly not their real names). My wife has a walk-on part as 'J' (not her real name).

I hope you like it. But first some condensed history.

Transylvania

—◆—

G ermans settled in Transylvania in waves beginning in the mid-12th century. This exodus from the west is regarded (by me, at least) as the basis of the legend of the Pied Piper. They were sought for their mining expertise and ability to develop the region's economy. Most colonists came from Luxembourg and the Moselle region. The term 'Saxon' was applied to all Germans in the region because the first to arrive were poor miners or groups of convicts from Saxony. The great majority of the Saxons embraced Lutheranism, with the result that there is an almost perfect equivalence of Lutheran and Saxon in Transylvania.

In the aftermath of the Mongol invasion of 1241–42 many towns were fortified with stone castles. In the Middle Ages about 300 villages were defended by *Kirchenburgen* with massive walls. Seven are included in the UNESCO World Heritage list.

Large numbers of Saxons emigrated to Germany after the fall of Communism in 1989. The pre-war population of 241,000 Saxons has fallen to 14,000. This figure includes Romania's president, and former mayor of Sibiu, Klaus Ioannis.

It is important to remember that until the Treaty of Trianon (1920) Transylvania formed part of the Kingdom of Hungary.

Bohemia and Moravia

———◆———

Moravia and Bohemia were ruled by the Luxembourg dynasty from 1310 until they passed to the Habsburgs in 1437. The period 1526–1620 was marked by increasing tension between Catholic Habsburg emperors and the Protestant Moravian nobility. In November 1619 Elector Palatine Frederick V was chosen as King of Bohemia by the Bohemian Electorate. On 8 November 1620 his army of 30,000 Bohemians and mercenaries was defeated by 27,000 men of the combined armies of Ferdinand II under Bucquoy and Tilly at Bílá Hora (White Mountain). In the longer term what the Czechs call the Dark Ages (Habsburg rule) began and night fell across Central Europe with the Counter-Reformation. Protestant nobles in the Czech lands were dispossessed and the vacuum – and the castles and châteaux we visited – was filled with those who had backed the winning horse.

The Zips of the iceberg: a note on the lost German tribes of Eastern Slovakia...

Germans settled in the northern part (present-day Slovakia) of the Kingdom of Hungary from the 12th to 15th centuries, mainly after the Mongol invasion of Europe in 1241, attracted by kings seeking specialists in various trades, such as craftsmen and miners. The main settlement areas were in the vicinity of Bratislava and some language islands in the Spiš region (German: *Zips*) and the Hauerland in the south. The settlers in the Spiš region were known as *Zipser Sachsen* ('Scepusian *[believe it or not]* Saxons').

South-west of Poprad is a mountain called Kozi Kameň, rising to 1,237 metres. Baedeker's *Austria-Hungary* (1905), confident that its readers would have been to Switzerland and would have picked up the reference, calls the mountain the Rigi of the Zips.

CHAPTER 1

A week in Transylvania – 2004

When Henry and I arrived in Vienna on 16 May we had half an hour to change trains. After dumping my luggage in the sleeper I hurried into the station concourse and bought an appropriately Habsburg novel: Joseph Roth's *Radetzkymarsch* which I first read about 30 years ago. As the train pulled out we asked the *Schaffner* the way to the dining car and discovered that, contrary to what we had been led to believe – not least by the published timetable – there wasn't one. A nice elderly Romanian lady with good English gave us a couple of rolls and the *Schaffner* sold us some packet bread and cheese and a couple of bottles of beer, and so we scraped together a dormy feast.

Murray (*Handbook for Travellers in South Germany and Austria* ['Austria' being interpreted as the Austro-Hungarian Empire], 14th ed. 1879) helpfully points out that in Hungary *Latin is no longer spoken*. The border guards came round at about 2 in the morning: first the Hungarians, who were fairly bored and, of course, ignorant of Latin, then the Romanians who were bored but numerous. One man prodded my bag: 'Souvenirs?' Other man: 'What is the purpose of your visit? Where are you going?' Thanks to Schengen you no longer get these personal touches in the EU.

We arrived at half past seven in the morning of 17 May (Monday) in Alba Iulia, *one of the most important towns of this Hungarian-influenced region... dominated by its huge citadel* according to the Rough Guide. It was grey when we arrived in the drizzle and we had to jump down several feet from the train to the platform. We had tickets from here to Cluj, but not reservations. Henry was delegated to buy them (on the grounds that 'you speak Hungarian'). The outcome was inevitable: we could only pay in *lei*, of which we had none. My turn to do some work. I went out onto the forecourt and accosted the first person not wearing a tracksuit. Do you speak English? Yes. (Very well, too). He paid for the reservations in *lei* and accepted euros in return, making a handsome profit which we decided we could not begrudge him.

The train was beautifully modern. We had a superb view of the long, winding journey through hills and moorland redolent of Wales and the Scottish borders with no fences or hedges. Every now and again we saw white specks in the distance which, as we grew nearer, turned into large flocks of sheep with shepherds and dogs, and each flock seemed to have a donkey in attendance. There were wells everywhere of the type you see in Hungary: Henry says they are called sweep wells. (The 'sweep' is the long pole which is lowered until the bucket on the end goes down into the well and fills with water). There were also very large herds of cattle. At one point, outside Teiuš or Aiud (I forget which) alongside the track there was what appeared to be a collection of large kennels which turned out to be hovels and which Sonia *[see below]* later said was almost certainly a Roma settlement. The villages in general seemed very poor, in many cases with dirt tracks instead of proper roads, although all the cottages had well-tended productive gardens. In the fields people appeared to be working large strips of land by hand.

Cluj

We reached Cluj at about 10, a little later than scheduled. Murray describes Klausenburg (Cluj) as *a pleasant, clean-looking town with wide streets diverging from the principal Platz,* which is true enough. *Up to the middle of the 16th cent. Klausenburg was chiefly inhabited by Saxons, but their distaste for the doctrines of Unitarianisam, which spread among the other townsfolk, caused them to retire to the south* [rather petulant, mmmh?], *and since then the place has been essentially Magyar.* This is no longer true. It is a majority Romanian city and the Hungarian element has declined to under 20%, in part perhaps because of the ferociously chauvinistic campaign being waged by Gheorghe Funar, the 'mad mayor', who is currently seeking re-election *[update: he lost].*

We were met by Henry's contact, Sonia, a tall young woman in her thirties with an engaging sense of humour. She is employed by the Presbyterian Church of Canada to teach English at a theological faculty (run by the Hungarian Reformed church).

She organised a taxi to our hotel, the Continental *[currently closed for restoration].* Before the war it was called the Hotel New York where, the Rough Guide maintains, Leigh Fermor enjoyed illicit cocktails with 'another man's wife'. Leigh Fermor himself says (in 'A Time of Gifts') that he and 'Angela', and 'István' cast in the role of gooseberry, sipped the barman's *amazing cocktail…with misgiving and delight.* For the record, they had three each then took *a hooded carriage* and *clip-clopped to a discreet Gypsy restaurant outside town* and later returned to their *fine vaulted quarters,* at which point 'István' was probably kicking himself for not asking 'Angela' if she had a 'sister'. At the end of the war the Continental was the German HQ in Transylvania.

It was a pleasantly pompous Habsburg hotel (built in 1885), with the generously large rooms and high ceilings of that era. Murray took a fairly dim view of accommodation in Hungary back in the 1870s. *The Hungarian inns are generally of one story* (sic), *planted in the midst of a court-yard* (sic) *ankle-deep in mud… Landlord and waiter are seldom at hand to receive a traveller when he presents himself; the attendance is slow and bad… A great portion of the inns are kept by Germans or Jews…* [In contrast to Baedeker, Murray was always at great pains to note the Jewish population of almost any settlement in Central and Eastern Europe] In our experience every single one of these statements is wildly inaccurate, and the notion that *leather sheets are desirable* may say more about Mr Murray than he would care to let slip.

The Continental's own brochure says, rather apologetically, that its *restaurant may meet all your culinary exigences*. So best eat somewhere else.

Sonia laid on a guided tour for us, starting with St Michael's Cathedral (built 1349–1487) on the main square, the Piaţa Unirii. The church used to be Protestant, with the office of *Stadtpfarrer* [town pastor] held alternately by a Saxon and a Hungarian. It reverted to Catholicism in 1716 and is now an exclusively Hungarian establishment. It has a fine baroque organ, dating from 1753, and a late baroque pulpit. It also has fifteenth century frescoes on the south wall. In front of the church is a statue of Matthias Corvinus (dating from 1902) with its inscription mutilated on Funar's orders. It used to read *Matthias Rex Hungarorum* but the last word has now been removed. Then on to the Greek Catholic Cathedral of the Trasfuguration and to the modern Romanian Orthodox cathedral, erected shortly after Transylvania had been absorbed into Romania proper after the First World War: polychrome, brassy and overbearing.

We moved on to the Romanian opera and, nearby, a farcically large statue of Avram Iancu (a rather pompous lawyer whose part in the events of 1848 seems to have consisted of raising a peasant army then doing absolutely nothing whatsoever to help Kossuth in his struggle against the Austrians unless the Romanians were given the right of self-determination in the new Hungary; result: defeat for the revolution). We walked along the 'mirror street' (where the buildings on the left perfectly resemble those on the right) to what Sonia called a 'convenience store' because I needed new shoelaces. The assistant was unable to give change for a 500.000 *lei* note.

As pangs of hunger gripped us we tried to get into a Romanian restaurant, the 'Roata', praised by the Rough Guide as being 'cosy, rustically styled' with 'sharp service and a convivial atmosphere', but, tough luck, it didn't open until 1 and this was 12.30. Then we tried a Hungarian restaurant which was full with a boisterous wedding party and, finally, the Lugano: Swiss-owned but locally run. Decent mushroom soup then stroganoff as the main course, with beer to start with, wine during the meal and coffee afterwards; it came to about €12 each.

After this we tried to get into the Corvinus birthplace but were thwarted by the unsocial times of the guided tours. However, the building does have a sign in Hungarian, as well as ones in Romanian, English and German. We walked past the Hungarian theatre, through the *Parc Central* and over the river (the *Someşul mic*) and up the daunting and exhausting *Cetătuia* (castle) hill past depressing flats to a lookout point with a view over the town (including traces of the synagogue, bottom left; sacked by the fascist Legionaries in 1927 and demolished in 1944). To the right, in the middle distance, there was a modern suburb of high-rise flats where Sonia lives. At the top of the hill where we were standing was the Transylvania hotel which I had almost picked from the guidebook.

Now what to do? Murray offers the following tip: *On the hillside just outside the town is a curious gypsy village; the dwellings are partly burrowed in the earth, and the inmates are mostly wild and uncouth-looking creatures.* This sounded promising, and reminiscent of my home town, but instead Sonia gave us the choice between the ethnographical museum and the Alexandru Borza botanical gardens. I wanted the former, Henry the latter. We settled on the former, on the grounds that Henry could see the botanics at leisure on Saturday, and hired a taxi. After a rather nerve-wracking, hot ride (Sonia says Romanians are superstitious about draughts of air, so only the driver had his window open) we reached the museum but discovered it was shut on Mondays. We should have known: Monday is a dead day for visitable sites all over Central and Eastern Europe.

We piled back into the taxi, again holding onto whatever we could to stop being thrown about (the seat belt has yet to be invented) and hurtled across town to the Botanical Gardens through the awful diesel fumes. The gardens, however, were pleasantly quiet and clean, and quite extensive. The administrative building surprisingly displays a plaque stating that the dreadful King Carol opened the gardens in 1931; odd that the Communists had not removed it. The Japanese garden would have benefited from having the pond filled with water, but I particularly liked the wonderful greenhouses, especially the palm houses where Henry and Sonia were stalked by a gigantic Venus fly-trap. There was a lookout tower in the grounds. Henry climbed to the top and took a photo of Sonia and me lounging on a bench as the temperature rose.

The changes of temperature are very great, Murray wrote. *The winters are long and intense, while in summer the grape and the watermelon ripen in the open air.* Not while we were there, but a not implausible scenario.

We wandered back down the Strada Bilaşcu to the city and its fumes and to the hotel and a trip to the bookshop just across the street. I wanted to buy a book on Saxon churches, but it was in a cellophane wrapper. As I tried to open the wrapper I was turned to stone by the Medusa-like glares of the female assistants.

We walked to the market, then on and down a couple of steps to a bar called the *Roland Garros* which, despite its name, is not a tennis-themed pub but has a riverside balcony. In summer you can sit on a terrace overlooking the river. We sat inside and had a couple of beers each which merged into a meal – rather dull pizzas – washed down with a couple of bottles of local Merlot. We had a rather pretentious conversation about literature, especially Canadian (where Sonia was at a distinct advantage), and less pretentious ones about the differences between varieties of English – the Canadians, for example, say *erbs*, not *herbs* – and about the Royal family (whom the others unaccountably seem to like).

A train trip

18 May (Tuesday): We had breakfast in the hotel, paid the bill, then took a taxi to the station. We paid for reservations – first class this time. I tried to make a reservation for Saturday, too, but was told to come back one hour before that train went. We bought rolls and water and the train, scheduled for 10.17, arrived a few minutes late.

First class was nowhere near as good as second class in Britain and certainly not a patch on yesterday's second class. We shared our compartment with two women in their forties who chatted incessantly and had to go out into the corridor every so often to smoke and chat again, an old lady with a black headscarf and one tooth who remained silent until she saw a friend in the corridor when she became very loud and voluble, plus a girl in her twenties who got off at Media.

The journey was enlivened by the presence of Roma. One man in his thirties went from compartment to compartment leaving shoddy trinkets on display and returning later in the hope that someone would want to buy one. The old lady looked at them in disbelief: keyrings, a purple fluffy dog... Then two small boys came round openly begging for money (our travelling companions told them sharply to clear off) a lad with a limp and, apparently, wearing two pairs of jeans, one of which he started to lower to show us his operation scars (our travelling companions shouted at him to go away); and a middle-aged man dejectedly trying to sell half a dozen cups and saucers.

The first part of the journey was Cluj to Teiu in reverse, and then we struck East to the unlikely sounding Blaj, then Copşa Mică, Mediaş and Sighişoara – which certainly looked interesting from the train. Near Sighişoara we decided to eat the filled rolls we had bought in Cluj – but in the corridor because the vendor had filled them with a strange relish which threatened to squirt all over us. After Sighişoara the line turned south-east to Cata, the scenery looking increasingly like the backdrop to a Renaissance crucifixion scene, then sharp south to Homorod, which sounds like a pain in the bottom, and sharp east where after a time it followed the river Olt very closely for a dozen kilometres, a river sluggish but swollen with dirty brown water. It had obviously been raining heavily up in the mountains. At Augustin we headed due south again, near but ignoring the wilful meandering of the river, to Braşov.

Braşov

We located where we were to meet the car hire man tomorrow and found a taxi to take us to our hotel. I was impressed by Henry's negotiating skills.

> Driver: You want taxi?
> Henry: How much?
> Driver: Two hundred thousand...
> Henry (marching on): No, that's far too much.
> Driver: One hundred and fifty thousand – it's the price of two beers.
> Henry: No! (Increasing his pace)
> Driver (pleading): One hundred thousand?
> Henry: Where's your car?

We arrived at the hotel (after a rather zig-zag ride which prompted Henry to ask sharply: 'You *do* know where it is, don't you?') and promised to phone the driver, a Mr Cristi, if we decided we wanted his services tomorrow. He had produced a pochette of photos of tourist traps and letters of recommendation from British and American victims.

The hotel Coroana – *the only place in town with real character* according to the Rough Guide (although the 2008 revised edition says it is *'muddy grey... concealing two rather careworn and rudimentary hotels'*) – was another establishment reminiscent of the Austro-Hungarian empire, an impression which faded slightly when a coachload of antipodean backpackers trooped in. We had been assigned massive suites: a large bathroom (again, without a shower curtain), a very large bedroom with absurdly high ceiling, and another room with, in my case, a TV, glass-fronted cabinets, a long oval dining table with six chairs, three other chairs dotted round the room and two three-man sofas; altogether enough seating to host a meeting of the central committee of the local party.

In Murray's day the population of Braşov (Kronstadt) was mixed: *beside the dominant Saxon, there are many resident Armenians and Sclaves, members of the Greek Church. One of the suburbs is inhabited by Szeklers and another by Wallachs.* However, the population was on the decline and *in fact, all over Transylvania, the Saxons are lessening in numbers, while the Sclavish race is on the increase.* I have no idea what he meant by the 'Sclavish race'. Surely not the Romanians – who appear elsewhere as 'Wallachs'. There were other treats for Murray's contemporaries: *A number of the Gipsy tribe are always to be seen mingled with the other varieties of people, and this singular race is everywhere welcome on account of their musical talent. The Czigány, or Gipsy band, is to be met with throughout Hungary[1], and the favourite air is the music of the Czardas, a national dance, which is the delight of prince and peasant alike.* This Ruritanian charm is far from reality. The Roma are certainly 'mingled with the other varieties of people', but despised by them and treated warily as beggars and potential pick-pockets.

After a brief freshening-up session we went for a walk. The map supplied by the hotel was completely useless so we bought a better one from a kiosk. Up pedestrianised Strada Republicii to Piaţa Sfatului (Council square) and leftish to the famous Black Church (Biserica Neagră), which looks old and grey rather than black and was shut, and off to the left past the German lyceum and the statue of Honterus (1498–1549), a famous reformer unknown to either of us ignoramuses. Apart from his Reformation activities, he was an important educationalist and he established a printing press. Then right into the Strada poarta schei, past the Jewish cultural centre

---

[1] Remember: when Murray was writing Transylvania was still part of the Kingdom of Hungary.

and the Neolog synagogue, built in 1901, and on to the Poarta itself which once marked the boundary between townies (Saxons) and peasants (Romanians – allowed in, at a price, only at certain times).

Then we turned right past the *Facultatea de Silvicultură* (dead easy language, this) and Catherine's Gate – a pleasantly green area – and right into Strada Barițiu. In the hill above we could see the *Turnul Alb* (white tower). Back along the road then into a courtyard announcing, in Greek, the Greek community of Brașov. At the back of the courtyard we went through an open iron gate and then into the Greek Orthodox church. No seats, except a few for the infirm around the sides. The church is dedicated to Saint Treime (Who? Actually it's the Holy Trinity) and is more what one expects of an Orthodox establishment than the others we have seen.

We went back down the street to the Piața Sfatului, where the Pied Piper and children are believed to have emerged, and the Casa Sfatului, the old German Rathaus. We wanted to see the History Museum but were told it was shut. We protested that the stated opening times were 10 to 6, but the attendant was adamant. 'Last entrance is 5.30 and it's 5.20 now, so you won't have time to see everything in ten minutes' 'But', we protested, 'if we come in now we will have forty – not ten – minutes to see everything'. 'No, it's not worth it' and there was nothing we could do. I only hope the museum was hugely dull and full of dreary pottery shards and coins. We went back down the road and peered through the grille of the church of Sts Peter and Paul, an uninteresting Catholic establishment.

Where to eat? According to Derek Patmore's 'Invitation to Roumania' (1939), *the various cafés and night-clubs, such as the Parisian-Grill, form a sophisticated contrast to the outwardly simple atmosphere of the town.*[2] The sophistication was not immediately apparent and so we returned to the Piața Sfatului and an early

---

[2] Patmore was related to the poet Coventry Patmore (1823–96), but Derek was more Solihull. These are examples of his banal observations: 'Roumanians as a race are deeply religious', 'At heart, all Roumanians are extremely kind-hearted and tolerant', 'Roumanians love music', 'the Roumanian peasant is a poet at heart' and 'The Roumanians have always been an art-loving people'.

supper at the Hirscher Haus [or Merchants Hall, which no longer exists]. We wanted to eat inside, as it was getting a bit nippy, but were told by the waiter 'Raus!' and so sat outside under an umbrella. The conversation rambled and dried up sporadically as we ate a decent meal: vegetable soup, a brochette of assorted bits of meat (already removed from the skewer), plus a salad and rolls, with the waiter making a great show of explaining that they were hot. He kept saying 'heiss, heiss' and mimed burning his fingers. I discovered that Henry loathes cucumber. This is a shame, as I have many cucumber recipes I would love to share with him; for example:

Concombre à l'ancienne

You will need: a potato peeler, a cucumber, a knife and a saucer.

Cut the last ½ inch off the cucumber, then cut off a section about two inches long. Use the potato peeler to remove the skin, then cut into thinnish slices. Place the slices on a saucer and eat.

Preparation time: 1 minute
Cooking time: -
Serves: 1

At a nearby table there were a couple of lads playing backgammon: one obviously English, with the blissfully gormless look and silly voice of the public schoolboy. The other could have been anyone, and probably was.

We returned to the hotel to arrange a driver – anyone but Mr Cristi – for tomorrow morning. The hotel recommended a man called John, who is very trustworthy according to the receptionist and wants only 500,000 lei (about €12) for the morning). Fine. We arranged for him to collect us at half past eight.

We breakfasted on the 19th in the rather daunting dining room: ham and eggs and coffee. John arrived on time and we set off in a north-easterly direction for a dozen or so kilometres to our first port of call: Hărman, or Honigberg. John is a neat little man in his late fifties perhaps, with silvery grey hair and a white moustache which makes him look older, and a striped jacket. Very deferential. We had not been driving more than a few hundred yards when he crossed himself three times. Henry thought it was because I had just mentioned the name of Ceauşescu, but in fact our driver crossed himself vigorously whenever we passed an Orthodox Church, which was fairly often.

Hărman (Hönigberg)

Hărman was erected in the fifteenth century and originally had three concentric walls, although the outermost wall has now disappeared. The inner wall is some 12 m in height with seven towers. We arrived a few minutes before the published opening time and so wandered about taking photos of the outside of the defensive wall. We tried getting in and were met by a young woman speaking only Romanian who indicated that we should follow her. She set off at a hand's gallop with us trailing behind. At length she returned with a man in his fifties, wiry, carrying lengths of timber over his shoulder, wearing a cap and with his front middle teeth missing. He spoke German and explained that the timber was to be used to repair part of the wooden fencing outside the defensive wall which local lads had broken in an idle moment. He may have been the minister – we didn't ask – but he was certainly very knowledgeable about the church, pointing out all its architectural features.

The church proper dates from 1293. There are clear Cistercian influences, and it has fifteenth century frescoes (discovered in 1920) with scenes depicting the Last Judgement and the Crucifixion.

There is one curious feature of the seating. The women sit on benches without backs in the centre of the church, the men in boxed pews on the periphery. In this way the men could protect the women if the church were attacked. The women's seats had no backs because in the past the women used to wear fairly voluminous skirts which would have been crushed. The side pews were decked with oriental carpets brought back by traders from Turkey. There are also Anatolian prayer rugs.

We asked how many ethnic Germans were still left in the village. *Vor der Revolution* – we became used to this accurate description of the events surrounding Ceauşescu's overthrow rather than the anodyne *vor der Wende* – there had been 1,002 Germans in the village; now there were only 122 – a decline of almost 90%. Most had emigrated to Germany, our guide said, but some of them still owned houses in the village and would come back for a period every year to see family and friends and, perhaps, keep alive the hope that one day they would return to their *Heimat*. The war memorial (Second World War) is full of German names, each man identified by a number which, our guide told us, was the number of his house (there are no street names in the village).

In the narrow confines of the neat *enceinte* workmen had arrived to spray the bushes and flowers with a poison designed to kill a pest which our guide described to us, but which we could not name. They seemed to be spraying at will but they, at least, were wearing masks. We bought guidebooks and postcards and shook hands with our guide. At this point I realised he had lost both his thumbs. I hope this was as a result of an industrial injury, rather than torture.

Outside, by the car John, the driver, was reading the racing results in the paper. He beamed and said: 'Very nice? Very nice!'.

Prejmer (Tartlau)

We agreed, got back in and drove on a few kilometres to Prejmer (Tartlau) which figures on UNESCO's world heritage list and is even more impressive, as a building, than Hărman. In fact the

Rough Guide refers to it as *'the most comprehensively fortified and perhaps the most spectacular'* of all the region's churches. It was originally built (completed 1225) in the form of a Greek cross but it, too, was later adapted to the Cistercian style.

Before entering the church we inspected the little museum. It had the usual artefacts: ploughshares, cooking implements, and some very fine local costumes. We spoke to the custodian, a young woman in her thirties. Henry was pleased to discover that he could converse with her in Luxembourgish, she could reply in Sächsisch and they could understand each other perfectly. Some words, however, inevitably had different meanings, she explained and, of course, Sächsisch does not have the French loanwords that Luxembourgish has, but by contrast has Romanian and Hungarian loan words. I asked her (in German) about the size of the Saxon population. She said Prejmer had suffered a worse decline than Hărman: from about 3,000 down to about 150, a decline of some 95% – but she, too, was resigned to it: *'Ja, es ist traurig aber es ist so'* (yes, it's sad but that's how it is).

We inspected the church, which is proud of its Gothic altarpiece depicting The Passion (1450–60). A panel explains why (in Romanian, German and English): *'This is the most ancient both-sised [sic] sacral item in Rumania. It was worked in Transylvania between 1450–1460. The dating being iconographically confirmed by the vesture worn by the personages. The head adornment reminds the local Saxonian costume'*.

Prejmer is larger by far than Hărman and, again, clearly in regular use even though the congregation is dwindling rapidly. Outside, the ring wall rises very high and is very thick, having been used in times of invasion as a place of refugee from marauding Tartars or Turks. Each family in the village was obliged to keep a week's supply of food in case of a siege and had its own dwelling – in effect a cave – with no window on the external façade (obviously) and a door on the side facing the church. Access to these dwellings was and is by means of rather rickety wooden ladders and walkways. I was not entirely confident that they would bear my weight. About half way round, however, we found stone steps leading up inside the walls to a defensive tower and a wall walk which at one time must have gone all the way around the defensive structure. It was dark, but there was some light coming in through slits.

Outside we walked round, trying to take pictures which would include the entire bulbous complex. It is possible to do this if you stand with your back to the new Orthodox church that is being built, the symbol of the chauvinist reconquista, just across the dusty road.

Back at the car John again greeted us with a 'Very nice?' and, again, we nodded. The agreement had been that we would have his services until midday, when he would leave us at the station, and since we had enough time in hand we asked him to drive us back into Braşov to try and look at the Black Church, allegedly the largest Gothic church between Vienna and Istanbul which – if you think about it – is a fairly meaningless claim. It took almost a century to complete (1383–1477), the work being interrupted by Ottoman attacks. Its nickname stems from an incident in1689 when the Austrian army, occupying the city, managed to start a great fire which blackened the church's walls with soot. The church is hung with mostly seventeenth-century Turkish prayer mats, donated by local merchants returning from the east.

Here we found encouraging signs that the German-speaking community still had some life in it (the German Lyceum had already suggested this): children's paintings of a trip organised by the (female) minister. There was also a competent and interesting exhibition on the history of the building, in both German and Romanian. As the Rough Guide says, despite its name the church is *'startlingly white'* inside.

John drove us to the station with several minutes to spare, Instead of the agreed 500,000 *lei* we gave him 600,000 (about €15) and he was touchingly grateful. We shook hands, parted, and went inside to lounge near the information office and await the arrival of the car hire man, Mr Popescu, due at noon. I wandered off briefly in the hope of finding a non-Romanian newspaper at one or other of the kiosks, but drew a blank.

A road trip

Mr Popescu eventually arrived about a quarter of an hour late and looking rather harassed. He had driven up from Bucharest. He looked Henry in the eye and shook *my* hand.

The car was a fairly modern black Volkswagen saloon. We had not paid in advance and had assumed we could use a credit card but Mr Popescu said this was not possible so we had to go back into the station to use the Bancomat machine. Just over half a million each: not very much in euros. We signed bits of paper and parted company with Mr Popescu who, we assume, had to get back to the capital.

Henry volunteered me to drive the first stretch. Finding reverse was tricky, and a crowd gathered to watch me edge closer and closer to a large and menacing obstacle. Finding any gear was not very easy as most of the knob on the gear stick came away in my hand within the first two seconds. The other feature of the car was that it reeked of elderly aunts' perfume. In the end, however, I manoeuvered it back out of the parking space, onto the station forecourt and off on the open road, guessing, successfully, the direction in which Bran lay. Henry the Navigator kindly forbore to comment on my driving.

The roads in Braşov itself were in a reasonable condition, while the roads outside town were of a much higher standard. This was our general conclusion. Henry's interpretation – that the national government pays for the main roads while the impoverished local authorities pay for roads in built-up areas – seems perfectly convincing. In any case, it mirrors the arrangements in Luxembourg.

It was about 40 kilometres to Bran – a flat road with the snow-capped Carpathians not far away to the East – and we passed Râşnov on our left rising sharply on an isolated hill.

Bran

In the village of Bran we found a guarded car park and walked to the ticket office of the castle, lurking in the far corner of what the Rough Guide kindly calls a *'hectic crafts market'*: Dracula t-shirts, crude wooden Count Draculas, gaudy ash trays and so on. But it also had a snack booth and we were able to buy a hamburger each, while resisting all attempts to have them sprayed with the bizarre mayonnaise we had encountered yesterday. The hamburgers were good enough, we bought our tickets and a selection of guidebooks and postcards and walked up the short, not terribly steep rise to the castle's main entrance. In contrast to the souvenir stalls, the castle makes no attempt to exploit whatever (tenuous) relationship it has with Vlad Ţepeş, although it would not surprise me to return in a few years' time and find it converted into a tasteless Disney-type theme park.

By the way, Romanians are baffled by the foreign obsession with vampires. For them, Vlad was a national hero, successfully defeating the Turks. He may have engaged in rather inventive acts of cruelty, but they were more or less normal for the times.

The castle was built by Saxons from Braşov between 1377 and 1382 to safeguard this vital trade route. Vlad is thought to have attacked it in 1460, but that's as far as the connection goes. Murray makes no mention of this. For him, Törzburg (Bran) is *in good preservation*. It once belonged to the Teutonic Knights *but they became so intolerable* [unfortunately he doesn't go into details: overzealous enforcing of the *jus primae noctis*, perhaps?] *that they were forced to leave the country*. It was donated in 1920 or thereabouts to the royal family and was lovingly – and tastefully and expertly – restored and maintained by Queen Marie as a proper residence. The castle was inherited by her daughter Princess Ileana who ran a hospital there in World War II. It was later seized by the state with the expulsion of the royal family in 1948. In 2005 the Romanian government passed a law allowing restitution claims on properties illegally expropriated, such as

Bran, and thus a year later ownership of the castle was awarded to American Dominic von Habsburg, the son and heir of Princess Ileana.

It contains just enough furniture to maintain the 'home' element without turning it into a museum, and the passageways and stairs around the fairly small central courtyard – reminiscent of many German mediaeval castles – are enough to satisfy any castle buff that it is the genuine article. While we were there a group of four French gendarmes, in uniform, were being given a guided tour in French. Apparently they have been brought in to help the local police stamp out corruption. All the evidence is that they will need major reinforcements.

At the foot of the castle and tucked away to the side is a small *Freilichtmuseum*, or folk museum, illustrating rural life in the vicinity: farmhouses and a fulling mill, about a dozen buildings in all. In contrast to most such museums in western Europe, where the houses have small, short four-poster beds where the inmates slept almost upright for fear of being mistaken by the devil for the dead, here the beds were open affairs, piled high with colourful rugs, more like sofas.

Râşnov

Back in the 'crafts market' we had a coffee, Henry bought tapes of folk music for the car and I bought a print, then we drove back up the road towards Râşnov in search of a way up to the castle. From a distance it looks like an Italian hill town and, at first attempt, it seems almost as inaccessible. There were signs outside the village announcing the presence of the castle, but no indication of how to get there. We drove past the shockingly bad road leading into the village then turned round frustrated and tried this very road. It lived up to the description in the Rough Guide: *'country roads... are poor and local roads are disintegrating'*. This one had several major potholes extending for the entire width of the road, in the first fifty yards or so. However, we managed it and drove up to a T-junction where, relying on guesswork, we turned right, then left where a sign pointed to the *četate* (castle). The road very soon turned into a gravel track, much like the ones you have to take to reach remote rented villas in Tuscany.

In Murray's day 'Rosenau' was approached from a deep ravine *overhung with luxuriant foliage, the birch and beech mingled with hawthorn.* Some of the more obvious potholes had been filled with sand to make the going even trickier; I soon exhausted my stock of colourful obscenities and had to drive the last hundred yards or so in a grindingly loud first gear, with the engine becoming alarmingly warm. We parked at the small, guarded car park and walked the last hundred yards or so.

Râşnov was built 1211–1225 by Teutonic knights. It was first mentioned in 1331 as *Rosnou* and again in 1388 as *villa Rosarum*. While the village was razed many times in its history by Tatars, Turks and Wallachians, the castle was conquered only once, in 1612 by Gábor Báthory. The present remains date from the fourteenth century. It rises fairly steeply from the entrance tower to a much higher vantage point from which you can see the plain on one side and the Carpathian mountains reaching 9,000 feet or thereabouts on the other. A lot of work is being done on the castle: largely consolidation of the remains, although a small museum has been created in the powder tower and a cafeteria has been opened in one of the buildings. Rather sparse documentation, but at least there was some.

My camera appears to have done the dirty on me, so I shall have to rely on Henry who has a fairly impressive digital affair. I must get one.

Murray comments that the district is *celebrated for its honey. Bee-keeping is an important item of industry in Transylvania.* While we saw no bees in the vicinity of Bran or Râşnov, in other parts of the country hives were very evident: square painted box-like affairs, sometimes in banks of twenty or thirty, in some cases mounted on trailers so that they could be moved about from one promising pollination point to another.

Moving on... slowly

We drove back down the alarming track, fortunately not en-
countering anyone daft enough to attempt to drive up, and the
bright hot sun soon turned into cold rain. At this point we
foolishly allowed our sense of adventure to get the better of us.
Instead of returning to Braşov and then heading west along the
road marked green on the map (no. 1 or E 68) we reasoned that we
could cut across country, pick up the road at Codlea, where there
is also a fortified church, and save ourselves a lot of time (15 km
instead of 31).

Ha, ha. For a start, we could not find the cross-country road (no
number according to the map) which went through Vulcan (another
fortified church; save it for next time) and so, feeling even more
adventurous, we decided to try the 73A which would take us to
Şercaia, thereby saving us even more time and effort (49 km instead
of 67). However, we had not realised just how bad a rural road in
Romania could be. We should have listened to the experts: *The
roads of Austria-Hungary, on the whole, fall considerably short of the
English standard, for the steam-roller is unknown in that country*
[Baedeker: Austria-Hungary (1905)].

It must have taken us at least an hour, if not an hour and a half,
to cover this short distance. The only thing in our favour was that
it was largely downhill, following the river Şinca, a tributary of the
Olt. But the surface was easily the worst that I had ever seen:
potholes and cracks everywhere. Worse, even, than Cheltenham.
For most of the journey we could only edge ahead cautiously,
weaving between the obstacles and zigzagging across the road to
find the best, or least worst, piece of surface, occasionally driving
through front gardens. There were very few other road users and,
of course, they posed no obvious danger since no-one could move
fast enough to cause an accident. Never again, although it has to be
said that the scenery almost made up for the nightmare experience.

At last we reached road no. 1. It took us through Făgăraş and on
to Avrig – which prompted a terrible joke about 'no mean city' –

and Tălmaciu along the foot of the mountains where every village
in the valley has its smaller counterpart up in the hills (thus, we
went through Sâmbăta de Jos, Ucea de Jos, Arpaşu de Jos and
Porumbacu de Jos while a few kilometres up the mountains we
were shadowed by Sâmbăta de Sus, Ucea de Sus, Arpaşu de Sus and
Porumbacu de Jos). Henry said 'I'm sure you will have guessed
what *de Jos* means'. Well, I hadn't, but I wasn't going to admit it. At
Tălmaciu the road became the E 81 and after another fifteen
kilometres of uneventful, easy driving we reached Sibiu.

Sibiu

Murray's description – *It has a scrupulously neat well-to-do air, like a
German town of the middle ages* – is not entirely inaccurate. Our
hotel, the Împăratul Romanilor (*a large, old-fashioned hotel in the
centre of the town, with enormous bedrooms, and the spacious furnishing
which recalls the easy-going days of the Austro-Hungarian Empire*:
Patmore; or *the furnishings are decidedly kitsch and the place is a little
shabby*, Bradt guide), was at the far end of a pedestrian-only street,
Str. Bălcescu, and so approaching it required an inspired guess
which proved right. We parked on the pavement where a sign
instructed us to do so, and a rather distraught young man in
overalls emerged from nowhere, gesticulating to us to drive round
the corner and park in front of the hotel. We did so and checked in.
Then I returned to the car and drove it back round the corner to
what turned out to be the hotel's guarded parking area which we
could use for two days for about €2. The attendant offered to give
the Volkswagen a wash, but I declined.

   We unpacked then set off in search of somewhere to eat. After
wandering about aimlessly – Piaţa Mare, Piaţa Huet and Piaţa Mica
– soaking up the atmosphere and being driven mad with hunger we
found a building with people sitting at tables in the window and a
sign saying 'Restaurant'. Gratefully we entered and flung ourselves
down at an empty table at the back. A girl brought the menu. We
turned it over and over: there was no mention of food. Slowly we

explained to her that we wanted something to eat. 'We do not serve food' we were told. After a time-consuming argument during which we pointed out that 'Restaurant' usually meant 'establishment that serves food to customers' we left and found a perfectly acceptable place called *La Turn*[3] where, after a brief struggle, we were allowed to sit where we wanted in a near empty cavern and enjoyed an excellent meal of which I can remember no details except that two bottles of wine were consumed.

The Luxembourg connection

We spent the morning (Thursday, 20 May, Ascension Day) looking around Sibiu. First stop: the *Casa Luxembourg* opened by the Grand Duke on a state visit to Romania in March. It was a very hot day and we had no trouble locating the building on the corner of Piaţa Mica and near the Podul Minciunilor, or Liars' Bridge. Legend has it that if anyone stands on it and tells a lie the bridge will collapse. Ceauşescu gave an entire speech on this site without the bridge suffering any adverse consequences.

The *Casa Luxembourg* building is neat, clean and recently restored. In the cellar there is a café and people were sitting at trestle tables underneath sun umbrellas (it was getting quite hot) drinking coffee as we stared at the building wondering how to get in: workmen appeared to be replacing the front door or the electric bell or both. After a few minutes a young man speaking *Hochdeutsch* asked from one of the tables if he could be of any assistance. We explained that we were from Luxembourg and were interested in looking around, if at all possible.

He had finished his coffee and agreed at once to give us a tour. It turned out that he is the curator or administrator. He showed us the offices of the Luxembourgish consulate – how many Luxembourgers come here, I wonder – still with exhibition material about Luxembourg and its language(s) left over from the

---

[3] 'La' is a preposition ('at' or 'on'), not a definitive article.

Grand Duke's recent visit; advertising materials from Henry's publisher Op der Lay (*lay* pronounced as in English and not as in German, Henry informed me: it means a school slate [cf. Dutch *lei(steen)*]). There was also a room for receptions and other events (where the Grand Duke had given a speech).

We went upstairs to see the offices of the *Siebenbürgen-Sächsisches Wörterbuch*[4], a project which had begun before the war, then lapsed but has now been revived with the official sponsorship of the Romanian Academy. It employs three people full-time: a lady in her late 50s/early 60s who is about to retire, plus two younger women, one of whom has only recently been taken on and to whom we were introduced. It is a lexicographer's paradise, with containers the size of shoeboxes and full of index cards piled high to the ceiling. Probably a race against time, with the Saxon community in Sibiu so sadly depleted. Baedeker says that in 1905 *of the 26,100 inhab., two-thirds are Saxons.* Not so today.

Upstairs again to see the guest quarters which can now be rented from the *Evangelisches Pfarrhaus*[5]: several large, well-appointed and nicely furnished guest rooms each with a decent shower and WC. They need to be booked some time in advance. Henry's eyes lit up. I imagine he is planning to come back soon. And upstairs to yet another floor: the *Dachboden*, or attic, to see details of its construction and the administrator's children's clothes hanging out to dry. Back downstairs again and into the cellar – the café – to see the earliest part of the building, after which we invited our host to join us for a coffee at one of the pavement tables.

He himself spoke Hochdeutsch, rather than dialect, although the latter was his mother tongue. His grandmother had spoken Sächsisch. As we were talking the lady in charge of the dictionary project came along and we invited her to join us, too. Very pleasant grey-haired lady with a gentle sense of humour and giving the impression that the future of the language depended largely on her. Despite the sponsorship of the Romanian Academy and the interest

---

[4] Transylvanian German Dictionary.
[5] Protestant manse.

expressed by the Luxembourgish government, funding has been a problem. At present she is paying the electricity and phone bills out of her own pocket. We were introduced to yet another German who is manager of the *Verkehrsamt* [tourist office] which is about to open in the ground floor of the building. It will have tourist leaflets in English, German, French and Dutch. He gave us a leaflet about Biertan.

We parted from the Sachsen feeling strangely elated and visited, just round the corner, the protestant cathedral (1320–1520). According to the Rough Guide it houses Romania's largest church organ and the tomb of Mihnea the Bad (Dracula's son). He was *voivode* of Wallachia for just three years before being stabbed to death in 1510 outside the cathedral. It was rather gloomy inside but we were glad of the cool air. It is *injudiciously restored, and many interesting monuments removed from their places* (dixit Murray. But if the monuments had been removed, how did you know they were interesting, eh?). The chancel's north wall displays a large fresco, the work (1445) of Johannes of Rosenau. The church also has the largest organ in Transylvania. Just saying...

We fought our way outside past a party of fractious school-children fighting their way in. Thence to the Ursuline Church for a second or two as a service was in progress. I made my usual light-hearted remarks about the Catholic church and was informed rather huffily by Henry that he had been brought up a Catholic.

We parted company (not because of any religious schism) to raid the local bookshops. I acquired a Romanian version of *Pride and Prejudice* for next to nothing, which I will pass on to any of my colleagues learning Romanian, and, in a different, allegedly German-language, bookshop, a handsome copy of Fabini's *Atlas der Siebenbürgischen Wehrkirchen*[6] which was to exercise my arm muscles for the next few days. After buying a disposable camera I rendezvoused with Henry again for lunch in the hotel dining room, a pleasant light and airy space (the roof retracts in summer) with

---

[6] Atlas of Transylvanian fortified churches: the definitive work on this subject.

gold and royal blue decorations. I ordered trout, Henry chicken, with mineral water for the two of us. 'No alcohol?' was the waitress's stunned question. Henry had been to the Brukenthal museum, named after Samuel Brukenthal, governor of Transylvania 177–87 with a particular interest in homeopathy.

After lunch, back to the Volkswagen where we were again asked if we wanted to have the car washed. Again, no, and so without further ado (sic) we wound our way successfully, thanks to Henry's navigating and despite the paucity of road signs of any description, to Cisnădie.

Cisnădie (Heltau)

Murray's 'village' has turned into a small town, although it is still *charmingly situated, and commanding fine views of the vale below* – and, of course, the snowy mountains in the distance. We parked in the main street and crossed the road to a post-box where I got rid of half a dozen postcards and where we were accosted by a middle-aged drunken ethnic German complaining about a variety of not entirely comprehensible problems. We crossed back to the tourist office, which turned out to be a shop selling *objets* for tourists. However, the lady was able to direct us to a gate in the church's outer walls where we could expect to find the custodian. We knocked on several doors and at last a good-natured man in his fifties with a balding head appeared and readily agreed to show us around the church. The Saxon community here, too, is dwindling at an alarming rate, although there is a service or event of some sort every day in the church, especially this morning (Ascension). Nevertheless, he was pessimistic about the future. Although the community still counted about 100 members the remaining younger members were tending to marry Romanians (hardly surprising if the choice from their own ethnic group is so restricted) and their children were being brought up as monolingual Romanians.

The church itself is fairly bare inside, although it has allegedly one of the three finest organs in Transylvania, the others being those in the Black Church in Braşov and Cluj. Outside, however, it boasts one of the Seven Wonders of this part of the world: the first lightning conductor to be installed in Transylvania (in 1795). Henry was enraptured.

We shook hands and left the church and discovered that our next port of call – Cisnădioara or Michelsberg – was only three kilometres away. But given that the temperature had risen to about 30° and we would be faced with a steep climb when we reached the village to get to the church, which is perched on a hill, and given that we were not sure about the opening times and, frankly, in my case at least, not looking forward to a walk in this heat, thank you very much, we drove instead across the gently undulating countryside, again with the snowy mountains on our left (the south side).

Cisnădioara

At the village it was not immediately apparent how we were to get up to the *picturesque ruins of a Romanesque ch. on a conical rock in the centre of a beautiful valley* (Murray). The one obvious route took us along a narrowing dirt track by a stream and away from the hill. We turned back and parked just off the village square where a couple with rucksacks, presumably jolly hikers, appeared to be taking a break. We asked them which way to the castle and the lady, obviously (now) a weather-beaten custodian rather than a tanned tourist, issued us with a set of keys and pointed our way through a gate and up a steeply winding track.

We passed, on his way down, a rather overenthusiastic German looking haggard and terribly keen to know our background: how many languages did we speak etc. We moved on having impressed him.

Henry, in charge of the keys, unlocked the gate of the *enceinte* and then the padlock on the door of the church itself. There is nothing outstandingly beautiful about the church which is surrounded by a defensive wall with three towers. Although the

West porch is attractive and clearly Romanesque (the church was built in 1223, according to the Rough Guide), the inside is almost totally devoid of decoration with the exception of tombs to several dozen unfortunates *gefallen für das Vaterland* at some point in the 1940s. No doubt about it, this had definitely been a German-speaking village. The enceinte is still in reasonable condition, despite centuries of neglect, and the site managed to withstand frequent Tartar attacks. We wandered round taking pictures, with Henry looking like an illustration from Arthur Ransome – dressed in whites with a white sun hat.

We returned to the car park and handed back the key, then set off back into Sibiu where I dropped Henry near the hotel and went in search of Cristian (or Grossau) on the E 68/71 on the road to Sebeş. I was exhausted by the heat and the foul diesel fumes of Sibiu's confusing road system, but the sight of Cristian from afar more than made up for this. It can clearly be seen as you drive downhill past the little airport on the left. The village is fairly nondescript but the German-speaking community is interesting in that those who are left are descendants of Austrian Protestants, rather than Saxons, who settled in the area to avoid Catholic persecution in the mid-eighteenth century. The church has a dual defensive wall system but, alas, was locked and there was no obvious way in, and no-one answered any of the bells I tried. An earthquake in 1850 partially destroyed the church.

Somewhat dispirited I returned to Sibiu and the hotel's guarded car park where, again, I came under pressure to have the car washed:

> Attendant: You like it washed?
> Me: No, thank you.
> Attendant: I make it like this one *[pointing at a gleaming vehicle with Dutch licence plates]*.
> Me: No, thank you.
> Attendant: But it's very dirty!
> Me: I know, but it's not mine.

I paid a visit to another bookshop where I did my good deed of the day. Two elderly Dutch couples were being pressurised by the owner to buy Alan Ogden's *Fortresses of Faith* – a history of the Saxon churches with black and white photos. I had given it a glance but rejected it, not least because the author thinks the plural of (lower-case!) *kirchenburg is kirchenburgs*. I explained to one of the Dutchmen, in Dutch so that the owner couldn't overhear, that a better bet if he didn't want too much detail was the book of coloured photos I had picked up in Cluj. He passed on the good news to the rest of his party: *die mijnheer* (glancing at me) *spreekt een beetje nederlands*. (This gent speaks a little Dutch). Een beetje! I thought it was quite good.

A decent meal

Meanwhile Henry, following the instructions of our guide at the *Casa Luxembourg* had located and booked a table at the town's best restaurant: the *Sibiul Vechi* [old Sibiu] in Str. Papiu Ilarian off Piaţa Mare, described by Bradt as *atmospheric* but by the miserable Rough Guide as *claustrophobic… its walls strewn with regional objects'* but with *the most authentic Romanian food in town'*. It was in a cellar and staffed by waiters and waitresses wearing bright local costume. We sat at the end nearest the kitchens, opposite a group of bored looking youths and girl friends who turned out to be the live music. Good, but very much 'folk light' as Henry called it, and we soon realised that we were the only people applauding. The food was also good: the by now usual preponderance of pork and chicken – typical backyard food for peasants.

I had a dish described as 'shepherd's purse': minced pork in a 'purse' (the sort with a drawstring) made of pasta, together with a slab of the almost unavoidable *mămăliga*, or polenta – very ethnic and it can be pretty horrible when it tries (but not on this occasion). We had a beer each to start with, two bottles of wine with the meal – during the course of which the conversation stumbled over religion and Marxism and other pretentious and portentous matters – and coffee with two rounds of *ţuică*, the local schnapps which tastes a bit like Luxembourgish eau de vie, the whole lot coming to the equivalent of about €25. And so to bed feeling pleasantly wrecked.

Another nice, hot, sunny day (Friday, 21 May). I bought myself another disposable camera – this time with a flash. The girl yesterday had omitted to point out that the cheaper ones were flashless. Henry's turn to drive, after resisting another desperate attempt to get us to have the car washed. Our targets for today: Moşna and Biertan. We gave the concierge's runner – the rather daft lad who confided in me that his name is Franz – a 10,000 *lei* tip and asked him for directions to the Sighişoara road out of town. He offered to come with us to the edge of town, then catch a taxi back, but I pointed out that this would effectively wipe out his tip. He took this in slowly.

We headed north spurning a number of other beguiling sites: fortified churches (seen from the road) at Şura Mare, Şeica Mare and Ruşi and a decent ruined castle at Slimnic, whose name was also given in German: Stolzemburg. I was strongly tempted to stop but decided that this might try Henry's patience. According to Sonia, bilingual place names are required in local authorities where at least 30% of the population speak a minority language (i.e. Hungarian or German). This seems an unnecessarily high percentage.

We drove on. After Şeica Mare the road starts to turn north-east towards what the Rough Guide calls *filthy Copşa Mică …probably Romania's most polluted town* thanks to a carbon black plant which opened in 1936 and finally closed down in 1993 and a lead smelter which for the last thirty years *has been spreading a cocktail of twenty heavy metals over the surrounding area*. The town certainly looks drearily industrial, but – with the windows firmly shut and the air recycling facility switched on – we noticed nothing of the pollution. Shortly after Copşa Mica we hit Mediaş which *despite the tanneries and chemical works feeding off the Târnava Mare valley's methane reserves, gets more attractive the further in you venture.* We were not aware of this, despite having ventured as far as, and slightly further than, the centre, looking for signposts to Agnita which, according to the *Atlas Rutier* boasts not one, but two fortified churches.

Moşna

We were not going as far as Agnita, but it was the direction we wanted, and after about 10 km we arrived at Moşna (or Meschen), an undistinguished village but with an imposing fortified church – with an eight-storeyed bell tower – in a potentially pretty setting.

We parked the car and climbed out into the heat. We walked round the building, and found a locked door to the site, but no bell. There was a flight of steps up to a house set in the walls. Henry went up and rang the bell. No answer. We wandered through what appeared to be a garden between the defensive walls, but there was no sign of life. Then we walked all round the outside of the building. A pretty young woman speaking German to a toddler in a push chair told us which house to go to in order to find a key from Frau something or other ('sie spricht Deutsch'). It was the house we had already tried. We tried it again, and, up a slight slope, the Evangelisches Pfarrhaus outside which there was a memorial to a Pfarrer. Still no luck, and we walked disconsolately back to the locked door and exchanged despairing glances, in between taking photos of architectural features.

We had almost decided to abandon our attempt to get in when a dapper little man in sports jacket and tie, reminding me of a nice teacher with a squint from my junior school, bustled up. He spoke only Romanian, but spoke it slow-ly and clear-ly and gave us to understand that he was the head of the local school (ah, yes, the rather drab building the other side of the rusty wire fence), that he had seen us trying to get in and that he would fetch the key from Frau X. Like Henry before him he bounded up the steps, rang the bell and emerged with the key plus the German-speaking lady who opened up for us. He was obviously determined to give us a guided tour, starting with a small but interesting exhibition about Saxon life in the village and a plaque set up on the wall commemorating a visit a few years ago by Prince Charles. The head was delighted to discover that we, too, were British and he sent the German lady hurrying away to the school.

She returned with another lady, very jolly, rather cropped hair and the faint outline of a ginger moustache, who announced that she taught English at the school. She would be delighted (she interpreted) to interpret for us. We said we were delighted to meet her. Although it is not difficult to understand isolated bits of Romanian (it sounds and looks like Dr Zamenhoff's first stab at Esperanto before it dawned on him that he could make it sound *really* daft), decent English was a lot better. We picked our way through the scaffolding (should we interpret this as an encouraging sign of restoration or depressing evidence of decay? We opted for the former) and into the church; 14th century Gothic but rebuilt in 1485. It had suffered an earthquake not so long ago, our guide said, which explained the wooden beams that spanned the nave and kept the pillars from leaning inwards. Most of the glass was still in the windows.

We had the impression that our interpreter had probably never been to an English-speaking country (the fell hand of communism) but her English was nevertheless impressive although, inevitably, a bit hesitant where technical terms such as 'flying buttress' were concerned. I doubt whether I could have done as well in German. We admired the organ (still intact) which had been brought here all the way from Vienna in the eighteenth century. 'Yes,' the lady said. 'We have an organon but we do not have an organon player.' – '*Organist*', Henry corrected. – 'Yes, yes! Thank you! We do not have an *organist player*'. We stopped while our hosts exchanged a few friendly words with a Roma girl who was obviously the cleaner.

We walked around the church outside. We were correct in our assumption that the scaffolding represented restoration. Wheelbarrows and other builders' implements were to be seen, plus a padlocked site office. Money had started to come in, apparently – from the World Bank – after Prince Charles' visit.

Our hosts were keen to show us the folk museum which the head teacher was in the process of creating on the wall walk and in the small rooms leading off it; it was intended to stress the importance to the community of the German element (almost all of whom now appear to have left; certainly no services are held in the church any longer). There were the usual inexplicable farm implements, beehives, butter churns and so on, and the pride of the head's collection – an old-fashioned plug-in telephone exchange. 'Does it still work?' we asked naively. 'Yes, it was in use until last year'. Ideal for repressive régimes: a device enabling – indeed, encouraging – the operator to listen in on any call.

But the visit had one last treat in store. In the farthest tower of the wall walk they had installed a museum of viticulture. White wine had been produced in this particular district for decades, if not centuries. Now they were diversifying with red. The Roma girl had been sent on ahead and had prepared four tumblers of this wine from a large plastic bottle. This was to celebrate the unexpected arrival of two Brits. Henry made it clear, as politely as he could, that he could only permit himself a sip as he was driving, whereas *'my colleague will be only too pleased to sample a glass or two.'* We clinked glasses, bowed slightly over the rims, and then began to drink.

It was immediately apparent why the locals had never bothered with red before: it was absolutely vile. But I was obliged to maintain a rictus grin and emit compliments and pleasantries until I had drained the glass, politely said how much I liked it and so had to endure another glass. Only then were we allowed to leave. We thanked our hosts and left after buying postcards and a map locating other fortified churches from the German lady. She assured us that the cross-country road via Richiş to Biertan was a good one and, trustingly, we set off.

The first half dozen kilometres of brown – on the map – road were perfectly acceptable, but the descent, although gentle, from there to Richiş was fairly appalling – almost as bad as a couple of days ago. However, after Richiş the last few miles down into Biertan (Bierthälm) passed without incident.

Biertan

The village is fairly large and well kept, with a certain air of prosperity, or at least of something-about-to-happen, which makes a pleasant change from most of the lifeless villages we have passed through. We parked in the centre in the least shady spot we could find (N.B.: Henry was driving), climbed out into the baking sun and set off slowly walking round the complex in the hope of finding a door or a bell. The site is quite extensive, with two or three, depending on how you count, defensive walls. We were accosted by two children, a brother and sister who asked for chewing gum, but we ignored them and they swore colourfully (I think) and ran away giggling. Having circumtraipsed the entire sodding site we discovered that walking ten yards in the other direction would have taken us straight to the porter's lodge, with a proper *Kasse* [ticket office] and a Germanophone attendant.

We paid and got in just before a group of elderly Germans arrived on a coach. The church (completed in 1522) is on a hill and is reached via a fairly steep covered wooden stairway. Part of the way up, the red wine having wrought its magic, I stepped out of the staircase into one of the baileys and had a welcome pee. I had just enough time to do up my fly before startling the *Gruftis* (from *Gruft*, a crypt) who were now inching their way up the steps. We charged on ahead and into the church, which is delightfully light and airy and in a reasonable state of repair, in time to be given a lightning explanation of its main features before the coach party arrived.

The guide drew attention to the polyptych altar (late fifteenth/early sixteenth century), the panels of which can no longer be moved. Behind the altar there is a crucifixion scene. As she pointed out, if you walk past it the eyes and the feet follow you.

The feet, eh? New one on me. The other main feature is the door of the sacristy which has an elaborate locking system of nineteen locks, although it is no longer in working order.

When the coach party finally dragged themselves into the building the young guide repeated the tour in a rather sing-song voice which made me suspect that German, or at least Hochdeutsch, was perhaps not her mother tongue. She explained the features again, in somewhat greater detail, as the old people nodded appreciatively, some slightly wary of our presence. *Die sind nicht mit uns, gel?* (They're not with us, are they?) Again, attention was drawn to the pews without backs to accommodate the women's voluminous skirts. The ladies in the party chuckled appreciatively. As the party went outside Henry and I broke free and walked round the first ring wall. The church was the seat of the Lutheran bishops for almost three centuries from the time when it became 'A.B.'[7] down to 1867, and their gravestones are on display in the Bishops' Tower.

After more photographs we went back down to the car and decided to try our luck in the Unglerus (named after Lucas Unglerus, first Lutheran bishop of Transylvania in 1572), described as a 'mittelalterliches Restaurant' in the brochure which we had received from the lad in charge of the nascent tourist office in Sibiu. It was very pleasantly designed with beams and odd staircases and we ate well. I have forgotten what we had except that we consumed a huge amount of mineral water.

At the other end of the dining room were two men talking German. We left more or less at the same time as them and fell into conversation. The younger man (fifty something) was the son of Donauschwaben[8] The elder man (in his seventies) explained that he had lived in the neighbourhood – not Biertan but another village – until 1959 when he had emigrated, or been expelled, to Austria. I think the two men were neighbours somewhere in the Bad

---

[7] AB = Augsburger Bekenntnis – Confession of Augsburg.

[8] Lit. 'Danube Swabians' – ethnic Germans from former Yugoslavia.

Homburg area. The older man said that he went back once a year to visit family (down to one female cousin) and friends. He was sad, but not excessively so, about the fate of the Saxons, and realistic enough to acknowledge that everything had started to go wrong for them when they had allowed themselves to be recruited, more or less enthusiastically, into the Wehrmacht during the war.

After the war almost all the Saxons had had all their property expropriated while several thousand had been sent as slave labour to the Soviet Union, not all of them returning alive. Romanians from other parts of the country had been brought in to fill the gaps, but they had no idea about agriculture, he said. The terraces we had correctly identified on the hillside above the village were, indeed, the remains of a once flourishing wine-growing industry but the incomers were not *bodenständig* (had no roots in the district) and *der Rumäne sucht immer den einfachsten Weg eher als den richtigen* (Romanians always go for the easiest option, rather than the right one) with the result that agriculture had suffered a catastrophic decline.

The trouble today, he said, was that the young men were tending to abandon their own folk and marry *Zigeunermädels* (gypsy girls). Yet he was not overly bitter. The two of them made a great play about the EU and overcoming hostility etc. and aren't you two brilliant linguists: *Sie sprechen fließend Deutsch – und akzentfrei –* which is what almost all Germans exclaim in wonder if you can manage anything more than *Guten Tag*. The older man was of the opinion that two-thirds of recent German émigrés would return from the Federal Republic like a shot if it weren't for the embarrassment of having to admit that they had not made a go of it in Germany.

We parted company and carried on along the white road – leaving the pretty red tiled roofs of the village behind – until we hit the main road west of Dumbrăveni (with an Apalfi chateau somewhere out of sight. To the west of Mediaş – *inhabited almost exclusively by Armenians* in Murray's day – there are a couple of former seats of the Bethlens) and we drove on the remaining twenty odd kilometres to Sighişoara, which is also on the UNESCO list.

We had booked into the Claudiu in the lower town – '*lovely, restful little hotel*', according to Mr Rough, but when we arrived, having discovered it miraculously through wild guesswork, we were told that the lady had made a mistake with the booking and it was not our fault.

Sighişoara

The lady was a beautiful young woman with a mane of chestnut hair, a permanent genuine smile and giggle and an acceptable amount of tanned midriff. She explained what had happened; the upshot was that she had booked us into the Casa Wagner ('*nicely restored*', says Rough) in the upper town in the Cetatea. Did we mind? Not in the slightest; it was what we had wanted in the first place. She said she would come with us to the other hotel so we had the further pleasure of her company as we wound up the side of the hill, through an arch, into the tiny main square and turned left. The hotel was the next building after Dracula's alleged birthplace. The manager of the Casa Wagner spoke to our companion in Hungarian and Henry, to my amazement, joined in. I knew he'd done the language courses, but I had no idea he was *this* good. Respect! He was obviously a great hit, joking with them and describing our itinerary. In the end Miss Hungary, unfortunately, had to make an exit and return to her own establishment. We parked the car in the hotel's back courtyard, checked in and I had a shower in one of the best bathrooms I have ever seen.

Immediately outside the hotel is the Piaţa Cetatii, where some sort of festival was going on. At the end, facing what I take to be the town hall, a sound system had been set up and there was a wooden, fenced stage on which some children, in Hungarian costume, we think, were about to perform. Half a dozen boys wearing what looked like aprons, but which were in fact very broad, flappy white trousers over black boots, came on and danced in formation as half a dozen girls, in two groups of three, took up positions at each end of the stage, each holding aloft a bottle. They sang a piercingly shrieky chorus as the boys danced. Then the girls joined in, too, bossily reminding each other of the steps. Because of the stress pattern we assume the music was Hungarian, too. The festival appeared to have something to do with a local hospital. Perhaps the idea was to raise money for an extension or for equipment. There were a number of stands selling traditional snacks, together with leather goods and jewellery.

But we had sights to see. We wanted to get to the *Bergkirche*, the Church on the Hill, before it shut, whenever that might be, which involved another steep climb up a covered wooden stairway, built in 1642, the Scholars' Stairs. There are 175 steps, in sets of half a dozen, followed each time by a sort of landing. About half way up a young woman was sitting on the steps playing a guitar.

We walked round the church to the west gate which a custodian was about to lock before showing a small party round. After verifying that we spoke German (much better than he did) he let us in to join a slightly surprised group of half a dozen middle-aged Austrians. We were lucky: the Rough Guide maintains that the church is rarely open. It also maintains that the church is 'austere', which is untrue. It was founded in 1345 and finished in 1525. Originally Catholic, it became Lutheran in the 1540s. It is light, bright and airy. The guide showed us tombstones inside the porch which (if I remember correctly) his father had discovered; the marks of the different guilds; the beautiful frescoes – so many remaining in different parts of the church that they must have covered the entire inside surface area at one time; the pulpit; more frescoes on the ceiling, this time of St Matthew, identified by the scales he was carrying (weighing souls), the altar and the organ.

Afterwards, when our guide had locked up and the Austrians had faded away in a very *k.u.k.*[9] manner, he accompanied us back down the steps; his house was at the church end of Str. Scolii. He spoke fluent bad German. He was not a Saxon and neither was his wife, but he sent his children to the local German *Lyceum*. Most of

---

[9] kaiserlich und königlich (imperial and royal, i.e. Habsburg).

the children at the school were non-German, but the parents saw it as a cut above the other schools with, of course, an entrée into a much wider world.

Murray says that *The inhabitants are all German* and, writing in 1939, Elizabeth Kyle said *It was all there; walls, towers, pinnacles, in the old German tradition; an amazing vision of medieval Germany transplanted, as by a miracle, three countries and three civilizations east of the land which had given it birth.*[10] We, however, were not aware of the town being all, predominantly or significantly German. We had the impression that there was a distinct Hungarian presence.

We asked the guide about the folk festival and he confirmed that it was to raise money for the hospital. 'They will also take your blood', he added. And this in Dracula's birthplace... We declined hastily and firmly.

Time for a wander about. The late mediaeval walls are still largely intact, with towers maintained in the past by the different guilds. Thus, there are (anticlockwise from the north) the Shoemaker's tower, Tailors' tower, Furriers' tower, Butchers' tower and Tinsmiths' tower. And, of course, there is the Clock tower. Each day, according to the Rough Guide, *one of seven wooden figures emerges from the belfry on the stroke of midnight* when there is no-one to see its appearance.

We split up and I paid to climb the clock tower to see the museum it contains. I was able to break the climb on the different floors, flattening myself against the wall as I went, as a party of partially sighted Croats gingerly felt their way past and over me, some coming back for a second go.

The museum contains the usual boring stuff about Iron Age man and what he got up to (not very much), with some later artefacts, almost all labelled in Romanian. However, there are some rooms with decent period furniture (eighteenth and nineteenth century) and one floor devoted to localish – born in Sibiu – Saxon hero Hermann Oberth (1894–1989). He is widely regarded as one of the

---

[10] *The Mirrors of Versailles* (1939), p. 99.

pioneers of rocket science, having discovered the idea of propulsion when he stepped from a boat onto dry land and the force of the movement propelled the boat away from shore (or so our guide at the church would have us believe; another version is that his interest in space was fired by reading Jules Verne's *From the Earth to the Moon*, a present from his mother when he was 11). Whether or not this folksy detail is true, there were photos of him well into an advanced age shaking hands with scientists, including Wernher von Braun who was his assistant in the thirties, and assorted spacepersons.

From the very top of the tower you can enjoy a view over the surrounding countryside and the featureless lower town. Brass plates screwed into the breastwork tell you how far it is to London, Beijing and other cities.

I descended and, on a necessarily brief wander back to the hotel, tried to find something, anything, to buy. The town certainly has souvenir shops, but the cult of Dracula is writ large, with T-shirts, dolls and mobiles, but nothing much that an intelligent adult would like to possess. I bought a booklet of photos of the town then saw, in a pavement café outside the Hirscherhaus (Casa cu cerb), the rather gormless looking public schoolboy whom we had seen in Braşov, this time with two companions. I confidently expect to find him in another few days' time with four companions then, late next week, with eight. And so on.

We had dinner on the small terrace at the back of the hotel. The restaurant '*offers an upscale take* (whatever that might mean) *on Romanian dishes*', says Rough. We were virtually the only diners and the two Hungarian waiters, Laszlo and Geza, closed in on us in a pincer movement[11]. This time we drank Silva beer, rather than the otherwise ubiquitous Ursus. Tastes pretty good, much like Bitburger and a cut above Luxembourgish beer. And so to bed after watching part of a film set in the eighteenth century, featuring Bernard Bresslaw, Sid James and Barbara Windsor but, alas, in Hungarian.

---

[11] A linguist's pun.

Back to Cluj

The next morning (the 22nd) Henry informed me that the film was 'Carry On Dick' (Turpin). Slightly worried about the driving conditions and the need to return the car to central Cluj by midday, we had intended to leave by 8 after an early breakfast, but discovered that the restaurant was not going to open until 8. So we left late after paying a derisory bill of about €32 each. The day was pleasantly warm and we found, without difficulty, the E 60 or road no. 13 to Târgu Mureş, the first 20 odd kilometres of which meander up through the type of semi-moorland we had seen from the train between Alba Iulia and Cluj.

Early on the trip we passed through the village of Şoromiclea with an interesting looking ruined castle. Nadeş, too, has a ruin, but a *Schloß* rather than a *Burg*. On through Chendu where the Romanian name has been sprayed out, leaving only the Hungarian Kendu. The villages along this road, and from Târgu Mureş to Cluj, are much more interesting than most of the others we have encountered. They look far more alive, with makeshift shops on the roadside selling basket ware. We passed a small encampment of four horse-drawn wagons, each with several iron hoops over which cloths and tarpaulins were slung. On each the male driver sat engaged in some sort of whittling while the womenfolk were elsewhere, working themselves into the ground.

Târgu Mureş (Marosvásárhely) – *the nearest stat. to the Baths of Barszek… The waters are considered to be efficacious in many disorders* (Murray) – has squares *lined with fine Secession-style edifices* (Rough Guide; 'edifices', eh?), but we saw none of this as we spent almost a dozen kilometres driving edgily along the road out of town, until we hit more or less open country. The countryside around here is heavily populated by Transylvanian standards, with villages scattered all over the plain of the Mureş river, and the small towns through which the main road ran made it difficult to get up any appreciable speed.

As the morning dragged on we became increasingly aware that

we would be late in returning the car, even though it had cost very little to hire and we could easily have afforded to turn up late, although this might have messed up Mr Popescu's chances of getting back to Bucharest before the wolves emerged from the forest. We drove on to Turda, once one of the wealthiest towns in the country thanks to salt mining, whose *wide main street...* *reminded me of Honiton* (Leigh Fermor) where we had intended to break our journey. The Lonely Planet notes that *Turda hit the national headlines in 1997 when hundreds of crows attacked the town, Hitchcock-style*. But we were not interested in this. We simply wanted to stand by the sign saying 'Turda' and take it in turns to photograph each other, oaf-style, concealing the 'A', a prospect which had had us cackling with schoolboy mirth back in Luxembourg. No such luck, however. The sign was quite high off the ground and we had little time to spare.

Cluj

After Turda the road turned into a very impressive dual carriageway for the last 30 km and we sped along overtaking everything, this time giving a very wide berth to the horse-drawn carts which are picturesque and charming everywhere else but a menace on a main road. We drove down into Cluj, past the massive signs erected by the loony mayor to remind all road-users that, in accordance with the Constitution, Romanian is the *only* official language, and past the sign welcoming visitors in a variety of *non-*Romanian languages, including Japanese and Hebrew (but not Hungarian). To my surprise I navigated us successfully to the Continental, where Mr Popescu was waiting and sneering slightly. We had made it with two minutes to spare, but with no time to fill up. He charged us extra for this.

Henry checked in and I dumped my luggage at reception and then, since we were early for Sonia, we had another browse through the neighbouring bookshop. I bought a slim volume (in Romanian but with an English summary) about the former royal family: the dreadful Carol II and the decent but outmanoeuvred Mihai, while Henry stocked up on unlikely looking titles in Hungarian plus dictionaries. Then we bought a bunch of flowers for Sonia and returned to the hotel lobby where she was already waiting for us.

The flowers having gone down well, we set off in search of the 'Roata', the restaurant we had missed on Monday. This time it was open and we sat in the shady front garden drinking beer and eating trout while poor Sonia had a simple salad to soothe her upset stomach. We strolled back through town dodging the cars with streamers: not a wedding but some sort of graduation day. We were treated by Sonia to a 'slushy': a North American delicacy consisting of flavoured crushed ice. Then it was farewells all round and I caught a lonely taxi to the station where I finally acquired a reservation.

Another beautiful new rail car. The booking clerk had a grim sense of humour and had crammed all six first-class passengers into adjacent seats in an open carriage designed to hold a dozen. As the journey proceeded we spread out. There were two elderly and courteous ethnic Hungarian men and a couple of nondescript women all travelling, as far as I could see, to Timişoara, the end of the line. I was only going to Arad, a journey of a mere four hours. I was rather tired and read in a desultory fashion and, when I had managed to move to a seat facing the direction in which we were going, stared out of the window at the rather damp scenery.

Arad

The line goes north west as far as Oradea, *a time capsule preserved for romantics in search of a simpler world* (Lonely Planet; pencil it in for next time), which is only eight miles from Hungary, before heading in a dead straight line south west to Salonta and then wobbling a bit before finally reaching Arad – *a trading town, of 32,729 Inhab., many of whom are Jews* (Murray) or *about the size of Guildford* (Leigh Fermor) or a *fine city of impressive buildings* (Rough Guide) or *not much to see here* (Lonely Planet) – and I saw precisely nothing. I had a four-hour wait in the station hall before my connection at 01.40.

At last the train from Bucharest arrived and I fought my way aboard past a score of young Czech hikers who expanded like Italians to fill every space on the platform. My sleeper was already occupied and a man in his sixties had got as far as removing his jacket, tie and shirt and was standing looking pitiful in his vest. The Schaffner – the same one as on the outward journey – said *Manchmal passiert das – zweimal gebucht* (That sometimes happens – double booked) and unceremoniously booted the other man out, for which I was most grateful.

Braşov: the main square with the black church

Râşnov castle

Bran castle – not a vampire in sight

Fortified church at Prejmer

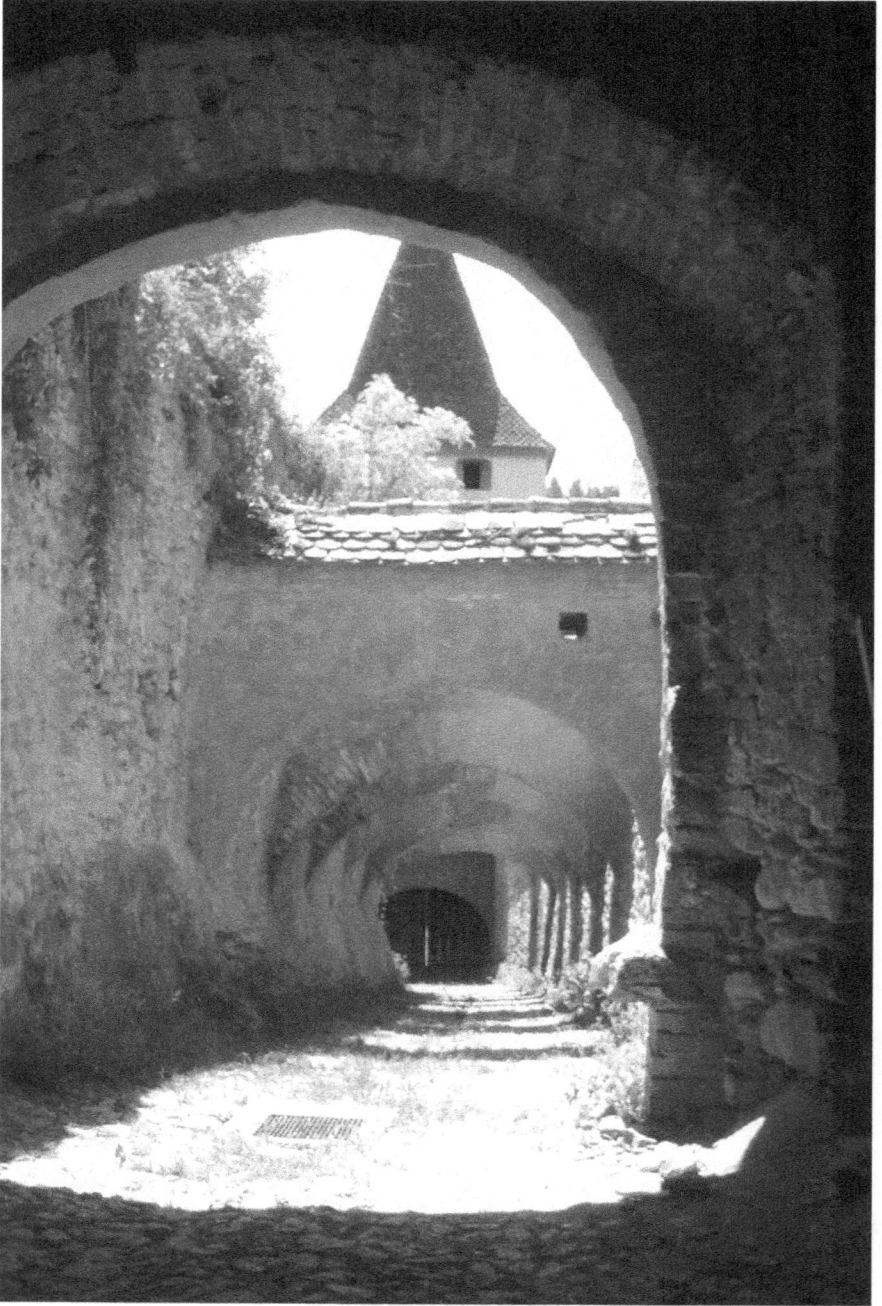

The path up to Biertan

Sibiu – Casa Luxembourg

Sibiu – Bridge of Liars

Sighişoara: the clock tower

Sighişoara: children performing a Hungarian folk dance

CHAPTER 2

Bohemian rhapsodies

—◈—

October 2004

Prague

We spent most of the day (4 October) book-shopping: together at first, then separately. On my way back to the Charles I stopped at the Reykjavik for a very late lunch, then crossed back over the bridge, first stopping at the Galerie U Křizovniku to take in an exhibition of postcards designed by Mucha on display in the brightly lit cellar. They are attractive but add little to an appreciation of the artist already fostered by the dedicated museum the other side of town. They have a period charm, but beyond that the pictures are simply smaller, much smaller, versions of what I have seen before.

We had arranged to meet at the Bazilika svatého Jakuba Většího (St James the greater) at just before 6 p.m. for a concert of organ and brass. It lasted a little over an hour and the eleven pieces ranged from the early sixteenth century (Melchior Franck) to the early twentieth (Max Reger), with obligatory visits *en route* to Vivaldi and Telemann. The church itself is very beautiful, and (interesting fact...) has the second largest nave in Prague after the cathedral. Having the players behind you (up by the organ) has the effect of making you concentrate on the music, rather than the musicians.

Hrad luck

The weather was decidedly hot (5 October) – low to mid-twenties – and we covered about 170 km on a leisurely trip down to Tábor via Šelmberk, which does not appear in the *Kammený Klíč* (Steinschlüssel)[12].

> As Wikipedia says: '*You can visit the ruins of a castle from the 13th century with a well-preserved bergfried tower as an observation tower that has survived to the present day. The castle remains are now a part of a historical-craft educational centre whose purpose is to inform the general public about craftsmanship of our ancestors. The centre includes multiple workshops, a forge, a pottery oven or, for example, a small herb garden*'. The educational centre wasn't there when we visited.

We could see the top of the tower in the distance and drove along tracks to a signpost with a place to park the car next to a more modern building. From here we walked past the latter's grounds, which included a mock-up of a wooden fort (perhaps it's a children's home), for a couple of hundred meters to the castle.

The remains consist essentially of a circular main tower, with the ruins of the curtain wall and a few other unidentified buildings. Plastic tape, signs saying 'Keep out' and posts indicated the recent presence of archaeologists. The information we had found on opening times proved to be hopelessly inaccurate and in fact the castle was officially shut while we were there, with a low-slung chain across the entrance. We solved this problem by stepping over it. The tower is supposed to house a collection of jewels or relics so perhaps this is why they bother with a *Kasse* and official opening times. Durdík[13] says the castle, of the *bergfritového*

---

[12] A handy guide to ca. 340 historical buildings in the Czech Republic, with notes on history and opening times, for example.

[13] Tomáš Durdík was the Grand Old Man of Czech castellology. Quotes from his work are from the English translation he provides.

typu[14], was first mentioned in 1318 but was abandoned by the seventeenth century.

We walked back to the car to find a motorcyclist also trying to work out the opening times. He commented on the beautiful weather which I failed to understand. He was talking about *počasí* (the weather) while I misheard it as *počítač* (computer). We had a meaningless conversation, then he smiled nervously, crossed himself and legged it.

Tábor

Tábor was named by the Hussites after the mountain of the Transfiguration of Christ in the New Testament. We parked in the old town centre and wandered up to the main square, Žižkovo náměstí, (Žižka square) with a statue of the great man on the northern side. Under Hussite rule all faiths were tolerated, with the obvious exception of Catholicism, although killjoy Žižka is said to have supervised the burning of members of the Adamite sect who went in for nudism during their religious ceremonies (trying to recreate the innocence of the garden of Eden, or so they said). We had a peek inside the Děkanský kostel, more extensive viewing being prevented by wires all over the place linked up to an alarm system. The tourist office on the square was shut, so we wandered about aimlessly then walked back to the car and set off to find our hotel, the Palcát.

One of its selling points, from the Internet, is: *'Capacity of hotel hall is 1200 persons'*. We assumed this meant a vast lobby which would take several minutes to cross, but this was not the case. The receptionist issued me with a card to put on the dashboard to indicate that we were bona fide parkers.

When we walked away from reception we noticed that everything was in hideous dark brown or dark yellow paint and the hotel's two lifts looked and felt very unsafe (sudden surges of

---

[14] In other words, it has a bergfrit (> German Bergfried) or keep.

movement). We cautiously took one each to ascend to our floor. Typical unreconstructed Communist-era hotel designed for visiting delegations from somewhere implausible like Mongolia: long, dull corridors with dusty plastic flowers in a bowl at one end and bedroom doors made of plywood. *'All rooms'*, the website claims, *'are equipped with toilette* [sic], *bathroom, TV set, telephone and radio'*. Not so: there is no radio and you can only call reception, not an outside line, from the super-ironic retro Bakelite phone.

I discovered the phone's limitations when I tried and failed to ring home. I then phoned reception and had this pointless conversation:

> Me: Hello? Reception? I want to phone my wife in Luxembourg?
> Reception: Moment......... brrrrrrrrr
> *Try again.*
> Me: Hello, I want to phone my wife.
> Reception: Moment.......moment .... [long pause]
> Other voice: Hello?
> Me: Hello, I want to phone my wife in Luxembourg.
> Other voice: Your wife is in other room -
> Me: Y e e e e e s,... in our house in Luxembourg.
> Other voice: Your wife not here?
> Me: No
> Other voice: She is in other room?
> Me: Chtěl bych zatelefonovat ženou v Lucembursku *[I would like to phone my wife in Luxembourg]*
> Other voice: You must come to reception. Only possible from reception [hangs up].

I went to reception and had an abridged rerun of this conversation, then phoned, obliged to half lean over the counter at reception to reach the phone, while hordes of teenage girls in their glad rags sashayed past on their way to a *Taneční kurz* in the big room at the back. This must be the hall that accommodates a thousand plus.

It then occurred to me that it might be a good idea to follow up on the idea of the *'safe, underground garage'* referred to on the website, so I tackled reception again.

> Me: You have given me a piece of paper for the car park, but can I use the underground garage?
> Receptionist: You want to park car?
> Me: It's already parked, and you've given me a piece of paper...
> Receptionist: You want piece of paper?
> Me: No, I was wondering whether I could use your garage?
> Receptionist: With piece of paper?
> Me (growing desperate and probably quite ungrammatical): No, look, err...chtěl bych že muj auto stojí v garaži... *[lit: I would like my car to be in the garage]*
> Receptionist (indignantly): I understood first time!

We decided not to give the resto a try, but instead set off in search of what had been our no. 1 choice hotel, the Dvořák. We had been unable to stay there because, after initially claiming they had no idea whether they had any rooms free, they decided they hadn't. It had only opened on 1 August so perhaps their computer had been having teething trouble.

The restaurant, however, was first class: a vaulted cellar seating about two dozen people at widely spaced-out tables, with another concealed room in parallel. The vaulting meant that we could make out with perfect ease a droning Dutchman boring his dinner companion to death about twenty feet away. I cannot remember what we ate, except that it was slightly on the *nouvelle cuisine* side, but the bill, including a tip, came to the equivalent of €100, helped along by deadly *apéros* and two bottles of Moravian wine to drown our sorrows at the hopelessness of the Palcát. When we came to call for the bill the young waitress misunderstood and assumed, not unreasonably, that we wanted a third bottle of wine.

We finished the evening with a visit to a low bar on the main square opposite the Děkanský kostel where we knocked back a couple of dirt cheap, but strikingly good, beers. And so, tired but legless, back to the Cosmonaut and its army cots.

Another encounter with the rubber world: we descended (6 October) to breakfast to find that the menu included scrambled eggs on a bed of onions. I imagine this was one of those traditional dishes based on something which Žižka may have eaten before a crucial battle, or perhaps it was just a joke. Instead we both opted for an omelette – which came with a massive side order of onions.

We had decided, before moving north, to give the local museum a whirl. It is largely devoted to the Hussite movement and, although the captions to almost all the exhibits (except the obvious ones) are in Czech only, it was worth the money; and we discovered that a *palcát*, the name of our surreal hotel, is the word for a mace, or club for use in battle. Along with the chalice it is one of the common Hussite symbols. The exhibition included battle tactics. A favourite ploy was to park the 'battle cars', primitive tanks, at the top of a hill and then use them either as a defensive wall to ward off cavalry attacks or as a point from which to rush down screaming and defeat the enemy in an ambush. It appears that the one-eyed Žižka (portraits, even contemporary ones, were not unanimous about which eye) never lost a battle, although one or two of his sieges had to be abandoned.

I was first down to breakfast on the 7th and ordered another omelette. It came without onions, presumably because I had left yesterday's offering. Ivor then arrived and made a great point of making clear to the waiter that he did not, repeat *not*, want onions with his omelette. When it came it was accompanied by two enormous gherkins, looking like bright green severed penises.

Střehov

Střehov (Ger. *Schreckenstein*) – is a Lobkowicz possession – about which Rough enthuses: *a dramatic nightmare fairy-tale pile built into a bleak, black, rocky outcrop high above the river* (the alliteration, the 'k' sounds, is pleasing, but the rest is misleading). There is nothing nightmarish about it whatsoever – and Karel Hynek Mácha (Bohemia's Byron) visited three times – except, perhaps, the plaque commemorating the fact that after a visit here and clambering about the ruins in the moonlight Wagner was inspired to write *Tannhäuser*. The 'fairy-tale' bit came later after we had hung around in the rain for ten minutes waiting for the guided tour to start.

The guide was a pleasant lady in her sixties with good, albeit slightly ungrammatical German (possibly the daughter of a German who had been allowed to stay on after the war). The tour was fairly uninspiring: only a few rooms can be visited, the first of which enables you to gawp in disbelief, from behind a rope, at crude papier-mâché models of (from left to right) the Devil, a vampire, a gaggle of witches and a few goblins. I tried to feign polite interest, because I didn't want to hurt the lady's feelings, but Ivor took a more honest view, with stage whispers of 'for God's sake let's get out of here'.

The guide also showed us a room in which there were reproductions of engravings of the castle and carefully explained each one, the explanation consisting of little more than reading out the captions, which, because not illiterate, we could do for ourselves. We clambered about a bit more up slippery, steep steps in the rock, took loads of photos and made our way back to the car.

Prague again

We were caught by a quite unexpected traffic jam on our way in – locals heading off for the weekend, I imagine – and at one point were crawling along a broad avenue named after Milada Horáková. She was a lawyer and MP for the unfortunately named National Socialist party after the war and until the February putsch. She had then joined an illegal bourgeois opposition group but had been arrested in 1950. The group were tortured into confession then made to appear in a show trial. Being brave, or foolhardy, and relying on her legal training she argued back in court, which simply enraged the Communists who hanged her in June of that year.

We decided to treat ourselves to somewhere special for our last night in Mitteleuropa. In the end we walked along Tomašska to the Waldštejnská hospoda on the near-eponymous square.

As it is slightly off the evening beaten track we had no trouble in finding a table, one of those affairs which always has an extra bar or leg to stop you getting close enough to eat in comfort. We had a meal consisting largely of game, preceded by *apéros*, washed down with copious amounts of local wine and ending up with a wickedly expensive brandy each in one of those novelty type glasses that make you feel like a dwarf. It was Ivor's turn to pay and the bill, including a tip came to about CZK3.700, which is farcically expensive for the Czech Republic, though not for Western Europe. He pronounced it the best ever meal in this country. As the resto's own propaganda rightly says: it is *'known for its perfect service and excellent cooking. Its Czech and international dishes, game and fish are certain to please even the most discerning palates'*. All true, although I wouldn't claim to have a particularly 'discerning' palate.

May 2007

We left Dresden at a reasonable hour on the 15th and headed out of town, back on to the motorway and eastward bound to the Polish border near Görlitz, or Zgorzelec in Polish. The city looks reasonably attractive from its website, with the German part to the west of the river; the Polish part to the right.

My old landlord in Bremen, Herr Praske, came from here. He had served in the Wehrmacht and been interned on the Isle of Man with Bert Trautmann, later goalkeeper for Manchester United. The only English Praske had picked up was 'bloody farking son of a bitch' and 'neffer meint, soon be Chrrristmas'. I imagine Trautmann knew a little more.

We crossed into Poland without incident and then headed south on the short cut into north-eastern Czech Republic.

Frýdlant

The trip to Frýdlant, a mere ten kilometers or so after the border, was quite straightforward, and when we hit the town we curved up the hill to the castle car park and there discovered that we would have to wait (it was about a quarter to twelve) until one o'clock for the next trip, despite my careful preparatory work. Nothing for it but to wander down into the small town.

A ten-minute walk took us down and across the river and into the old town square. Like so many places in rural Bohemia, the German origins of the town were unmistakeable, although now it is rather drab. We wandered round the town, finding nothing much to do, then wandered back up to the *zámek* in time for the guided tour, and had to wait again.

The Rough Guide claims that Frýdlant could well have been the model for Kafka's castle, which seems quite plausible. He was very fond of it. It looks slightly gloomy from the outside (the weather not helping), with its fading yellow walls with the trompe l'oeil stonework painted on, but we were glad to have got there since it is one of *the* sites for castle buffs. We entered one courtyard then had to climb steeply up to the upper courtyard and through another courtyard before the tour proper could begin.

We had the German guided tour and the young female guide recited names and dates with the enthusiasm of a robot with a dying battery. *Hier sehen Sie Friedrich von Räääädern – hier sehen Sie Katharina von Räääädern … Hier sehen Sie Melchior von Räääädern* and so on. The Von Rederns bought the lordship in 1558 but made the mistake of being on the losing side at the battle of the White Mountain and their estate was confiscated in 1620 and given to the rapacious Wallenstein. After his assassination in 1634 it passed to the Gallas family and then the Clam-Gallas branch. The last male heir, Franz, died in 1930. Another series of dates followed…

The family took the revolutionary step of opening the castle to the public over two centuries ago (in 1801). When we toured the kitchens one member of the party (there were a number of elderly

Ossies) said that on his previous visit – in the mid 1950s – he had been shown round by the last Princess's cook, who had been allowed to stay on, or at least show people round, after the Communist coup d'état.

The castle is very richly decorated with period furnishings, arms, paintings and so on, and there is a whole flight of rooms on the top floor, one opening onto another as far as the eye could see – suites for visitors – with another row of rooms above them under the roof, all arranged in such a way that guests could move about unnoticed as they indulged their affairs. Everything seems to be in an extraordinary state of preservation. The state has obviously pumped money into it; it is one of the top attractions of the Czech Republic.

Frýdštejn

From Frýdlant we drove southward through the outskirts of Liberec, German Reichenberg (seat, for a few weeks, of the short-lived Deutschböhmen province of Austria in 1918; also birthplace of Henlein, the Sudeten German 'Führer'), and on very minor roads which wound down to Frýdštejn, a ruined mediaeval castle reached up a very steep path from a car park beneath the site. When we finally made it to the ruin itself we still had to climb a set of metal steps to a desk where an old guy was happy to take our money and issue us with little folders showing, on one side, a photo of the ruin as it is today and, on the other, an artist's impression of what it might have looked like in its heyday (ca. 1500).

Building began in 1320–1340, although the first written record of the castle dates from 1385. The best known (but not to me) owner was Bohuš z Kováně (1406–1460), who supported the emperor Sigismund during the Hussite Wars and helped in the defence of Karlštejn. One of his successors was the sibilantly alliterative Zikmund Zápsky ze Záp. By 1591 the castle had been abandoned. For 130 years (1653–1783) it belonged to the Augustinerkirche of Vienna (which had become the Imperial court church in 1634).

What remains of the castle is on several different levels on the hillside, all – and the tower, too – reached by rather scary open metal stairways. The living quarters must have been fairly cramped at the best of times, but at least the occupants would have been pretty fit from all that climbing up and down. There are wonderful views over the plain towards Trosky (where Ivor and I went years ago) and a number of other castles.

Litoměřice

When I had confirmed the booking on 24 April, offering my credit card details, the Hotel Salva Guarda had replied, with what sounded like offended dignity, *'We would not like your credit card details. Necessary steps we will dispose and make understood till at your payment.'* They had also enclosed a note saying:

> **Reservation only to the 17 clock around.**
> **Late carriage-drive is necessity**
> **In advance announce. From 17 clock around evolution place**
> **other interested person.**

Can't say fairer than that, so I phoned the hotel from Frýdštejn to say we would be arriving a little later than 5, more like 6, which did not appear to be a problem. The drive took us south west then a north west stretch, jerking to the left, then right again as we skirted dismal Terezin until we hit the Labe, crossed it and found ourselves in Litoměřice, *'arguably the most appealing town in North Bohemia'*, according to the Rough Guide, and I certainly wasn't prepared to argue. Most of the population (Leitmeritz was overwhelmingly German-speaking) were expelled in 1945, but today it is a bustling little place.

We crossed the river, turned right and then veered left past the old town walls and up Dlouhá (Long Street), past the kostel všech svatých (All Saints Church) and hit Mírové náměsti (Peace square), essentially a car park, with the hotel on the left on the corner of a street leading to the town's theatre. The Salva Guarda is unmistakable: an attractive sgraffitoed building named after the sixteenth century owner (the emperor's bodyguard). We took the hotel's remaining parking space on the square, Ivor having to get out and struggle with the bollard marking the spot.

Just as well we had alerted the hotel to our late carriage-drive, as two middle-aged north American women were being turned away as we arrived. The reception area was comfy, with a very large teddy bear reclining on a chaise longue (probably been on his feet all day), and there were broad stone stairs leading up two flights to our rooms. Mine was at the front of the building, an oriole affair with windows looking onto pieces of Peace Square from three sides, and translucent orange curtains to rob me of the chance of a lie-in.

The hotel issued me with a parking permit with the stern warning that *'A car-park can't be insured against a stealing'*.

Before retiring for the night (or simply 'going to bed'), I had a look at the folder of bumf about the hotel in my room. It had evidently been used by partisans, or dyslexics, since one entry said: *'Hotel SALVA GUARDA can accommodate only a fully registered resistant'*.

I would note in passing that Karel Hynek Mácha died here in 1836, exhausted no doubt from having visited just about everywhere else. Last year in Prague I bought a bilingual version of Macha's *Máj*, but regret to say I have not got very far with it. Mind you, there's quite a nice feel to it.

Bezděz

Off north-eastwards on the scenic route to Bezděz. There we parked in the little car park in the village near the fishpond at the bottom of the hill, then hiked our way to the top, passing a series of wayside shrines: Stations of the Cross, I suppose. The Rough Guide is a bit odd: *'tour in English... you get to explore it without taking a guided tour'*.

It was founded by King Přemysl Ottokar II in 1264. At one time it was a prison housing the young Václav II (1271–1305) and his mother, Queen Kunhuta, then later became a monastery and subsequently a pilgrimage place (which would explain *les gares de la croix*). Needless to say, Mácha had been there. The owner from 1610–1620 was Václav starši Berka z Dubé (Wenceslas the older berk?) whose estates were confiscated after the Battle of the White Mountain and it was subsequently snapped up by greedy Wallenstein. On his death the monks took over, losing all their valuables (tee hee) when the Prussians occupied the castle in 1778, until 1789 when it reverted to the Wallensteins, before being taken over by the state in 1918.

The walls still retain a lot of the original white render. The chapel is in a reasonable state of repair, with new glass in the windows. It still has its roof, as does the bailiff's quarters, a three-storey affair, and the Great Tower with a magnificent view, not just across the valley but also down onto the ruined outworks. We took photos of every conceivable feature, before setting off again back down to the car.

About halfway down, between Stations, I managed to slip, despite wearing walking boots and despite the fact that the path was reasonably dry; but the stones were very uneven. Oddly enough, I managed to fall forwards, hurting my left foot (slightly), my left palm (slightly) and achieving a nasty deep graze on the left shin. It hurt like hell, but I insisted on carrying on walking to ensure that I could in fact walk. Yes, I could. Talk about brave.

Karlovy Vary

And now for some unbridled luxury. It is a fairly straightforward journey to Karlovy Vary if you happen to be a crow, about 145 km, which is quite a lot at the end of the afternoon. The town was named after the emperor Karl IV. According to the legend... but no,

I won't bore you. *Prominente* started arriving in the late 17th century to take the waters. Bach came twice; Goethe 13 times between 1785 and 1823. Marx wrote part of *Das Kapital* here between 1874 and 1876.

The road winds down, down and ends up in what must have been the old centre with the Grand Hotel Pupp right in front of us: *'They don't come better (nor more expensive) than this outside Prague'*, says Mr Rough and, of course, has to spoil it by adding *'though the decor is pretty stunning, the service is not as good as it should be for the price'*. I can't agree, but since I got a special rate through Booking dot com, perhaps the service was commensurate with the price.

We pulled up outside, unloaded and handed the key to a flunkey who drove off to God knows where (in fact, the private car park round the corner), while we filled in the usual forms and went up to our rooms. Mine looks straight up the river – Stará louka to the left, Nová louka to the right – towards the colonnade in the distance ('louka' means meadow…). We luxuriated in our rooms although, wait a moment, for this money you would expect a bathmat: *I* would, because I always flood strange bathrooms.

I read the hotel notes and discovered that *'We have to ask you to wear formal suite* (sic) *in our restaurants'*, signed by a lady called Andrea Pfeffer-Ferklová. We descended to the restaurant and its *'unrivalled Neoclassical decor'* (Rough). There were few other diners, and most of them seemed to be Russians who had ignored Peppa Pig's request: various forms of casual wear (track suits, tee-shirts) with overpainted mistresses (not fat enough to be wives). The meal was excellent. We had a table overlooking the street and could smile in a superior way at people from cheaper hotels wandering past with their umbrellas up.

We had a brief walk afterwards then decided we would rather stay dry. The hotel was used as the setting for the gambling scene in the 2006 remake of 'Casino Royale'. I went in search of the casino. It is not the same as the one in the film – perhaps only the hotel's façade was used – but is concealed from public gaze. I strode in and was immediately stopped by a burly bouncer who wanted to see my passport, which he passed to a bored young woman who carried out a security check. Finding me blameless, she issued me with a plastic card which says 'Czech Casinos' on it and is apparently not transferable, although since there is no sign of my name on it this seems rather odd. I then wandered about the casino. The atmosphere was anything but glamorous. There were a few tables with gamblers (mainly Chinese and Russian) but no blondes in low-cut dresses, no whiff of excitement, no hushed expectation as fortunes were won or lost, just a lot of bluish cigarette smoke hanging in the stale air as the bored middle-aged punters killed time and themselves. It is hard to imagine a more lacklustre pastime than gambling.

Ascension day (the 17th) and, after ascending, we descended to breakfast, a buffet affair in what looked like a part-time ballroom. Not many guests, and most of them Russian with fractious children.

Bečov nad teplou

Off south on the 21 km via Horní Slavkov (cf. Horní Bolíkov, which we found a few years ago on the road from Telč to Jindřichův Hradec) to Bečov nad teplou, which the Rough Guide fails to include despite the fact that it has a very decent zámek, with a ruined castle attached. It is at the end of the village's main, or only street, just before it swings to the right, so if you park (as we did) up the street and look downhill you see the iron railings of the zámek with domestic buildings to the left and right (those on the right now housing the ticket office, toilets and a souvenir shop) with a gravel path sweeping on past formal gardens up to the entrance of the manor.

Access was, of course, by guided tour only and, of courser, we had just missed the last tour before lunch, which left us having to eat in the one decent eatery just up the road (the imaginatively named Restaurace U Zámku), which looked from the outside as if it might be popular with bikers, but was full of middle-aged foreign (mainly German) culture seekers like us. We had a decent meal for just over 400 crowns. It was still drizzling slightly when we moved outside and back to the zámek to buy our tickets. We killed time by wandering around the formal gardens and taking photos.

> The castle was founded in the early fourteenth century, the first documentary evidence dating from 1314. The village was given a municipal charter in 1399 (but even today the population is under a thousand). Its main source of revenue was tin mining which made it a very rich town. It was confiscated by the Emperor Ferdinand I in 1547. Two quadratic towers were added to the tower in the sixteenth century and, as an Imperial garrison town, it was seriously damaged in the last year of the Thirty Years War by the Swedish General Königsmark. The Baroque octagonal Schloss, built partly on the foundations of the mediaeval fortifications, dates from 1750–1753. It has been open to the public since 1996; only the Schloss can be visited, not the Burg (which looks quite interesting). In 1813 it was acquired by the Belgian aristocratic family of Beaufort-Spontin in whose possession it remained until 1945 when the last count had to flee. Unusually for a Czech aristo he was on the side of the Nazis.

The interior consists of collections of *objets d'art*, paintings and tapestries formerly belonging to the last owners. The octagonal chapel with its frescos has been restored and is worth a visit. Bečov's selling point – for the simple minded – is the Romanesque reliquary of St Maurus which Alfred de Beaufort had acquired for 2,500 francs and had restored. When the family fled in 1945 they buried it in the garden. Following a tip-off that a businessman was offering money to have it dug up and transported out of the country, the police managed to find the shrine which is now on display in a special treasury in the Schloss. This cost extra and we were not remotely interested.

Plzeň

The Hotel Irida has four stars, and it may be that because of this hint of luxury it is not included in the Rough Guide (although the Pupp in Karlovy Vary *is*, so that theory collapses almost immediately). The front of the hotel has guarded parking (the receptionist showed us the 24-hour surveillance cameras) next to a building site which, in turn, is next to a footbridge over the Mže. The hotel is quite pleasant, although the leaflet shows all the rooms bathed in a reddish-orange glow which lends it the popular image of a brothel, and the inner rooms face onto a narrow courtyard perhaps only 15 to 20 feet across. The rooms were OK with the usual excess of furniture.

We dumped our stuff and set off over the footbridge onto a busy (I first typed 'busty') highway which we ran across, then climbed up into the city to náměstí Republiky and the cathedral with its 'bile-green' spire (Rough: for God's sake, man, try to *like* something).

We wandered round the city – the centre is really quite compact and easily manageable – looking for somewhere to eat mentioned in the leaflet we found at the hotel. Most of the places that looked promising turned out to be pretty full, but at length, on Pražská (right at the end, so only just 'on' it), we came across a bright modern hotel, U Zvonu (the name rings a bell), with its own restaurant. The dining room was elegant and largely empty. We had an excellent meal, and returned at a leisurely pace to the Irida where, to show willing, we had a couple of glasses of wine in the bar. And so to bed. In my room I managed to bang my right shin on the corner of a piece of furniture that had been lying in wait and so, combined with my scar from Bezděz, I look as though I bear some unusual stigmata.

Saxon-Bohemian Crusade (October 2009)

We skirted Bautzen which, because it was illuminated, looked very attractive. Walter Kempowski and his brother, incarcerated there for eight years from 1948 to 1956, probably found it less appealing. The road wound on to Zittau at which point the directions seemed to go wrong, or I was tired or, more likely I find it increasingly difficult to read small print. Then there was a slight altercation as to whether we were going to Bertsdorf or Hörnitz. In the end, no surprise to me, we arrived at the latter and the Schloßhotel Althörnitz in soft but persistent rain.

We parked the car, checked in and went straight to the restaurant: *2001 wurde dem Haus das blaue 'F' der Feinschmecker verliehen*, as it said in the folder in my room. The maître d' was a stolid-looking character a bit like the good soldier Schwejk, and possibly a former nightclub bouncer. I had pavé de saumon; Ivor, a *Rinderfilet*.

At a neighbouring table a party of half a dozen locals, some men, some women, seemed to be having a jolly time trying out every alcoholic drink on offer, laughing loudly and slapping the table.

Schloß Althörnitz was built 1651–1654 and purchased in 1881 by Hans Rudolf von Sandersleben, a *sächsischer Kammerherr*. The family were dispossessed in 1945 and *von 1948 bis 1991 wurden Ferienurlauber des Gewerkschaftsbunds der DDR hier unter einfachen Bedingungen betreut*. The *Bedingungen* are no longer so *einfach*: I had a large and pleasant room with sliding-door windows taking up the whole of the exterior wall. On the other hand, there was not much to see out of the window. About twenty feet away an earth embankment rose up ten or fifteen feet, with roofs and smoking chimneys in the background. In 1990 the Schloß was restored on the initiative of Rudolf von Sandersleben (relation), banker and honorary Swedish consul (and new owner), and it has been functioning as a hotel since February 1996, having been given three-star status in November of that year.

Up early and into the breakfast 'Atrium' by 8.30, a stylised traffic light in the *Gästeinformation* having alerted us to peaks and troughs. I had the full Saxon breakfast: sausages, bacon and scrambled eggs plus loads of bread, cheese and ham. This may sound greedy (in fact it sounds *very* greedy), but we have decided, as on previous occasions, to eschew – rather than chew – lunch and concentrate our time and efforts on castles. The neighbouring revellers from last night sat a few tables away, looking slightly, but only slightly, chastened.

We settled up and drove off into enemy territory: a brief visit to Poland then into the Czech Republic and a lousy road into Hrádek nad nisou (German *Grottau an der Neisse*) where there seemed to be road works everywhere and we had to take four or five sides of a triangle and guess our way to the main and only square, the Horní náměstí. We visited the tourist office where a young woman showed us on a map the route to take to get to Grabštejn – the Liberec road.

Grafenstein

We drove to the castle – *der Grafenstein..., eine sehr alte und noch bewohnbare Burg mit Kapelle aus dem Jahre 1387. Vom 50 m hohen Turme schöne Aussicht*[15] – arriving at about half past ten. Ivor and I walked up the steep path to the *hrad* for our 11 o'clock guided tour with Kateřina Koudelková with whom I had corresponded.

The *hrad* is being repaired. We crossed the inner courtyard to use the toilet (very clean). Roofers were throwing broken tiles and bits of loose masonry down into a roped-off section of the courtyard.

We went to the *pokladna*, bought tickets (CZK100 each) and arrived almost simultaneously with Kateřina Koudelková, which spared me from trying to explain in broken Czech to the attendant exactly who we were. Kateřina was a very pleasant, under-age looking girl, although with a *magistra* under her slender belt she couldn't have been that young. Her English was very good, but she didn't realise that a royal representative is a viceroy and not a vice-king (we explained what this might mean and she giggled), and she thinks it possible to use the word 'author' instead of 'painter',

---

[15] Josef Rabl: Illustrierter Führer durch Böhmen, A. Hartleben's [sic] Verlag 1913, p. 252.

'sculptor' etc. Had she had any other visitors today? – Only three soldiers. Every nice girl loves a soldier.

The precise origins of the castle are not known. In the second half of the thirteenth century, says the guide book, it came into the possession of the Dohna family who held it for the next three hundred years, although after a protracted feud (1385–1402) they had to surrender most of their possessions in Germany to the rulers of Saxony. In the fifteenth century it successfully withstood a siege of several weeks by the troops of the *Sechsstädtebund* – six towns in Upper Lusatia (including Bautzen and Görlitz). In the latter half of the sixteenth century the Dohna family were obliged to sell up to the imperial vice-chancellor, Dr Georg Mehl of Strehlitz (or Jiří Mehl ze Střelic), who converted the gothic castle into a Renaissance residence from 1564 to 1569, although in 1586 he was forced to sell up because of *die sich verschlechternde Stellung am Hofe von Kaiser Rudolf II*. [What does this mean? That he fell out of favour, or that the Kaiser was becoming increasingly odd?] *sowie finanzielle Schwierigkeiten*.

The castle suffered considerable damage in the Thirty Years War (when the main tower was gutted by fire). After a series of owners, Graf Johann Wenzel von Gallas acquired the castle. In 1818 Graf Clam-Gallas had the new château built in classicist style. The last Clam-Gallas in the male line, Graf Franz, died aged 76 in 1930, *und mit ihm auch die alten Zeiten*. I note the absence of *guten*.

Franz's marriage to Maria von Hoyos-Sprinzenstein had produced seven daughters. 'Lucky man', said Kateřina brightly. Ivor (two daughters) and I (one daughter) exchanged pitying glances. At one time the family owned large parts of northern Bohemia including Frýdlant.

With the expropriation of the family after 1945 the castle fell into decline and a report in 1979 highlighted the urgent need for repairs to prevent its complete ruination. It was opened (partially) to the public on 15 June 2001.

The castle has the usual representative rooms of the eighteenth and nineteenth centuries, a portrait gallery and – the high point – a chapel. It also contains a lot of contemporary furniture, overspill from the North Bohemian Museum in Liberec. Our tour, however, started with a trip down into the cellars where brightly lit glass cases contained samples of bits of gemstone to be found in the region. This is the castle explorer's worst nightmare – being invited to take an interest in something that is intrinsically dull. Other things in this category would include reproductions (not even the real thing) of Greek statues, the late duke's coin collection and a display of lady so-and-so's fans or combs or hair-brushes.

Georg Mehl was a well-travelled man and he was responsible for commissioning the murals in St Barbara's chapel, which bear the dates 1571 and 1579. The guidebook maintains that they are comparable to the best of contemporary Viennese courtly art and similar in style to the works of the Italian-Dutch painter Friedrich Sustris (1540–1599), a pupil of Vasari. The chapel had only just been restored when we arrived, and there were bits of plastic sheeting, buckets and rope still lying around. The chapel has an upper gallery which the guidebook keeps quiet about. But when there is something to say, the guidebook seems to repeat the same information over and over again. But enough! The murals are very beautiful, marred only by the fact that in the Last Supper Jesus, or one of the disciples, seems to be doubled up in agony.

The portrait gallery contains, inter alia, a painting of Josefine Clam-Gallas, née Clary-Aldringen, to whom Beethoven dedicated one or several works. *Ah! Perfido* (Op. 65), 'Aria composta e dedicata alla Signora di Clari di L. v. Beethoven', was definitely inspired by her, and the Sonatinas in C minor (WoO 43a) and C major (WoO 44a), the Adagio in E flat major (WoO 43b) and the *Theme and Variations* in D major (WoO 44b) may have been written 'pour la belle J.', as inscribed on an autograph copy of the *Adagio*. He must have really taken a shine to her.

There are also two paintings – 'Nachtlager' and 'Überfall' – by Francesco Casanova (1730–1805), younger brother of *the* Casanova.

The whole castle was taken over after the war by the Czechoslovak army, and the Czech military still occupies the newer building which appears to have been repainted fairly recently.

At the castle we had picked up a leaflet about other places to visit in Northern Bohemia. We decided to give Sychrov a try, the only place reasonably near that appeared to be open. We had never heard of it. It lies between Liberec and Turnov.

Sychrov

Shortly after leaving the motorway, a pleasant drive of a mile or two along a winding road with tall hedges – it could have been deepest Surrey – took us to a huge open village green and car park with the château off to the right. We arrived at a quarter past one and were told – Czech, gesticulations and the number '14.00' scrawled on a piece of paper – to come back at 2 p.m. We realised we had almost no Czech money between us so we rejoined the motorway, turned off at Turnov, a bit of a turn-off (joke), where we found a cash point. This time I withdrew a more plausible 2,000Kčs. Then we drove back to Sychrov, still with time to spare, wandered round, relieved ourselves next to trees planted with some forethought a century and a half ago by Duke Kamil then visited the cafeteria – *U Konradu* – just across the car park. We ordered two coffees and the waitress, with an amused simile, said *Vše?* (is that all).

We paid for tickets to the *zámek* – *trasa* A (CZK100 each); other tours were not available at this time of year – and for permission to take photos (CZK50 each) which meant displaying a nice badge, then wandered through the courtyard, looking at the coats of arms displayed in stone around the tops of the walls. The former owners, the Dukes of Rohan, originated in Brittany but had left France at the time of the Revolution, becoming citizens of the Habsburg empire. During the war the Germans set up a puppet government in Brittany which was presided over by a member of this family. The last resident owner – Alain Anton Joseph Adolf Ignaz Maria de Rohan (1893–1976), third prince Rohan, 13th duc de Montbazon and duc de Bouillon, 14th prince de Guémené, prince de Rochefort et de Montauban – was expelled in 1945, of course.

> According to my 1943 edition of the *Almanach de Gotha*, the family were major landowners with properties in, e.g. Böhmisch-Aicha (Česky Dub – the one name a literal translation of the other; 12 km from Liberec), Lomnitz an der Popolka (Lomnice nad Popelkou; near Liberec), Swijan (Svijany: 8 km west of Turnov and bought by the Rohans in 1820, the year when they acquired Sychrov), Ilovy (which I have not been able to locate... although there is a place of this name on Madagascar) and Siebendörfel (also unlocatable).

We wandered out of the courtyard and stared at the park landscape, then went back into the courtyard where we exchanged friendly nods with a German couple who had arrived at Grabštejn just as we were leaving.

Sychrov is a neo-Gothic pile built on an earlier foundation, a baroque chateau built 1690–1693. Karl Rohan bought it in 1820 and extended it in Empire style, while his successor, Kamil, carried out the conversion work in the mid-nineteenth century (1847–62). He was also responsible for the *anglický park*. There was an almost unbelievable succession of state rooms and the owners must have been enormously wealthy.

The guidebook afforded the usual innocent amusement. The tour starts in the chapel where we were invited to admire the woodcarvings of Petr Bušek (1824–94), influenced by Pugin. He worked for the Rohans from 1856. His work is indeed admirable, and present everywhere in the château. *Carver Bušek* (cf. Carver Doone) *made not only pews and pulpit for the chateau chapel but also organ, which, during his visits of Sychrov, played Antonín Dvořák a world-known composer*. Mmmh. Still, turn the corner and what do we find? *Staircase hall was main access to social salons in the first floor of the chateau*. A staircase! What a brilliant architectural wheeze.

Up we go to the southern wing and, inter alia, the Salon of Royal Apartment with a portrait of Louis XIV, called *'King of the Sun'* and the inevitable Chinese Room *(got its name according to its equipment, which was brought from China or Japan)*. The next room is the Duke's study with a portrait of 'Kamil from Rohan' who succeeded to the property in 1846 and *grew very rich by excellent management*. But he was also a scientist: *Botany was big duke's hobby*. Next door is his bedroom, and next door to that the Duke's Salon. But, look: ... *two yellow vases on the floor are from Míšeň and they only imitate oriental style*. Fairly tame compared with the organ downstairs. At length we reached the private rooms of the duchess, and in particular the bedroom *which prides with one of the most beautiful stucco ceilings in the chateau*.

The Large Salon seems to have posed quite a challenge for the translator, although one can only applaud his or her efforts: *Owners of the chateau saw their guests in the salon, who, when nice weather, entered by glassed door directly from the park. After festive admission the duchess left with ladies to fireplace salon and the duke with men to game room*. Ah, the *vie de château* with festive admission indeed.

The Game Room boasts wallpaper *made from pig's skins* which is truly odd.

Třeboň

We drove on what seemed like an interminable journey but finally made it to Třeboň, passing round the *Altstadt*, out through the Hradecká gate and into a bus lay-by where we desperately consulted the map and were on the point of ringing the hotel when we saw, on the lamp-post ten paces or so away, not a mirage but a sign directing us to the left where, after a couple of hundred yards we found the Hotel Romantick.

It was basic, albeit nice and bright. Each room was named after a flower, a painting of which appeared on the wall. Mine, room 34, was *Šafrán sličný* (Crocus speciosus); Ivor's, room 35, was *Chrpa* (cornflower). The young man (this makes me sound like an old man) at reception explained that breakfast was from eight – holding up one splayed hand and three fingers of the other – until – two splayed hands – ten.

There was a note in the bedrooms explaining that clocks would be going back at 3 a.m. on Sunday morning, so *Central Europeans ... will be able to contribute*. The Czech verb used in the note was *přispát* which I correctly guessed (since *spát* means to sleep) means 'to have a lie in' whereas the Czech for 'contribute' is *přispět*. Not as simple as it seems, this translating lark.

Jindřichův Hradec

The next day (the 24th) our target was Jindřichův Hradec. We found the centre – Náměsti miru – with no trouble. Then I blindly fed a parking meter with unfamiliar coins until I had inserted about 110 Kčs – probably more than most people earn in a year – entitling us to park until mid-morning on Monday. A short walk took us down to the *zámek* where we bought tickets for the first guided tour of the day at a quarter past ten. Interesting fact: it was the second town in Bohemia (after Prague) to have electric street lighting.

We wandered around taking photos until the appointed hour. Other people were assembling in the courtyard speaking an unrecognisable language. Our consensus view: if they're Europeans, dark-haired and you can't make out a word, it's probably Hungarian. If blonde, then probably Finnish.

> Vítek z Prčice (or Witiko von Prčice) controlled large parts of Southern Bohemia in the twelfth century which, on his death in 1194, were divided amongst his four sons. The eldest, Jindřich I. z Hradce (Heinrich I. von Hradec), founded the branch of the Witigonen which held this town and castle. The castle was originally known as the *novum castrum* but by 1410

had acquired, in Heinrich's honour, the name of Jindřichův Hradec. It was besieged (unsuccessfully) by Jiří z Poděbrad (Georg von Podiebrad) in 1467. The Neuhaus/Hradec family died out in the male line in 1604 and town and castle passed by marriage to the ubiquitous Vilém Slavata z Chlumu a Košumberka. In 1654 the town had 405 inhabited houses, which made it the second largest (after Prague, of course) in Bohemia. Today this is almost inconceivable. The Slavatas in turn died out in the male line in 1693 and town and castle passed by marriage to the Černín z Chudenic (Czernin von und zu Chudenitz) family who held it until their expulsion in 1945.

The last owner, Otto Rudolf Theobald Ottokar Maria Graf Czernin von und zu Chudenitz (1875–1962) had been a senior Austrian diplomat before and during the First World War (including a posting as minister to Sofia). In the 1930s he became a Nazi sympathiser and in 1933 published, in *Der Stürmer*, a piece entitled *Pan-Juda im Kleide Pan-Europas*. Not many people will have mourned his expropriation. By contrast, his estranged son Manfred (b. 1913), who lived with his mother in London, became an RAF pilot – and squadron leader – and, from 1943, a member of the Special Operations Executive (SOE). His mother was a daughter of the second Baron Grimthorpe.

Neuhaus, as Jindřichův Hradec, was known in German, had a population in 1930 of 10,467 of whom only 551 (5.3%) were Germans.

We had booked for *trasa* A – the only one available at this time of year (again, CZK100 each) – and found that we were the only two people in the group. The guide – a beaming, duffle-coated girl in glasses who looked about 12 – ushered us in dumb show from one room to the next while we followed from the printed German text. No photography was allowed, unfortunately, as the

Renaissance interiors are stunningly beautiful. The tour covers the representative rooms of the first floor of the Renaissance wing, built in the latter half of the sixteenth century by Adam II. of Hradec (1546–96), Supreme Chancellor of the Bohemian Kingdom (1585–93) and Burgrave of Prague from 1593. In addition to the interiors there are many paintings.

The *'extended property crisis of the debt-laden family'* prompted the sale by auction of the most important part of the Černin collection in 1877. Very few of the paintings that were spared this fate made it to Jindřichův Hradec, but they include the inevitable White Lady and a canvas by Petr Brandl apparently entitled 'Joseph of Egypt Lets His Brothers Recognize Him' (as the castle's website puts it, or 'Joseph of Egypt Makes Himself Known to his Brothers', in the guidebook's excellent English). Brandl (1668–1735) is allegedly the best-known Czech Baroque painter. The National Gallery in Prague, has an entire hall devoted to his works.

All castles and chateaux of the Vítek family are associated with the White Lady, Perchta of Rožmberk, who lived between 1429 and 1476. She was married to Jan of Liechenstein who was an absolute swine. On his deathbed he was said to have asked her for forgiveness but she refused. Jan then laid a curse on her: for her obstinacy, Perchta is said to have to appear as a 'spectre in the domains of her ancestors until they turn to dust' (the domains, rather than the ancestors, I imagine).

The tour takes in the Rožmberk Corridor – essentially the art gallery – which has a couple of large paintings with animal themes and works by Philipp Peter Roos (1651–1705), aka Rosa di Tivoli which seems to invite crude jokes. One shows the animals leaving Noah's Ark after the flood, with two dappled grey and white horses dominating the foreground, a reindeer (back right), a flamingo and leopards and various other grateful species.

Passing on, we enter the anteroom, or Renaissance Green Room, and are almost knocked out by the magnificent wall paintings and panelled ceiling, with an Allegory of the Senses by one Raimund Paul. There is a particularly beautiful photo in the official guidebook, and the wall paintings look as though they could have inspired Burges or Ludwig of Bavaria. This room was one of the few Renaissance chambers not destroyed by fire in 1773. The Černin dining-room has a rare set of Habán majolica from the sixteenth and seventeenth centuries and Holíč ceramics from the eighteenth. But these are quite uninteresting by comparison (and not terribly interesting in their own right, it has to be said) and they are nothing compared with the painted walls and ceilings – bright colours and an almost edible riot of detail.

Beyond the fairly small castle garden is the roundel, or music pavilion, built 1591–1596 by a team of Italian architects and builders under Baltazare Maggi (in fact Italian Swiss from Ticino) and Giovanni Mario Faconi. The interior is interesting for its acoustic properties. As serfs, in effect, the musicians could be heard but not seen: a basement was constructed for them under the floor of the roundel, with a narrow opening emptying into the hall. *The opening was covered with a thin bottomless vase transferring the sound from the basement to the listeners, dancers or feasters. The great fire of 1773 largely reduced the social life in the chateau of Jindřichův Hradec and its use by the family of the Černíns of Chudenice. In the 19th century, the Roundel was used as a larder, woodshed and even, for a short time, as stables. Its former splendour finally shone again after its reconstruction in 1990*, as the castle's website says.

Back in the main square, we attempted to find a bookshop, to satisfy the cravings of my colleagues in Luxembourg. However, this being a Saturday, the shops – even the tourist information office – were due to close at 12 so we, and they, were out of luck.

Excursus: Landing in the shit

Vilém Slavata z Chlumu a Košumberka (1572–1652) is famous as one of the defenestrees of Prague of 1618 along with Jaroslav Bořita z Martinic (1582–1649) and their secretary Philip Fabricius (later ennobled by the emperor and granted the title *von Hohenfall*, which is a fairly feeble joke). As representatives of the Emperor Ferdinand II they had been arguing in the Hradčany with a larger group of protestant noblemen who neatly settled the dispute by throwing them out of the window. All three survived by landing on a convenient dung cart, although some gullible Catholics believed they were saved through the intervention of angels. Vilém went on to write a history of Bohemia in the period 1608–1619 in Bohemia, but I bet he kept quiet about the dung.

One of his descendants – a confidant of the Archduke Franz Ferdinand – makes an appearance at a château in Bánffy's Transylvania Trilogy, where his host cannot help wondering why the man's ancestor had not done the decent thing and died of shame. In 1729 Slavata's great-great-great grandson, Josef Graf Waldstein, married Bořita's great-great granddaughter, Josefa von Trautmannsdorf. Another descendant was Sophie Countess Chotek, the morganatic wife of Franz Ferdinand.

Červena Lhota

There are lots of places in this part of Bohemia with the 'lhota' component (or just this component) in their names, so it would be worth finding out its significance. Wikipedia to the rescue!

> *Lhota is a popular name of Czech villages, founded during the Middle-age colonization… The inhabitants of newly founded villages had obligations towards suzerains, but those duties were usually suspended for a certain period (such as 5–8 years) as a compensation for felling of forests and making the land available for agriculture. This period used to be called "lhóta"…* Err… Thanks for that.

The drive was very pleasant and when we reached Červena Lhota we discovered, to our complete lack of surprise, that the zámek would not open until 2 p.m. so we wandered about. The restaurant where we had had a cuppa a couple of years ago –

inevitably 'U zámku' – was full with a wedding party, so we went to what looked like a shack next door and had a coffee. Ivor noticed that the place also sold becherovka, schnapps (various) and bottled beer and said: 'You could have a really nice time here' – an inanity that made us both laugh uncontrollably.

As its name suggests, if you have a basic knowledge of Czech colours, the castle is bright red (červena). There is a convenient legend to account for this: the daughter of a former owner turned against religion and threw her crucifix out of the window and into the lake. The devil carried her off and with his claw painted a scarlet cross above the window. To cover up this sign the entire building was repainted red. Yeah, right.

Outside we tried the toilet block and discovered it was closed for repairs. We walked through the grounds of the restaurant to try their facilities. Locked. Meanwhile, the bride and groom were being invited to take part in various embarrassing traditional rituals: she darning a sock, he chopping wood.

The wedding party was breaking up, with final photos at the shore end of the bridge to the castle: stocky men with grizzled grey hair stuffed into suits that had seen no use since their own weddings; rather overweight and overlubricated women; gawky young men awkwardly seeking to make eye contact with the girls. A stray cat. My camera packed up.

The *pokladna* (this time admission was only CZK90 each) had no batteries, but Ivor suggested trying the lady at the cafeteria and, sure enough, she produced her last two batteries. In gratitude I took a photo of her but she shied away. She reminded me of a friend's alcoholic sister in Berlin.

Right, time for the guided tour and another chance to don floppy felt slippers at the top of the first flight of stairs.

The guide book says that some people *falsely condemn the attractive appearance as a non-historic construction of romanticism of the 19th century*. I can't see why. We certainly didn't condemn it. It only looks (slightly) nineteenth century to the dull, uninformed observer. It is nicely compact and feels very homely.

The earliest written record dates from 1465 (an inheritance matter) Later in the sixteenth century the owners were clearly not on speaking terms: two hostile branches of the same family occupied the castle – *the setting of many quarrels, skirmishes and personal attacks, during which a punch often seemed to be a better solution than words.* The Glaswegian approach: If at first you dinna succeed, first the boot and then the heid.

In 1621 it was occupied, and later sold in 1630 for 38,500 guldens to one Antonio Bruccio who *generally contributed to the settling of conditions* in the aftermath of the Thirty Years War. He died childless in 1639.

> *Oh, oh, Antonio*
> *He's gawn away.*
> *Left me on my own-i-o*
> *With his icea creama cart*

as my mother used to sing.

The castle passed, almost inevitably, to Vilém Slavata and subsequently (in 1693) after the failure to produce any sons, to the Windischgrätz family. They *drove the manor into great debt thanks to their obsolete manner of management* (manor > manner > management), and there was a fire in 1774 which destroyed all the farm buildings and damaged the château. Two years later Baron Ignacio Stillfried (who sounds like a character in a rather poor comedy) bought the castle and gave shelter to Mozart's friend Karl Ditters von Dittersdorf. The castle was ultimately sold in 1835 to the Dukes of Schönburg-Hartenstein who occupied it until 1945, after which it became a children's sanatorium until 1949 when it was opened to the public.

The last noble resident of the castle, (Prince) Karl (or possibly Carl: the guidebook says the former; Google, the latter), died childless in 1972 at the age of 71 in Vienna. His mother was the rather repetitive Sophie von Oettingen-Oettingen und Oettingen-

Wallerstein. One of his brothers-in-law was a Frankenstein: a monstrous thought. The current head of the family is Johannes (b. 1938). Karl's uncle Eduard Aloys (1858–1944), whom he succeeded, had been a Habsburg general (latterly c-in-c of the 6th army in Northern Italy) who later became Minister for the Army under Dollfuß. In 1918 Kaiser Karl had toyed with the idea of making him Prime Minister with semi-dictatorial powers. He was married to a Colloredo-Mannsfeld

The guided tour is largely confined to the apartments on the first floor: boudoir, gentleman's bedroom, dining room, guest room (comfy and cosy), and salon. Each is pleasing, fairly low-key and of manageable proportions. There were probably a dozen to twenty of us in the party which was just the right number.

The guide was keen to point out several works of art, including Jakub Seiseneger's 1529 portrait of Joachim and Zachary of Hradec. Just a moment: we saw exactly the same painting this morning in Jindřichův Hradec. So, which is the original, and which the copy? The party were already trailing off to the next room when I collared the guide and confronted him with this great mystery. No mystery to him: ours is the original; theirs is the copy. The castle also has a portrait of the ugly duchess Markéta Pyskatá ('thick-lipped'), better known (to me, at least, and this is my story) as Margarete Maultasch. Tenniel must have modelled the Red Queen on her.

Only the state rooms were open at the time of our visit and not the attic or cellars, which will have to wait for a return match.

Třeboň

After a relatively early breakfast we packed and paid the next morning and were at the pokladna of the château with plenty of time to spare. Far too much, in fact (the next guided tour was at 11), and we were obliged to have a walk out past the brewery (the place was already fairly full of locals 'at leisure'), and out over the dried-up moat (with grazing deer) across the road and up the embankment to admire the lake.

My little guidebook – mysteriously entitled *Places and points of in the Třeboň area* – says that the first fish ponds in the region date back to the time of Charles IV, but the person largely responsible for developing the network of ponds was one Jakub Krčín of Jelčany – the 'immortal regent' (never heard of him, but Wikipedia has this to say: 'He was a prolific designer and founder of fish ponds'. Is that *all* you have to say?), who ran the town on behalf of the Rožmberks, completing the largest pond in the Czech Republic – also called Rožmberk – in 1590. There is a statue to him at the side of the lake, with informative panels in Czech, German and English.

Back to the *pokladna* where we bought tickets – a mere CZK35 each (what's wrong with this place? We soon found out) – and whiled away the last remaining minutes before the tour started by taking interminable photos of the courtyard; the trees; the trees in the courtyard, and so on. Then we waited impatiently in the inner courtyard (treeless) until the tour started.

> In the fourteenth century the stone castle (first mentioned in 1374) was purchased by the Rožmberks. The Hussites twice laid siege to it, unsuccessfully, but both town and *zámek* suffered terrible damage during the fire of 1562. After the death of the last Rožmberk (1611), the Švamberks were briefly the owners until they found themselves on the wrong side at the Battle of the White Mountain (1620). The emperor took it over, but sold it on to the Schwarzenbergs in 1660 who held it (it was run as a hotel after 1920) until 1940 when it was confiscated by the Gestapo. The state took over in 1947.

We soon found out why it had cost such little to get in: the interior – or, at least, the part we saw – is profoundly dull. We had been issued with an English language text which took little or no time to read, but the guide – a youngish woman who should have known better – droned on and on in every room, drawing attention to the most uninteresting of *objets*. The only light relief came in the large and gloomy entrance hall where, after an interminable lecture delivered in a monotone by the guide, a child knocked over one of the brass stands holding up the barrier rope. The guide was furious and hastily ushered us into the next room, and the next…Still, here's something interesting: the kitchen. No, not at all interesting when you are given an idiot's guide to crockery spotting.

There was a room in which we were required to express our admiration of scientific and alchemical instruments, but this sort of thing soon palls and we were glad to be released back into the community and the twenty-first century.

Back to the hotel to pick up the car then out onto the road again, back down towards České Budějovice then north-west on road 20 towards Pisek, on past the turning (the no. 4) down to Strakonice and its bizarre chateau (with permanent exhibitions on motor-bikes, bagpipes and fez collection which we saw a few years ago) and on to Blatná, which looked sufficiently intriguing with its moated chateau to prompt us to stop and see if it was open. It was, but not for an hour or so of course. Never mind, we're used to this.

Blatná

We parked the car and wandered through the courtyard of the château (a bit like Gormenghast) and out the other side across the moat into the deer park. A photo opportunity, then back through the courtyard. We were still too early so we strolled slightly uphill past the teeming trout farm on the other side of the road and up to the town itself and the one square.

On the right, set back from the road and slightly sunken, was a building with a plaque dating from before the First World War, saying

> Královsti České
> Město BLATNÁ
> sidlo c.k.
> okres. Hejtmanstvi
> a c.k.
> okres. soudu

or 'Royal Bohemian city of Blatná: seat of the k.u.k. district *Hauptmannschaft* and k.u.k. district court'. This was obviously an important place at one time, although now it exudes an aura of hopelessness.

In the past Blatna was renowned for rose-growing. Today it is distinguished by having the most depressing hotel I have ever seen. It may have been a successor to the *Weißer Löwe* or the *Herrenhaus* referred to by Rabl. It is at the end of the town square on a corner. The walls are covered in drab stucco and most of the windows look either broken, missing or dirty. It is almost impossible to imagine commercial travellers coming here in the town's heyday, if it had one, perhaps to admire rose cuttings, and to think of them forced to spend a night here with absolutely nothing to do except drink or go mad.

Back to the *zámek* where we paid CZK100 for the two of us, and a guided tour at the top of the steep stairs with two families with young children.

The earliest record of Blatná dates from 1253, and the oldest part of the castle is a well-preserved Romanesque chapel dating from about 1220. This was not part of the tour, however. What we saw was confined to the late nineteenth century and early twentieth century representative rooms, although the elderly lady guide managed to make it interesting for the children by getting them to try on helmets, for example.

In 1798 the castle was purchased by the Hildprandt von Ottenhausen family who were clearly not Nazi sympathisers. After the war they were allowed to stay on in the estate, albeit in a barn, until the early 1950s when the Emperor Haile Selassie was on a state visit to Czechoslovakia. The count's father-in-law had been an ambassador before the war and knew the Ethiopian Imperial family quite well. Haile Selassie used his influence to have them resettled in Ethiopia, where the countess became a teacher, until the revolution when they went to live in Bavaria. The castle has now been restored to the family.

I have no idea how much of the entire complex – it's in the shape of a blunt arrowhead with two long walls which are joined by a small wall near the drawbridge – is inhabited We only saw one of two floors of the wing that is on the right as you go through the drawbridge. It looks lived in: comfortable, rather than grand, although there are a few sticks of furniture which look as though they are worth a bob or two. There is also, not surprisingly, an Ethiopian room with various artefacts dating from the fifties onwards until the brutal overthrow of the monarchy. The castle also houses the study of Jan Evangelista Purkyně (1787–1869), a savant who published several works on human anatomy. He was the family's house tutor in Blatná from 1809 to 1812. He was also an accomplished singer and violinist.

We left and crossed the road to stand with our noses pressed to the windows of a vinothek which, perhaps fortunately, was shut, before heading off on a rather long and tedious trip to Pilsen via the almost unpronounceable Lnáře and the small town of Nepomuk, with the abbey of Želená Hora up on a low hill to the right. Nepomuk is the birthplace of the eponymous saint. Nearby there is a former Cistercian monastery sacked by Žižka's men.

Back to Plzeň

Rabl singled out the fact that Plzeň had *die älteste und zweitgrößte tschechische Sparkassa in Böhmen* (p. 71)

Up and not terribly early on the 26th, and after breakfast we headed off on the wrong road, thanks to my brilliant navigating. We turned south at a desolate crossroads, headed down the 180 towards Město Touškov, where the bridge over the Mže was being repaired, then west on the 605, turned off at Plešnice, through the village and under the railway line where we parked then changed into walking boots (one of my laces snapped, of course).

A walk of 40 minutes or so downhill took us to a hamlet where there are several holiday homes and an old water mill, the Zámecký Mlýn on the Mže, which was pretty enough, but no sign of a *zámek*, or even of the *hrad* we were looking for. However, when we turned around there it was – Buben – on an accessible hill a couple of hundred yards away.

Durdík gives Buben reasonable coverage, including several attractive photos and a ground plan which shows an elongated castle, the whole complex about 100 m long, and perhaps 35 m wide at its broadest point, with traces of outworks. The first written record dates from 1349. It was held by the Lords of Jeřeň. *Further holders were either their relatives or new people. Either ones did not care about the castle too much.* Further steady deterioration resulted in it being abandoned from the mid-sixteenth century. *Like most castles, Buben too was founded on an elongated site preceded equally by a bailey. A nuchal ditch* [a WHAT? The Czech text refers to a šíjový příkop – literally a 'cervical ditch'] *cut into the rock was guarding the front of this castle segment.*

Volfštejn

We walked back up the path to the car and made our way back to the 605, then into silvery Stříbro and out on the 230 for a dozen kilometres until we reached the rather dreary settlement of Černošín where we turned left and parked near the football pitch where we had to walk another kilometre or so through the sodden woods until we reached the ruin of Volfštejn. I hand over again to Durdík.

> Dendrochronological data suggest the castle was built in the first half of the thirteenth century, although the first written record is from 1316 when it was owned by one Beneda, son of the assassinated Ctibor of Volfštejn. The latter's coat of arms included a wolf's head – hence the name of the castle. The castle remained the property of the family *through all its existence.* In 1452 they succeeded in gaining the neighbouring Třebel Castle – *a site much more important and much prettier.* The prettiness is belied by Durdík's own photos, but the importance bit I am prepared to accept since the family stopped using Volfštejn as their seat.

It is believed that it was significantly damaged in late 1479 and it is referred to as desolate in a text dating from 1527. It was a fairly small castle – perhaps 50 x 15 m, in a sort of elliptical shape. *The inner core's periphery was demarcated by a vigorous wall* and there is a rounded freestanding bergfried poised above yet another 'nuchal ditch'. Durdík is slightly miffed at the lack of accurate dating but consoles himself with the thought that. *Whichever its construction development may have been, one thing is certain: it has always kept features typical for the very vivid bergfried type.*

Baffled by the presence of all these nuchal ditches in this part of Western Bohemia, we returned to the car and drove back to Plzeň.

I had a wish list of books for three of my colleagues. Two proved no problem. However, Monica's choice – *401 Czech Verbs* – proved entirely elusive. I must have gone to half a dozen bookshops but it was nowhere to be found – and yet this is a university city. I finally gave up after experiencing the following Kafkaesque dialogue in the last bookshop I tried:

Assistant: There is no such book.
Me: Yes, there is. I have a copy at home.
Assistant: That is impossible. It does not exist.
Me: Could you check on the computer, please?
Assistant: That would be pointless: it does not exist.
Me: But I have a copy!
Assistant: That is not possible. I have worked in six different bookshops in this city and I can assure you that this book does not exist.

There was nothing I could do, short of beating her to death, but Ivor thought that might be against the law.

Andělská Hora

We left and headed up the 20, or E49, to Karlovy Vary, stopping on
the way to visit Andělská Hora, which I had briefly looked at last
year – but from the car park below, as a group of knuckle-trailing
local youths had looked rather menacing. This time there was
safety in numbers.

From the road it looks very impressive and close-up, too, it is
impressive, particularly after one has panted up a wet path with no
safety rail to speak of from the car park by the church. The site
must be about 150 m long and perhaps 40 wide. It is elongated with
several sets of buildings still standing.

The castle enjoyed or endured the usual changes of ownership.
For example, and here I must rely on the mighty Durdík once
again, *Several holders were taking turns until the 1460s… The lords of
Plavno gained the castle in 1466, but as soon as three years later it was
conquered by royal troops. However, lords of Plavno got it back again
pretty quickly.* It remained occupied until the seventeenth century
then fell into decline. The Swedes captured and looted it in 1635
and it was devastated by fire in 1718. *Public could start visiting it in
1889.*

As to the stages in its construction, Durdík is none too sure. *The
large ruins preserved prove that the construction development of the
castle was quite complex and still offering many questions to answer,…
We still know neither what the fortification looked like, nor how large it
was… We still hesitate when trying to describe appearance of the second
gate… Neither are we very certain about looks of the inner build-up of
the eastern part of the site.* No matter – it looks impressive and feels
as a ruined castle should, with steep bits to climb, slippery bits to
beware of and unexpected vantage points to look out across the
countryside toward Karlovy Vary. Goethe visited Andělská Hora on
his 37th birthday when he was staying in Karlsbad.

We drove into Karlovy Vary, or *Karlsbad, ein Weltbad im vollsten
Sinne des Wortes* (Rabl, p. 181), where we spent a pleasant hour or
so walking up and down the main shopping drag trying, in my case,

to find some item of jewellery to buy for J and failing. Signs in Russian everywhere, particularly in estate agents' windows. A lot of flashily-dressed, tarty-looking beblinged women who I assume (meanly) were Russians.

Hauenstein

Out on the 13 (E 442) to Duchcov, passing Ostrov. About 6 km later, in a dog's leg bend we saw signs to Hauenstein. About 1 km off the road. We parked in the car park (we were the only vehicle) and walked up the path to the castle. Rabl refers, without comment to, *Schloß Hauenstein, in der Mitte eines schönen Gartens gelegen.*

A brief description of its history – in English – appears in *Vergessene Burgen, Festen und Orte* (No. 28). It was founded (probably) by Přemysl Otakar II in the second half of the 13th century. *For long centuries it used to be a small castle constructed in a old mountain style with half-timbered walls and high gables.* In 1320 Blind King John ceded it to one Mikuláš Winkler, [S]*ince then the owners changed with amazing speed here.* It later became the property of Grand Duke Ferdinand III of Tuscany, brother of the emperor Franz I, who sold it in 1839 for 400,100 gulden to the Counts of Longueval-Buquoy who held it until 1945. Soon after this purchase, Countess Gabrielle began to remodel the entire castle in the English Gothic Revival style, although the German (and longer version) of the castle's history in this booklet suggests it could have been inspired by 'Mad' King Ludwig's castles, for example Hohenschwangau (but I thought that was largely the work of Ludwig's father).

The surroundings and the valley became a romantic park, which is perfectly feasible, but the castle itself is an absolute ruin. After the war it served as offices and accommodation for the workers of a mining company before becoming a home for problem children, who seemed to have had no problem wrecking the place. It was sold to a group of private individuals in 1994 who are bravely attempting to restore, or at least repair, the castle.

Gabriella (née) von Rottenhan (her mother was a Czernin z Chudenic) (1784–1863) was the wife of Graf Georg Franz August (1781–1851). Their son, Georg, married Princess Sophie Therese Wilhelmine zu Öttingen-Öttingen und Öttingen-Wallerstein, whom we have met before. Their grandson, Graf Karl-Georg (1885–1952), the last owner, was tried for collaboration but acquitted, although he remained interned *aus politischen Gründen* and died in Brno-Mírov prison hospital.

You enter the castle, unsurprisingly, through the gatehouse and turn left and up some stairs to the first floor where you ring a bell and hope someone answers. So far, so good; the masonry is intact and you don't feel bits will fall away as soon as you look at them. But, having paid the entrance fee and bought guidebooks from a smiling young woman who then disappears to help with the restoration, you are on your own. Whether you go up or down you enter areas where either the floor, or most of it, is missing, or there are gaping holes in the wall. The *Rittersaal* is a joke. You can pick your way through rubble to the windows and try to imagine what the place must have looked like when Gräfin Gabrielle's project had been completed, and then you are reminded of what a desperate task the new owners have undertaken.

Without a massive injection of time and money (volunteers and a limited amount of money have come from enthusiasts in Saxony), I see no hope of this building ever being anything other than a sadly, collapsing shell. However, I admire the owners tremendously. They have done what I would dearly love to do: buy a castle, although they have perhaps not yet realised that they have bought a castellated pig in a poke.

CHAPTER 3

Châteaux – March 2008

———◆———

Weather conditions were severe, or simply horrible, until Nürnberg. They were particularly bad in the Saarland where there was a horizontal blizzard raging over the Autobahn. I drove on towards Pilsen as the temperature gradually rose from 0 (or minus 0 in the Renault's quaint counting system) to about 6°. The familiar advertising hoardings for Mattoni appeared. I thought this was an Italian import, but a gem of a book I acquired in Prague (*Almanach Českých Šlechtických a Rytířskych Rodů* – a sort of Debrett's of the baronetage) says that the Mattoni family originated in Milan but settled in Karlový Vary in the late 17th century. They were ennobled in 1889, but the *Almanach* gives no date after 1940. On the plus side, the *Almanach* lists not only the Rilkes but also a family called Wanka of Rodlova.

As I passed the 666 km point in my journey I was reminded of Jonathan, so stopped at the next service station for a coffee and rang to say I would be with him in an hour.

We had a walk in town. I bought a disposable camera in a shop in Celetná – *We have two colours: red for ladies and grey for gentlemens*. I also bought a Guardian in case the conversation flagged… as Jonathan stared gloomily into jewellers' windows trying to find something for Zoë. His comment at one shop: *I'm not paying that much for my daughter*. On to Wenceslas Square, with its smelly fast-food stands, and to the Dům Knihy for a happy half hour's browsing: Jonathan looking at the English books, me pretending to understand some of the other stuff.

Dobříš and beyond

For some inexplicable reason the Rough Guide doesn't think Dobříš worth mentioning. The website, however, says: *The rococo chateau with its expressive plastery descends from 1745–1765, when its reconstruction realized Jindřich Pavel Mansfeld. His daughter Marie Isabella got married with František Gundakar Colloredo. This was the foundation of the noble stock Colloredo-Mannsfeld...* (Or, to quote another website: *Thus uprised the aristocratic family Colloredo-Mannsfeld...*).

The zámek is a rococo, three-wing, two-storey building with mansard roofs. It remained in the property of the family until 1942 when Vikard Colloredo-Mannsfeld refused to declare himself German, rather than Czech. It was used as a residence by Karl Daluege, Heydrich's successor. Colloredo-Mannsfeld joined the resistance movement and returned to Dobříš in 1945 with Col. Bělov's partisan unit. After the departure of the Soviet partisans it was confiscated again and the poor owner died shortly afterwards, in 1946, at the early age of 32. (Source: guidebook no. 1 in the 'Small Guides to Local History' series – quite good English). *The nowadays owner is Dipl. Ing. Jerome Colloredo-Mannsfeld.* And if you want cultural activities. *They are thrown irregular: concerts* [the musical branch of the family go under the name of the Colloredo Beatles...[16]], *theatre, exhibitions and others.*

I had organised the tour by corresponding entirely in Czech with a Ms Renata Semová, who seems to be in charge of bookings. I was quite pleased with this, but also slightly worried that I might have made a spectacular linguistic gaffe and she would be waiting for us with a stuffed otter and a gypsy band. But no.

We had a few minutes to kill in the castle shop before crossing the courtyard to the door on the left – *I mean the left door of the middle doors* – to meet our guide, a schoolboy of 17 or 18 with a vacant smile, a slightly oriental tone of voice and poor language

---

[16] Joke.

skills. Ms Samovar had offered a tour in German in response to my tentative query of 'English or possibly German?', but the guide, on learning that we were Brits said his English was better than his German, but he would nevertheless do the tour in German as arranged because he *hadn't learnt the English text*. He was pleasant enough and on the whole we were able to resist the temptation to give him a clip round the ear.

We were given a brief historical introduction – the place has been restored to the Colloredo-Mannsfelds and the present owner spends a couple of days a month there. Any questions? No, on we go.

We mounted the staircase, turned left into the corridor and donned castle slippers that make movement well-nigh impossible. The corridor is lined with rather dull prints *showing various corners of Prague*. Our guide started out reasonably confidently, but after about a minute the gaps in his German became painfully apparent as he asked, rather too frequently, 'Was heisst [English word] auf Deutsch?' We urged him to switch to English but this, too, deteriorated as we moved from room to room: *This man had many childs*, for example. Another previous owner had had a string of daughters but no sons, so had encouraged his wife to drink lots of red wine (supposed to work; you can try it at home), but no luck. Only daughters. 'Still no questions?' in a rather disappointed voice.

Oh, look at this (in the Tapestry Room, if I remember correctly): a chessboard – a gift from a countess to her husband, but unfortunately she had a limited grasp of the game so the board is ten squares by ten.

In the Italian drawing room our attention was drawn to the *jewel among the vedute, an oil painting on wood of the Grand Canal in Venice attributed to the famous Canaletto*.

Jonathan: Whatever it is, it's definitely not a Canaletto.
Guide: But all experts are agreed…
Jonathan: Your experts are wrong.

The Gentleman's Bedroom has a portrait of one Prince Evžen Savojský (friend of the Džůk ov Málbr[17]). Then on to the Hall of Mirrors with ceiling and wall frescoes dating from 1746 by the Czech painter Jan Petr (or Johann Peter) Molitor (1702–57). Molitor, a German, settled in Prague around 1730. In addition to Dobříš there are frescoes by him at the chapel in Ho ín and the Capitular Hall in Osek. His 'Portrait of a young man with a lute' appears on the Czech 26-crown stamp.

At one end of the room is a full-length portrait of the builder of the present chateau, Jindřich Pavel František (Heinrich Paul Franz), and, at the other end, his wife Josefína (née Czernin), an elderly widow in black standing next to a table with a small dog on it – a puppy, the symbol of fidelity; 'was heisst *loyalty* auf Deutsch? 'Treue'. 'Jajaja, Treue. So this picture represents loyalty'. However, no dog figured in the portrait of the lady's husband at the other end of the room. (He had had a number of childs out of wedlock, apparently.)

And here we have another portrait of a lady and 'das ist das Symbol der Eitelkeit. Was heisst Eitelkeit auf Englisch?' 'Vanity'. 'Jaja, volity'. And pictures of two dowdy spinsters. Our guide's comment: 'Better remain celibate than marry one so ugly'. Never mind, here is a portrait of James I of England.

> Jonathan: No, it's Charles I.
> Guide: But the experts are all agreed...
> 'They're wrong', we yelled.

The Library, while pleasant and comfortable, reflects the slightly middle-brow tastes of its owners: the Encyclopaedia Britannica, Palacký's *History of the Czech Nation* and the works of Alexandre Dumas, along with a few Almanachs de Gotha (one of which I have), and several photographs of family members from the early part of the 20th century fill the shelves. Apparently, the

---

[17] Another joke.

library contains about 4,000 books, mostly in German, French and English with only a few in Czech.

As the tour drew to a close our guide said conversationally: 'So you are from Luxembourg, and you [turning to Jonathan] are from...?' 'Oh, he's from England'. By the time we had reached the bottom of the stairs he said 'So, say hello to Luxembourg and' [turning to Jonathan] 'say hello to Finland'.

Orlik

On and then to the left, as we geographers say, so that I could show Jonathan Orlik – described by Rough as having been turned by the Schwarzenbergs into a *'pseudo-Gothic money-waster'* – from the outside. We paid to leave the car at the castle car park and wandered down the slope and were amazed to find the castle open with a guided tour (in Czech) starting in five minutes' time. We shuffled round the castle dragging our feet in the *Filzpantoffeln*, but glad of their warmth because the building was freezing cold, and clutching our copies of the *anglický* text, although I found I could understand about 30% of what the guide was saying. Rough claims that *[t]here's nothing among the faience, weaponry and Schwarzenberg military memorabilia... to hint at its seven-hundred-year history*. Really?

There is an awful lot of history in the well-illustrated guidebook (1993). Like the Colloredo Mannsfelds, the Schwarzenbergs had a genuine claim to anti-fascist activity, which helped in restoring the castle to them. The present prince's predecessor, Karel VI, was the author of a declaration of Czech noble families defending the country's historical border which was presented to President Beneš in 1938. As a result, the Nazis confiscated his property. In 1945 he was the first head of the 'National Committee' in Čimelice (southwest of here where the family owned another château), but this didn't prevent the Communists from expropriating the property in 1948.

The guided tour starts in a smallish room with some rather dull medals and things awarded to various members of the family (but does include the Order of the Golden Fleece, for example). It passes on via two Empire salons (note the portraits by people you've never heard of), all very interesting, of course, and into the Teska hall. This contains the real attraction of the tour – the wooden coffer ceiling, doors and wall panelling by the woodcarver Jan Teska, a cousin of the painter Mikuláš Aleš (there's a gallery dedicated to his work at Hluboká), executed in 1885–89, the design being based on a fragment of a Renaissance ceiling in Zvíkov.

The objects displayed in the Hall of Knights [*sic*] reflect a *fancy for the Middle Ages and the past in general*. Fair enough. Admire the pewter ware, candlesticks and weapons and on to the 'Small Armoury': more weaponry including duelling pistols.

From here to the library which was founded by Karel I with 8,000 volumes and has grown over the years, and indeed it was *beeing* [sic] *supplemented until 1948*. It now contains about 18,000 volumes, including some in Czech and also 'worthy of attention' (Why? Oddity value?) an Italian version of Schiller's *Wallenstein* from 1854. A large part of the rest of the château is taken up with corridors hung with skulls of dead deer, each one bearing the name of the person who killed it and the date; it reads like a guide to the aristocracy of *Mitteleuropa* of a hundred years ago. All slightly repellent, but not as grotesque as Konopiště which I remember from thirty odd years ago.

We drove on via Milevsko, lured by the promise of the basilica of Sv. Jiljí (Rough: *it's currently in a desperate state*; actually it's been done up recently, but there is nothing of interest in it) and the pre-menstrual tension – sorry! Premonstratensian – monastery which, alas, was shut. However, it was a bright day and parish-ioners were busy in the cemetery cheering up the graves with pretty spring flowers. We amused ourselves with coining names for family tombs: Legova was fairly obvious, and Rolmiova only slightly less so.

Český Krumlov

We had booked into the Hotel Růže, which Rough surprisingly describes as *the hotel of choice* – surprising in that it's comfortable, large and fairly sumptuous, all the things Rough doesn't seem to like very much.

After breakfast (23 May) up to the castle for a guided tour in English for 10.

Past the bear pit – they are not *unfortunate animals*, Rough, but happy creatures at play, and not *incarcerated* –, to the assembly point for the tour to start: a young Francophone couple, two North Americans, several Germans and us. Welcome, up the stairs and first stop St George's chapel where the guide, a speccy young woman rather on the plump side, fixed Jonathan and me with a suspicious, disapproving look. I was half expecting her to shout out 'That's the pair, officer'. To be fair: she was competent and interesting with a good command of English. except that in the first two state rooms we were told that these had been reserved for the *rooers*. 'Pardon me', said Howard, the elderly American, 'what was that?' The guide repeated *rooers* and Howard nodded, politely and uncomprehendingly. I assume the guide meant 'rulers' – the owner's family. 'If there are no questions, we will advance', the guide said (and repeated in every room). Apart from the *rooers* and the mispronunciation of 'symmetry' as 'psymetry', I have no complaints.

The chapel was first built in 1334 and reconsecrated in 1576 after being rejigged in Renaissance style. Andreas Altomonte (1699–1780) gave it its present rococo appearance. He worked in Vienna, producing work for the riding school and also, aha, here's the connection, designed the Schwarzenberg palace orangerie. The organ dates from 1753 and is still in its original condition. *The remains of St.Calixtus are a precious component of the Altar*, the castle website says, but I don't remember seeing them.

We moved on, spiritually refreshed, for a brief lecture on the founding of the castle by one Vítek who died in 1194 and, look: the picture – 'Division of the Roses' – shows the legend of how he divided his estate among his five sons whose coats of arms, the five-leafed rose, had different colours to distinguish them. But, as the guide pointed out, Vítek only had four sons. When the Vítkovci died out, the Rožmberk's took over in 1302.

Nearby there was a painting of one Ulrich (the Mendacious?) who used to go round claiming he owned estates which clearly weren't his. Worth a try, I suppose.

On to the first Renaissance chamber, the first of five (a bedroom): *'Is anyone able to guess vich item is not Renaissance?'* Well, obviously, I'm no expert, but it must be the baroque stove, so a gold star for me. Renaissance chamber two is a dining room. It has the inevitable Brussels tapestries, and a finely carved chest. Renaissance chamber three has a painted panel ceiling by Gabriel de Blonde (1577)[18]. And then, of course, Renaissance chamber four – another panelled ceiling and frescoes made to look like tapestries. More rooms followed. We saw the room where a mad prince had been confined after hurling his girlfriend and her father out of the window.

We glanced down the corridor with the Rožmberks' coats of arms painted on the vaulted ceiling, then up to the second floor and the Schwarzenberg Baroque suite, the key feature of which (for me) was the Eggenberg hall. After the Rožmberks had died out, with Petr Vok the last representative, the castle reverted to the Habsburgs who granted it in 1622 to Johann Ulrich von Eggenberg. On the death of the last Eggenberg (Johann Christian II) in 1717 the castle and all the family's possessions passed to the Schwarzenbergs.

In 1638 Johann Ulrich's son, Johann Anton I (1610–1649), took part in a diplomatic mission to the Vatican to inform Pope Urban VIII that Ferdinand III had been elected Emperor. The following account is savagely and unashamedly adapted from the castle's website.

---

[18] Gentlemen Prefer Blondes.

Johann Anton set off from Vienna on 21 March 1638, with a retinue of 200. They went overland via Ljubljana to Trieste, then sailed on the 26th to Ancona, left there on 3 May, and arrived in Rome on the 9th. After a month (doing what?) at the Ceri palace of the Cardinal of Savoy, Johann Anton set off on 8 June for the Vatican palace for his first public audience, accompanied by 50 coaches drawn by six horses each. The audience was marred by a number of incidents which make life at Gormenghast sound fairly relaxed. Nobody told Johann Anton to remove his gloves during the audience (OMG!) and he was left waiting in the hall accompanied only by the butler, not by the Cardinals. Nobody helped him to stand up when he was kneeling in front of the Pope, and then he was left to stand, while all the Cardinals and other envoys were seated. You wouldn't think this would be terribly taxing for a 28-year old man, who looks fit enough from his portrait. On top of this, the Pope kept him waiting quite a long time, when he knew Eggenberg was the Emperor's special envoy.

The Papal nuncio was obliged to go to Vienna to resolve this diplomatic incident, although this took five months. Johann Anton took advantage of this time to organise a new procession, so that the first audience might be forgotten. His priority was to make a special carriage for the Emperor's gifts: the Golden Coach designed by Giuseppe Fiochini. It was made of gilded walnut wood and the metal parts were covered with gold plated silver. The interior of the coach was upholstered with black velvet with golden embroidery.

On 9 November 1638 Johann Anton tried again. The procession was led by four messengers dressed in scarlet robes, followed by 60 footmen leading 60 mules, divided into five groups of 12. each animal shod in silver. The procession continued with 12 servants dressed in silver-edged scarlet robes. Behind them walked seven trumpeters, similarly dressed, playing silver trumpets hung with squares of material bearing the Eggenberg coats of arms. These were followed by the 25 soldiers of the Duke's personal guard, followed by two regiments of the Papal guard, the Cardinals on their mules, and 24 pages, all in scarlet and silver robes. Behind them were four thoroughbred horses, followed by representatives of the nobility, clergy, and ordinary citizens of different nationalities. Then came the city drummers, the Pope's trumpeters, and 30 Eggenberg footmen, then, finally, Johann Anton von Eggenberg himself, accompanied by the Pope's majordomo and the Swiss guard. The Duke's robe was embroidered with gold and his horse had golden horseshoes. At the end of the procession was a carriage decorated with green velvet. At the public audience in the Vatican Pope Urban VIII apologised for the July misunderstanding, and both parties settled on a date for a private audience. It was on 16 November 1638 and the procession from the Ceri palace to the Vatican was as grand as that of 7 November.

When the Emperor's envoy began his journey home on 3 January 1639, he took the coach with him. He wanted to present it to the Empress Maria Anna, but finally decided to keep it for himself.

So, after a round trip of getting on for a year, Johann Anton had
  (a) managed to inform the Pope that there was a new Emperor and
  (b) bought himself a nice coach.

The guided tour ended with the Masquerade Hall, built by Altomonte in 1748, and with decorative frescoes all round created by Lederer (who appears in a minor role as 'man drinking coffee') who was employed by the Schwarzenbergs from 1746–1749. The main theme of the paintings is a group of aristocrats enjoying themselves at a masked ball, joined by Negroes, Chinese, Turks and characters from the Commedia dell´Arte such as Harlequin, Colombine and Pierrot. Most are quite lifelike, but all seem to have more or less the same rounded, well-fed face as if they were inbred. The hall is used in summer for concerts.

On the way out Mrs American – whom Jonathan has dubbed Maybelle – clutched my arm. 'Did she [the guide] say the chandelier was from Meissen?' I said I thought she had. 'Because, you know, we live in California in an ultra-modern house, of course, but Howard did buy me a genuine Meissen chandelier and it looks totally different to this one'. She was genuinely puzzled, so I suggested there might be different styles of Meissen, which seemed to put her mind at rest.

We hung around the various gift/book shops, sat on a bench as a young Czech guide gave a tour in Japanese – including a much appreciated joke (respect!) – then drifted along past the *jizdarna* or manège (which I remember used to contain a decent restaurant) and on through the blazing sun past parked coaches, and down the steps to the Krčma Marketa (Margaret's pub; interesting etymological note: the German surname Kretschmar is cognate with *krčma*) where we had a beer and an evil-looking red sausage (Jonathan's inspired suggestion) and I killed a wasp which came too close. Then back through the gardens to the theatre in time for our tour.

> Plays had originally been performed in Krumlov in the Jesuit seminary and in the Masquerade Hall. Prince Johann Christian von Eggenberg, a great patron of the arts, ordered the building of the Baroque theatre which was completed, to plans by Italian architects, in the period 1680 to 1682. The castle had its own repertory company until 1691. Theatrical activities seem to have ceased after Johann Christian's death. Under the Schwarzenbergs the theatre was converted in 1765–66. In the eighteenth century it was placed at the disposal of travelling companies, or local amateur groups, but in 1897 it was closed for safety reasons (it's almost entirely

made of wood and illuminated by naked candles). It was used briefly in 1903 and 1906, then again for the South Bohemian theatre festivals in 1958–1966. Restoration started in 1966. There are occasional performances today, but visitors can take the tour we took.

Useful Tip: To get a good impression of what it must have been like in its heyday, watch the DVD of Giuseppe Scarlatti's *'Dove è amore è gelosia'* (Jonathan's translation: 'Doves like ice cream'), a live performance from the theatre. One of the extras featured on the DVD is an interview with the toad-like Prince Schwarzenberg, runner-up in the 2013 presidential election.

The party was slightly more select: six Brits (possibly one family), a young American woman and us. We were told to perch on the original wooden benches (for retainers and peasants; the Fürst and his family sat up in boxes behind us). One of the Brits, a small, elderly lady, found it impossible to get up onto the bench. We were shown a video of the restoration of the theatre. This included shots of the scenery made to look like boats rocking on waves. The American was intrigued: 'Did they know how to make the wave effect?' Yes, dear, you've just seen it on the video. Jonathan claims that God created Americans to make the Brits seem clever.

We were invited to try out sound effects – wind, rain etc. – (Jonathan leaped at the invitation) then taken through a narrow door backstage, or rather understage, to see the intricate scenery which, in expert hands, could be changed remarkably rapidly. The guide had better English than the lady this morning, but didn't seem terribly well genned up

Hluboká

I had discovered that *exceptionnellement* the château at Hluboká (which means 'deep') would be open today, despite it being a Monday, so we headed there next, past lakes or ponds to Dasny where we joined the main road and found our way to Hluboká for an

English tour, as promised, *at about 1 p.m.*; in fact, at exactly 1 p.m. I refilled with fuel – carefully noting how much it cost in order to pass it on to my navigator – and then we drove into the townlet past an enormous fishpond and a much smaller one called the Židovský, or Jewish, pond.

A Jewish community was founded in the late seventeenth century but there was no synagogue until 1907. Hluboká consists largely of one long shopping/eating street (Masaryková, of course) with a relaxed spa-town atmosphere about it.

On the town's website the mayor suggests: *You may be interested in visiting the Raft Museum in Purkarec.* Well, not really. We're here for the château.

The girl at the information office told us it was not possible to drive up to the château but we should park in the main street where a traffic warden wearing orange on a bike would flog us a ticket (or, possibly, wearing a ticket and selling us an orange. Not easy, this language lark). He did, we got out and walked – slowly – up to the *zámek* and joined a guided tour in English for which we probably had to wait 15 minutes or so.

Useful Tip: I can thoroughly recommend the loos at Hluboká.

The château dates from the mid-thirteenth century. The Schwarzenbergs bought it in 1661 and rebuilt it in baroque style in 1707–1721. However, after they had transferred their main residence from Český Krumlov, the building was transformed between 1841 and 1871 in Neo-Gothic style by Prince Johann Adolf II (1799–1888) and his wife Eleonore of Liechtenstein (1812–73). The result is a rambling pile, white like Orlík, and slightly reminiscent of Neuschwanstein

Our guide was frighteningly odd: a bloke in his thirties, leaning to one side, left hand in pocket, right hand clutching a set of keys, pronouncing some words with absurd precision, others in a loud voice and repeating words for no obvious reason: e.g. 'So, here we are in an **anti-camera**, camera'. There were about a score of us: an

American couple, a family of three Brits from somewhere Up North, us and about a dozen Dutch people, whose children had to interpret the guide's poor English for their parents' benefit. Some wood was described as 'e Bonny' – a nice touch for the Northerners – and in one room there was a 'Haydn door', or rather 'hidden'.

Up the stairs (formerly an open courtyard, now hung with military trophies) to the so-called Entrance Room where *The complicated architectonic development of the chateau is documented by some of the objects on display*, as the château's website helpfully says. It was after a visit to England in 1838 that Johann Adolf and Eleonore decided to remodel the château. The key name to remember is Eleonore of Liechtenstein, who seems to have been the driving force behind the nineteenth century conversion, but it was impossible to make out what the guide was saying. It sounded like Zlawrnyung. Naughtily, we entered the bedroom of the princess: a private prayer alcove, with panes of glass rescued from other Schwarzenberg properties, the usual solid bed, an Italian chest of drawers, tapestries and a series of Madonnas. From there and through her dressing room to the Hamilton Cabinet – the princess's study – named after John George Hamilton, who came from Scotland and liked to paint animals, especially horses: the Stubbs of Southern Bohemia. He was in the service of the Schwarzenbergs from 1709 to 1718.

It was roughly at this point that the guide announced: *I heff **problem**, problem*. At last, we thought, he's owning up to it, but the problem was that the Czech guide before us was only a room away and we were in danger of catching up.

On, now, to the Morning Salon – sunny and typically English, it seems – for some harmless fun. In 1732 Prince Adam František organised a stag hunt at Brandýs nad Labem during the course of which he was shot and fatally wounded by the Emperor Karl VI. You can imagine Karl's embarrassed message to the new widow: *Err... terribly sorry, love, but ... err ... you'll be one short for supper tonight*. Karl was taught music by Fux (*sic*) and was responsible for the Pragmatic Sanction. His other claim to fame was that he died from eating death cap mushrooms, about 1,700 years after another emperor, Claudius, suffered a similar fate.

Humbled by the fate of this poor man, we trooped into the Reading Room which is circular and stuffed full of Delftware showing the months of the year and typical peasant activities associated with each month, and thence to the Little Dining Room. The portraits in the room represent several leading ladies of the Schwarzenberg clan, including Princess Ida, née (another one) von Liechtenstein, who in the period 1906 to 1910 installed a personal lift and a lift for transporting food and later introduced electricity throughout the chateau.

And now, some information on the tiled stoves. The servants, our guide told us, shoved wood in the backside. Jonathan's shoulders started shaking uncontrollably... The back passage wood insertion was designed so as not to distribute (possibly 'disturb'?) proncess l'Nora.

The Smoking Room, with its backgammon tables, is chiefly famous for the stately fireplace of white granite bearing the gay family motto 'NIL NISI RECTUM'. We could only speculate on what this might mean.

This is followed by the Reception Salon where the atmosphere begins to get rather oppressive and it's hard to stifle a yawn. But then we reach the Great **Dining** Dining Hall, hung with magnificent tapestries showing well-known proverbs. They were completed in 1644 to designs by Jordaens. Our guide took a particular interest in a tapestry showing a farmer, farmer shoving a cow into a pond. The moral was lost on us.

As I continued to ponder this we moved on and into the magnificent Library, and another chance to play 'Spot the book in Czech'. Previous owners were keen on Diderot, the *encyclopédiste*, Adalbert Stifter (who appears to have been an all-time favourite of Johann Adolf and Eleonore), Defoe and Agatha Christie. Did they buy it by the yard? They seem to have been far too busy supervising the construction of canals and sugar-beet factories, defeating Napoleon and dressing up (Cardinal Friedrich von Schwarzenberg, for example). The guide pointed out an original copy of *'Die Biene Maja und ihre Abenteuer'* (1912) by Waldemar Bonsels. Quite what it is doing here is beyond me. After the book burnings of 1933 the press published an article by Bonsels entitled *NSDAP und Judentum* (The Nazi party and Jewry), describing Jews as the 'mortal enemy' of the movement. It is hard to believe that his views found favour with the Schwarzenbergs. The father from Up North was having difficulty pronouncing the book's title: 'Dye bean Madge?' he said slowly, with a bewildered look.

The château had been confiscated from the Schwarzenbergs by some types called 'nayzees'. This may have been the Germans' revenge for the fact that when President Beneš visited the area in the Thirties the then Prince Schwarzenberg handed over one million crowns to be spent on improving fortifications against the Reich.

We were released back into the community and decided to pay a visit to the *Alšova jihočeska galerie* (named after the painter Aleš; see above) which was hosting a temporary exhibition of Russian academic paintings from the early twentieth century – serfs, boyars and what not – which we ignored and concentrated, instead, on the small(ish) permanent display of Gothic art, some of which was stunningly beautiful. And most of it was from this region. I was particularly struck by a seated Madonna from St. Tomaš, with her cloak and hair blowing in the wind. Interestingly, it dates from 1510–1520, which is far later than anything considered Gothic anywhere else.

Coffee in the cafeteria afterwards, then we drove into České Budějovice, strangely deserted, and had a wander round. I pointed out the *Zvon* and the *Malý pivovar* where I have stayed and we went upstairs to the latter's *cukrarna* for Kaffee und Kuchen (Sachertorten), and very nice too. The town was unbelievably deserted and bleak. I had no idea that they would make such a big thing about Easter. In the *Malý pivovar* I asked 'Do you have a leaflet?' – 'A lift? It's over there'.

At length we returned to Český Krumlov where we decided to

give the advertised concert, with its slightly lewd title ('the finest horns'), a miss and wandered around aimlessly until supper time.

Excursus: The Schwarzenbergs

The Schwarzenbergs were the most powerful and the wealthiest family in this part of Bohemia. Rewards for loyal service to the crown – members of the family were statesmen, diplomats and, *rarae aves* in the Habsburg empire, successful generals – and chance inheritances left them owning huge tracts of land.

I bought from an antiquarian bookseller in Ungelt, the square behind the Týn church in Prague, the *Fürst Schwarzenberg-Jahrbuch* for 1913. It lists, for both the senior line (Krumlov) and the junior line (Orlik), the stately homes and territories owned and also their domestic staff and other employees. The senior branch owned a dozen or so lordships with a total of almost 184,000 hectares. They also owned some 30,000 hectares in Styria (where they had originated). The Orlik line were relative paupers, with only about 90,000 hectares, but combined with the senior branch the family together owned land in excess of the size of present-day Luxembourg. Between them the two branches owned 24 châteaux (many of which were used to house their staff) and 13 ruined castles. In addition to forests and farms they owned breweries and distilleries. They employed 3,586 people (including a private bodyguard of grenadiers at Krumlov: one officer, one sergeant and 26 men – one of whom had a medal for 40 years' loyal service) and were paying pensions to a further 144.

Small towns of Southern Bohemia

Dačice (the first place in the world where sugar lumps were manufactured, in the nineteenth century) has a blue château (the 'New Castle', originally renaissance but redone in Empire style in

1816 by Riedl of Vienna). It was owned by the Dalbergs until the family died out in 1940, when it passed to the Salm-Salms; I repeat, the Salm-Salms, and was taken over by the state in 1945. The château's website has the intriguing claim that *It was the Dalbergs' prerogative to come first during the knighting ceremony on the occasion of the Emperor's coronation.* It was shut but seemed devoid of interest. It may have something to do with the colour. Red is acceptable (and cheerful) while blue simply looks as though the owner has bought the wrong paint. We peered through the door of the nearby St Lawrence church which *can be seen when coming to Dačice from all sides.* We came from only one side but saw it nevertheless. Beneš and his wife visited the town in 1946 followed a mere half century later by Havel in 1997.

Founded on the wealth from silver mining, the *Sprachinsel* of Jihlava (or German Iglau) suffered heavily with the expulsion of the Germans after 1945. The town has a broad main square sloping upwards (or downwards if you approach from the other side, of course). We parked on the left, then headed off further to the left to the *Minoritský kostel* (minorite church) which dates from about 1250 – Romanesque pillars and mediaeval frescoes. Then to the top of the square and a look at the *muzeum Vysočiny*, the regional museum. 'Vysočina' means 'Highlands', so we were expecting bagpipes and tartans, but not a bit of it. The museum is worth it, as Rough says, if only to see the lovely interiors. It was one of the few Renaissance houses to survive a fire in 1523.

We had a near silent guided tour, the guide's function appearing to be to fling doors open and usher us in with a smile. A pleasant, elderly lady, although she forced us to listen to the audio display, of which she was inordinately proud. I clicked on 'Buildings' and learnt about 'vite vash' (rhymes with 'cash'). Afterwards we tried two churches, Sv. Ignác (Jesuit of course) and Sv. Jakub. Rough says it is best *admired from afar*, which suggests the interior is disappointing. But both churches were shut. We decided – on seeing some of the paintings on display – not to risk the local art gallery.

We headed off to Kutná Hora, turning off at exit 62 and heading for Tynec nad Labem where we crossed the road and took the wrong turning, thanks to my refusal – based on bitter experience – to believe the navigator. Turn round and back on the right road for another dozen kilometres and down to Kutná Hora.

Kutná Hora

We found the hotel – the Zlatá Sloupa (Golden Pulp-Mill; look it up) – with no problem and the owner, Leon Pelikán (sic), at the reception desk. Our rooms are on the second floor. Leon beamed at the inconvenience: *Der Fahrstuhl ist nicht*, he said in his best German. Forty-six steps later we reached our *stylish and comfortable accommodation* – an accurate description. We had a restorative raid on the minibars then set off on a walk round town for *orientace* purposes, ending up with a meal (fish platter for two – excellent value) at the hotel, in a curtained off area just for ourselves: the English milords in their private dining suite as buxom serving wenches bustled past carrying foaming pitchers of ale.

Off-season I reckon you can do Kutná Hora in half a day. This is because a number of sights are shut and only two others are really worth seeing: the cathedral and the Vlašsky dvůr. Having said that, however, the cathedral (St Barbara's) is an absolute must for any visitor to the Czech Republic.

Kutná Hora was built on silver. The first silver deposits were discovered in 1260, there was a 'silver rush' in 1290 and by the end of the century the mines were producing one third of all silver mined in Europe. At the turn of the fourteenth and fifteenth centuries the 'Osel' (donkey)[19] mine had reached a depth of half a kilometre, making it the world's deepest mine. In 1300 Václav II enacted the *Ius regale montanorum* (codified mining law). At the same time he established the central mint of Bohemia in the town and the Prague (or Bohemian) Groschen, with a fixed silver

---

[19] Cf. German 'Esel'.

content, helped to stabilise the monetary system. So, a Pretty Good
King Wenceslas.

> In 1300 and 1303 the Habsburg Emperor Albrecht tried
> unsuccessfully to capture the town and shut down the mines.
> On both occasions it was German-speaking miners originally
> from Jihlava who defeated him. The late fifteenth century
> saw the town siding with the king against the Hussites, and
> in fact throwing large numbers of them down the mine shafts.
> Increased silver production in Germany and, even more so in
> America, the ravages of the Thirty Years War, followed by the
> arrival of the Jesuits effectively wound the clock back several
> centuries. Mining stopped, although the Nazis revived it
> early in the Second World War and lead and zinc ore
> continued to be produced until 1991.

Conflict between the monastery of Sedlec (now a suburb of
Kutná Hora) and the miners led to the latter deciding to build their
own cathedral in 1388. The first Clerk of Works was Jan Parler, son
of Peter Parler the builder of St. Vitus' cathedral in Prague – which
St. Barbara's was supposed to rival (it was originally planned to be
twice its present length). It was effectively completed by Benedikt
Ried in 1558 but work did not finish until 1905.

It is a light and friendly place and incredibly beautiful.
Although very large it is not at all oppressive. The vaulting of the
nave and presbytery are worth driving a long distance to see and
Rough is quite right to say it is *arguably the most spectacular and
moving ecclesiastical building in central Europe.* There are stunning
frescoes in the Minter's chapel and in the other chapels behind the
main altar, in particular the Smíšek burial chapel. Michal Smíšek
was Clerk of Works in the late 1470s and early 1480s. He and
members of his family are portrayed preparing the altar for mass.
The ceiling has an orchestra of angels playing period instruments,
and in another scene a sylph-like Queen of Sheba is portrayed
meeting Solomon.

There were a number of other tourists, mainly Brits, or at least Anglophone, with a few Japanese, including an elderly man with complicated camera equipment and a stick hobbling about like Blind Pugh.

Always game for an adventure, we decided to have a look inside the Corpus Christi Chapel. The door was locked. Back to the tourist office to complain... and to be handed a key, which the young woman on duty bent down to retrieve from a drawer, inadvertently revealing an orange thong. Tut tut.

While the cathedral easily scored 10/10, the Corpus Christi Chapel is worth no more than 2/10. It dates back to at least 1300, was not used after the Jesuits were suppressed in 1773 and was later sold to a private owner who installed a roof garden on it. It changed hands several times in the nineteenth century, ending up as an organ factory which disappeared after the last war. Some 20 million crowns were pumped into restoring it from 1970 to 2000 but, to be perfectly honest, there is absolutely sod all to see. There are four cylindrical pillars supporting nine cross-ribbed vaults. And that is all that can be said.

The Vlašský dvůr, by contrast, merits 7/10. Its name means 'Italian court' (as opposed to vlašský salát = Russian salad) and it was designed as a palace for Václav II, later housing workshops and a chapel. We went on a guided tour, just us and the elderly Japanese. The guide was a lady with reasonable English except for her pronunciation of 'smississ' (smithies) and her, consistent, references to 'in 1491 year', for example (CZ: *v roku*). Worth singling out is the royal chapel (dating from 1386) with its full-relief altarpiece (Nuremberg, before 1497) of the dying Virgin Mary. When the chapel was restored in 1904 it was decorated in Art Nouveau style by František Urban (1868–1919), who also designed some of the stained glass in the cathedral, and his wife Marie.

After a break for lunch (6/10) – we thought we had better pace ourselves – we decided to visit the Museum of Alchemy in the cellar of the information office. The museum's flyer describes it as 'fascinating and exciting', where you can 'STIMULATE your

IMAGINATION'. Nonsense. It is quite breathtakingly dull, so only scores 0/10. Don't go there. Ever.

But this still left loads of time on our hands, in a town that seemed to be shrinking by the minute. What to do to fill the hours? We sought refuge in the Museum 'Unveiling of the mysterious face of Kutná Hora', advertised as *real crimes and filth* which is in the cellar of the Vlašsky dvůr. The 'filth' was the selling point, of course, but it was a disappointing mistranslation (of what?), consisting almost exclusively of instruments of torture used to punish alleged witches. I gave it a generous 2/10 for the ludicrous English versions of the captions.

After that, and after trawling the bookshops (where I acquired a bilingual version of the *Hound of the Baskervilles*) it was back to the hotel to punish the minibar for an hour or so before we set off in search of a meal.

Lobkowicz châteaux: Nelahozeves

An hour and a half's drive took us on the 27th to Nelahozeves. A more careful study of the map – who was navigating, mmmh? – might have got us there quicker and reduced the wear on the back axle but, as they used to say in Russia, you can't complain.

> The château was built in the 1550s but after its owner picked the wrong side at the battle of the White Mountain it was acquired in 1623 by Zdeněk Vojtěch, first Prince Lobkowicz (chancellor of the Kingdom of Bohemia under three Emperors – Rudolf II, Matthias and Ferdinand II) and husband of the fabulously wealthy Polyxena, née Pernštejn, widow of Vilém of Rožmberk. The last reigning prince, Max (whose photo shows him sitting, his hands clasped together with a rather sinister stare), was an ardent supporter of the First Republic and the exile government's wartime ambassador to the Court of St James. This led to confiscation of his property by the Nazis. After the 1948 Communist coup he fled to the United States

and went native. His grandson, William, and wife Alexandra – all teeth and a mad glare in the guidebook photo – opened the château to the public after its restitution.

We had arranged a guided tour with Petra Dolejšová (possibly from *dolejšek*: bottom, or lower part) and we waited for her in the shop. She herself showed us round. The tour started by crossing the courtyard diagonally and mounting the stairs which took us in from the bitter cold. Ms D led the way, shedding her jacket as she went – *We're onto a good thing 'ere*, as my navigator remarked with a leer – and causing a momentary fantasy on the lines of *Ooh la la, eet ees so 'ot in 'ere, ah must take mah clothes off... But what are you looking at, you naughty Eenglish?* We had recovered by the time we reached the library with its 65,000 volumes in Greek, Latin, Hebrew, Italian, Spanish, Italian, German and, believe it or not, Czech.

However, the real purpose of visiting Nelahozeves is to admire the Lobkowicz family's magnificent collection of paintings – the largest private collection in the country. The rooms themselves are worth seeing, with their period furniture – *Please don't touch the dining chairs!* – cabinets inlaid with ivory, pietra dura and mother of pearl, and also rather dreary hunting trophies and guns – but it is the paintings, a fully representative selection of Western art with Cranach, Dürer, Rubens, Bruegel the Elder ('Haymaking') and Velázquez, that are the true focus of attention. It came almost as a relief to inspect the earlier, more sober works in the chapel and note Petra's only three mistakes in English: 'pajan' (rhymes with 'cajun') for 'pagan', in contrast to the Baby Cheeses, a truly yoonick work. These are minor quibbles. We had nothing but praise for Petra: she was charming, enthusiastic, interested in her job, well-informed and blessed with excellent English.

After an obligatory raid on the shop – there are several versions of the guidebook available, but none of them (except the Russian version) tells you much about the château itself rather than the paintings – we decided to lunch in the Zamecké restaurant. Rough doesn't mention it, so it must be a fairly recent fixture, but it's worth a couple of stars. I had spaghetti carbonara – absolutely wonderful and quite delicate – and Jonathan had a chicken Caesar salad. It is one of the best restaurants ever in the Czech Republic: food as it should be, and easily the equal of most places in the West.

Mělnik

We drove the 20 odd kilometres across country to Mělnik, with its château visible for miles. We had booked a wine-tasting preceded by a visit to the château, but my Czech wasn't up to explaining this to the lady at the cash desk, so we just booked for the tour and set off around the building. Despite Rough's claim – *Visits are by guided tour only* – it is, I think, the only stately home in the Czech Republic which you can visit without a guided tour, although there are National Trust battleaxes in every room whose job is to stop you enjoying yourself too much. There are the usual paintings (recently returned to the present owners), sticks of furniture and porcelain. It has belonged to a cadet branch of the Lobkowicz family since 1753 (after previously being owned by the Czernins).

> There has been a castle of sorts here since the eleventh century when Václav I built a Romanesque edifice, which was subsequently used as a dower house for royal widows. In 1542 it was granted to Zdislav Berka of Duba who turned the Gothic castle into a Renaissance château with arcades in the north wing. In 1577 Rudolf II swapped it with Jiři Lobkowicz for Křivoklat. Jiři lost it in 1593 following his participation in a plot against the emperor. It was granted to the Czernins in 1646 and when Countess Maria Ludmila married August Anton Lobkowicz in 1753 it passed into the possession of the latter family who were expropriated by the Communists in 1948, but who recovered it in 1992 as part of the restitution programme. The king of Thailand visited the château in 1934, and the king of Romania in 1936.

Wine has been produced here for centuries. The present owners[20] are Jiři and Bettina Lobkowicz. She appears to be in charge of wine production, while he runs a minor liberal party which has one seat in the Senate. They have no children, so they have adopted their nephew Peter as their heir. This seems to be a fairly common practice amongst the Bohemian nobility.

The large bedroom has a portrait of George Christian Lobkowicz, who died in 1932 in his Bugatti on the AVUS racetrack in Berlin, a painting by Karel Škréta of Humprecht (an unlikely name) Count Czernin, other family paintings and baroque furnishings. This is followed by Prince August Longin's study with writing desk and some inlaid odds and ends. The dining room has David with Goliath's head (ca. 1720), one of Peter Brandl's greatest works (the website claims). On through the Grand Drawing Room in Rococo style, with a lot more porcelain to take in, followed by the Big and Small Halls. Ahha, something more interesting: the rooms have coffer ceilings and the walls are hung with 17th century maps and views of what were in those days major European cities – the usual suspects plus Verona, Bologna, Stralsund, Königsberg and Magdeburg. There is also a lot of largely 17th century armour.

The Concert Hall has a sunken floor and is crammed with spindly tables and chairs waiting for the next audience. At the end of the room are portraits of the present owners (the princess looking slightly like Picasso's Girl with Dove, but only slightly) by the Czech painter Tomáš Císařovský (Wikipedia tells me that 'he works in thematic cycles. He painted a series of political paintings, notably a painting entitled *Lover in Prague* (2004) which is a portrait of Goebbels').

Then the Grand Dining Room with Baroque furniture and original 18th century china. The chairs around the main dining table date from 1740. There is also a bust of Napoleon. And here we are, at last, in the 14th century Gothic chapel, built by the fourth wife of Karl IV, Queen Elisabeth, who died in 1393 in Mělník. The

---

[20] They divorced in 2021.

chapel was initially dedicated to St. Louis. After being badly damaged in the Thirty Years War, it was recreated and rededicated in memory of St. Ludmilla. There is a Baroque altar, a number of relics and portraits (some by Škréta) of patron saints. The most notable works of art are the three paintings in the back right corner of apostles by Peter Brandl and the painting above the Renaissance chest entitled Flight from Egypt by the Italian painter Bassano. Jonathan pointed at a painting of Christ on the cross and said in a quavering old man's voice: *I say, this chap Inri doesn't seem to have much luck, does he?*

Back to the shop where the lady, whose face had now softened slightly, said: 'Are you Mr Cole? Cos the princess wants to show you around herself'. Yes indeed, so we were led out to the door of the Princess' office where she appeared after a few minutes.

Bettina Lobkowicz appears in most photos to be wearing an Alice band, with swept back hair. She was wearing a tweed jacket and what looked like riding breeches, which gave her a look of *Mädchen in Uniform*. In fact, she's attractive and absolutely charming with a good sense of humour.

We started off in the fourteenth-century cellars, the monotony of the gigantic million litre barrels relieved by a large papier mâché dragon lurking on top of one of them. What does that symbolise, we asked. Absolutely nothing (laugh), it's there to give the tourists a photo opportunity.

We asked about the sort of tourists they get. A lot of Russians, apparently. Russians, eh? How does that go down with the Czechs?

'Oh, I *love* the Russians!'

'Why?'

'They spend lots of money!'

What about other nationalities?

'We get lots of Japanese'.

What are they like?

'Oh, I *love* them – they like to have a good time... and they spend lots of money.'

What about the Dutch?

'I'm not so keen on them'
Why not?
'They don't spend much money' (shriek of laughter) 'Do you
see a pattern building up?'

Indeed we did. The Brits could be loutish, the Swiss dour (BL is
of Swiss origin) and the French – 'Well, the French are French
whether in France or anywhere else...'

Enough of this idle banter, though; give us a drink, woman. Back
upstairs to daylight, across the quad and into the vast restaurant
with its panoramic view over the Labe (Elbe). It was opened in the
Thirties. It is light and airy. We sat at a table at the bar end, the only
guests, apart from an old codger a few tables away. A waitress called
Theresa served us. BL had lined up half a dozen wines for us to
taste.

We started with a Ludmila White (2007) – a 'light wine for
everyday consumption'. I'll drink to that. No nonsense about
pouring most of the glass into the large silver bucket on the table.
Swallow the lot. Did you like it? Yes, we did. So how about a
Château Mělnik Blanc? According to the notes, it has a 'lively
bouquet'. Too lively, alas. BL took a huge swig then leant forward
with her hand to her mouth: 'Quick, QUICK, the bucket!' and spat
the lot out. Another, better bottle was produced and we were able
to enjoy its 'balanced complexity', whatever that might mean. We
followed this with a Rhine Riesling. BL explained how she had had
no family connection with wine-making – her father was 'in
textiles' – but a degree in economics plus an interest in drinking
lots of wine had proved sufficient qualifications. When she and her
husband had taken over the estate following restitution she had
rationalised business practices and turned it from a rather dozy
state-run lame duck into a lively enterprise which now exports to
other countries.

Before we got on to the red, the old Kodžer a few tables away
tottered over to chat with BL. She explained afterwards that he is
the local piano teacher who comes in every Thursday afternoon to

fortify himself with half a litre before having to face his unwilling and untalented pupils. We complimented her on her Czech; we discussed languages, the EU, Jonathan's jobs, how long we have known each other, and polished off some Pinot Noir and St Laurent Barrique, when BL's mobile phone rang. It turned out to be the parish priest – 'one of our *best* customers' – renewing an order for communion wine.

We asked how they got on with the elder branch of the Lobkowicz family at Nelahozeves. She gave a rather distant look and replied, slowly: 'W-e-e-e-ll, William is an *American*, you know. So apart from the obvious family festivities, we don't see much of each other: I don't think he really trusts us.' At length we had drunk the place dry, so bade BL farewell and brought a few crates of her wine from the shop, before staggering the 100 yards or so to the hotel.

Prague

Our drive to Prague (on the 28th) was fairly uneventful apart from my navigator's bizarre belief that, despite approaching from the north-west, we would need to cross the Vltava three or four times before reaching the hotel.

We walked up the hill, past an Antiquariat on Neruda, and on up to the castle when we wandered down again to the Lobkowicz palais and art gallery to continue the theme established yesterday morning. The Rough Guide is out of date, referring to a *hotchpotch historical collection… marginally more rewarding [than the toy museum]*. Not so; it is a continuation of Nelahozeves by other means – room after room stuffed full of art, probably not as impressive as Nelahozeves, but containing some interesting archive stuff (bog standard portraits of members of the princely family, for example), plus two views of London by Canaletto – 'The River Thames on Lord Mayor's Day' and 'The River Thames with Westminster Bridge'. The Lobkowicz Events Management website describes it as *one of the most beautiful and significant cultural sites in Europe*, and they are right. The family regained it in 2002. The present exhibition opened on 2 April 2007. We zapped the shop then went into the café (the museum ticket entitling us to a discount of 10%). I was last here in December 2006 when my daughter bought me lunch.

Next stop: the Betlémská Kaple (completely new to me, and pretty new in absolute terms). The first sermon was preached (praught?) here in 1394, and in Czech, thereby breaking the German domination of the Bohemian church. It is essentially a memorial to Jan Hus, but nothing, absolutely nothing is left of the original chapel building or of its successors. It was rebuilt from scratch about a hundred years ago. Inside, the chapel is square, bare and with a few inscriptions: possibly original, more likely copies. It is fairly dull. The only thing the chapel manages to convey is a sense of how many people Hus could have preached to (roughly 3,000 – a three-loaf job), if the building was full, at any one time.

We walked briskly over the Charles Bridge and off up Husova to an Italian restaurant, the Bellini, which we had reserved earlier. Jonathan ate here on his first night, alone, and has been raving about the size of the antipasti portions ever since. This turned out to be quite accurate and we had an excellent meal (lasagne for me, a pizza for him), good service (despite only one waiter and one waitress) and very good food. Pricier than average, but worth it.

I was up in time for an early breakfast with Jonathan before he left by hotel taxi for the airport shortly after eight. I managed to fill my time profitably.

First, a walk along Tomašska to catch the no. 23 tram up to the castle area. The hotel sold me a ticket and the tram was jam-packed with small Italian women who squealed excitedly whenever the tram lurched round a corner.

I bought a ticket for the evening's concert at Sv. Jilji.

Still with time to kill I found a place called the Monarch wine bar – not far from Betlémská Kaple – which offered a special deal: an enormous plate of ham and salami, plus bread, plus a glass of red wine for about CZK150. Excellent. It claims to have over 1,000 vintages, but I had time only for one.

And so to the church, where I sat in darkness until, just in time, I realised the concert was in an antechamber – the chapel of St Zdislava (this lady, a noblewoman from Brno, spent her short life irritating her husband by caring for the sick and feeding the poor. She was canonised in 1295).

The artistes were Hana Jonášová (soprano; she is a soloist with the Prague State Opera and, surprisingly, has appeared in Luxembourg), Zuzana Němečková (must be in her fifties) on the organ and either Jan Valta or Tomáš Vejvoda (the playbill was not clear) on the violin. Whoever the violinist was, he was a bit screechy at times and the Adagio by J.S. Bach was on the painful side, while the largo from Handel's Xerxes was simply over the top – a lot of melodramatic sweeping and bowing. Apart from this my brief notes on the other 12 items read either 'very good' or 'excellent' (the Soprano singing Biblical songs 8 and 10 by Dvořák and a humoresque by the same composer). Afterwards I hung about on the church steps like a stage door Johnny until the artistes appeared and thanked them profusely, which rather surprised them.

Excursus: Your Hundred Best Tunes

The programme included 'Winter' from Vivaldi's Four Seasons,. Gounod's Ave Maria, Mozart's Ave Maria, Schubert's Ave Maria and Mozart's Alleluja. Had I stayed on a couple of days longer I could have heard 'Summer' from the Four Seasons, Mozart's A Little Night Music, the Blue Danube and Schubert's Ave Maria in the Lichtenstein palace or, on different nights but in the same venue, Vivaldi: 'The Four Seasons. Selection', Pachelbel's canon and Mozart's A Little Night Music, plus a suite and the toreador aria from Carmen.

On the 30th I could have gone to the Baroque library hall of

St Michael's monastery for a concert which included A. Vivaldi: The Four Seasons I. (presumably Spring), Pachelbel's canon, Mozart's Little Night Music and an Ave Maria each from Bach (J.S.), Gounod and Schubert, plus the overture from Carmen. While I was sitting comfortably (*20° heated*) in St Giles, the monastery of St Michael was performing Winter from the Four Seasons and Aves Mariae from Bach, Schubert, Gounod and Mascagni. St Havel's church, by contrast, was offering A Little Night Music and Schubert's Ave Maria. Throughout the month Prague Castle had hosted gala variety concerts of Pachelbel's Canon, Mozart's Divertimento D (KV 136) and all four of Vivaldi's seasons. Throughout March the Obecní Dům was offering The Four Seasons, Eine kleine Nachtmusik (German title to fool the unwary) and highlights from Carmen.

Obviously, there's a little more to it than just this, but the circumstantial evidence does suggest, m'lud, a certain dumbing down to attract foreign tourists.

Before leaving Prague on the 30th I visited the Klementinum, a former Jesuit college, which covers an area second in size only to the Castle. Jesuits were summoned to Bohemia in 1556. Dientzenhofer rebuilt the church of Sv. Kliment (hence the name) for them. I had not been here since we were first in Prague in 1975. There was a guided tour for just three of us, a young German couple and me, and the tour was in English, rather than German although I asked the Germans if they minded and they said no. It reminded me of a trip to Křivoklát a few years ago with Ivor when we were part of a group of half a dozen or so, including a young German and his Czech girlfriend. The guide started by asking what language everyone spoke. Everyone knew German, so he decided to do the tour in English and we had to interpret into German for the young couple.

You get to see the Zrcadlová Kaple (mirror chapel), the Barokní sál (Baroque library, from a safe distance) where the guide pointed out a sculpture containing some numbers which, she said, was an early sudoku [joke] and the Astronomická věž (astronomical tower). The guide was a sweet young thing, whose English was dreadful: another instance of a Young Person having learned the set text parrot-fashion, but quite unable to answer – or even understand – any questions. A shame, because the enthusiastic, but rapidly disillusioned young German male had a whole barrage of intelligent and interesting questions up his sleeve.

Instead of paying CZK220 for the guided tour, a better bet is to buy the well-written and lavishly illustrated guidebook for CZK100 and read it in a congenial bar.

I returned to the hotel, mounted my steed and was off like an Ageing Lochinvar on an uneventful trip to Kynžvart:

Kynžvart

The original castle dates from the latter half of the thirteenth century. After the battle of the White Mountain it was confiscated, then granted to the nephews of Lothar Metternich, Elector of Trier. The family held it until 1945. The renaissance keep was replaced with a baroque château between 1681 and 1691 which in turn was remodelled between 1820 and 1833 in the Viennese classicist style: a very pretty pinky white building, and I had had the sense to ring yesterday to check that it would be open.

I had an excellent guided tour given by a girl who announced herself as Marie and who spoke absolutely perfect German.

> The best known Metternich owner was Klemens (1773–1859) who was Austria's Minister of Foreign Affairs from 1809 to 1848 and Chancellor from 1821 to 1848 and whose repressive conservative rule inevitably led to the revolution that obliged him to go into self-imposed exile in London for three years. He was married three times: firstly to Marie Eleonore, Countess Kaunitz-Rittberg, by whom he had seven children (three sons who all predeceased him and four daughters)

secondly to the beautiful Marie Antoine, Countess of Beilstein who died tragically two years later after bearing him a son; and, thirdly, to Melanie Marie, Countess Zichy-Ferraris, who bore him three sons (one of whom predeceased him) and two daughters (one of whom predeceased him). His youngest child was born forty years after the eldest. Apart from running an empire and procreating he seems to have read a great deal, as will become apparent.

The guided tour takes in 25 rooms. The first few are rather dull unless you are keen on minerals and metals: bronze sculptures, a vase made of Ural porphyry (a gift from Tsar Alexander I), malachite vases and tables inlaid with *pietra dura*. Then comes the Blue Chamber with Napoleonic memorabilia (Metternich stitched up Bonaparte's marriage with the unfortunate Marie-Louise of Austria) The next room, the Chancellor's study, becomes more interesting, and even the dozen or so other members of the tour party – glazed-eye elderly Germans with grey plastic shoes and dodgy hips – began to liven up. It has portraits of Metternich's wives, the middle one, who died ten days after the birth of her son, being quite a stunner. The room also contains the *very same desk* which Metternich used at the Congress of Vienna, a souvenir, no doubt, a gift from the organising committee. Others further down the pecking order – the Danish minister, for example – would have been lucky to walk away with a blotter.

But enough of this, since we must move on to Richard's Library, created in about 1870 by Metternich's son and heir (and son of the stunner). It has about 6,000 volumes, the emphasis being on contemporary French and German literature. Adalbert Stifter was Richard's private tutor. The Green Room is green, of course, thanks to its brocade wallpaper, and there are portraits of members of the family and the Imperial family. The Billiard Hall contains, yes, a billiard table, another gift, but from a different Tsar, Nicholas I. Dotted round the room are card tables and tables for board games. The Great Hall is dominated by a replica of Canova's 'Amor and Psyche' (the artist himself made the replica), a portrait of Tsar Nicholas I and the Austrian Emperor Franz I.

Now look out of the window at the English landscape park with ten ponds and *many Romantic structures*.

What else? The Dining Hall (glimpse through the doorway only), the Smokers' Room with four 1510 panels by Bernard Strigel showing the legend of finding what the guidebook calls the *Holly Cross* and then the Music Chamber with a grand piano that belonged to Princess Pauline, wife and first cousin once removed of Richard Metternich. She was instrumental [pun] in introducing Wagner to the court of Napoleon III. Then there is the Oriental Room where, traditionally, my interest flags, and the Armoury with the usual halberds, sabres and arquebuses, which can get rather tedious.

But just as the visitor stifles a yawn he turns a corner and enters the Karl Huss exhibition. No relation whatsoever of the famous Reformer, this man was the last executioner of Cheb, having succeeded his father and uncle, a renowned local historian and first custodian of the Metternich museum where he lived from 1827 until his death in 1838, having abandoned his cutting-edge local authority job. He also practised traditional medicine (grimly muttering 'One way or another I'll finish the buggers off'), collecting obsolete coins in payment – the beginnings of his numismatic collection. There is a visitors' book signed by Goethe himself. The Chapel is much as one would expect from this period, after which we hit the *serious* libraries.

First, there is the Chancellor's library with 24,000 volumes including an Old Testament fragment dating from the late eighth century and 145 incunabula including a manuscript by Lope de Vega. Some of the manuscripts were brought here after the suppression of the Benedictine monastery of Ochsenhausen in Swabia. Most books are in Latin, French or German, a few in English and Italian and *[O]ther languages appear only seldom*, so no Czech. The Chancellor's library (II) has a bust of Homer and various graphic works. The next library – Paul's library (named after the pre-war owner of the château) – has about 5,000 volumes, mainly from the turn of the twentieth century.

Reeling with all this dusty learning, we enter the Old Curiosity Cabinet – the castle museum – most of which is just junk: for example, a rhino horn, a Chinese Parasol, puppets wearing various forms of national dress, locks of Beethoven's and Cherubini's hair, a fragment of Charles V's coffin, a prayer book belonging to Marie Antoinette, remains of an undersea telegraph cable, samurai armour and Alexandre Dumas' writing desk. This takes one seamlessly into the Egyptian Cabinet where, amongst other things, the uncritical visitor can admire a 3,500 year old mummy of Ken Amon (or Kenneth Amon, if you haven't been introduced), guardian of Pharaoh Thutmosis III's treasure.

I headed back to Plzeň and the Zvon, checked in, had a walk round town and decided to eat in the hotel restaurant – a wise move since the food is excellent (as was the service – I was the only diner) and residents get a 10% discount. Another short walk, a read of the paper and off to Nodsko[21].

In the morning (the 31st) I went to the tourist office – reasonably helpful young women, provided you don't want any information about anything – then bought another disposable camera and took a few snaps like the tourist I am.

Plzeň: the brewery

The weather had perked up enormously and was quite warm, so I set off on foot to the brewery – ignoring the wildly inaccurate instructions from the receptionist and collaring a passer-by – for a guided tour at 2 p.m. The brewery complex is vast and the visitor centre is in a new building through the triumphal arch, not far from the entrance and on the left. Beer has been brewed here since the Middle Ages, but the present brewery was erected in 1842

---

[21] Skotsko = Scotland, so Nodsko = land of nod.

following serious civil unrest in protest at the crap quality of the stuff then on offer.

The guided tour started at quarter past. There was a glum-looking young Brit and his very enthusiastic Czech girlfriend, a weedy North American couple and me, feeling like a disreputable uncle as I laughed at all the guide's feeble jokes. Or at least I think they were jokes. We were ushered upstairs to a vast cinema where we huddled in the middle for a film – not the *gloriously tacky video show* as Rough has it, but a rather tedious piece of advertising, the essential message of which was that Plzeňsky Prazdroj (or Pilsner Urquell) is the finest bottom-fermenting beer (whatever that may mean) ever devised by the wit of man. It went on quite a long time. Then we were let out into the open and boarded a bus which drove us all of 200 metres to the (new) main brewery. It is now owned by SABMiller, a South African conglomerate which has started to produce Pilsner Urquell in Poland and Russia. This doesn't seem quite right to me.

Český Krumlov

Bezděz

Hotel Salva, Litoměřice

Hluboka

Červená Lhota

Kozel

Nebílovy

CHAPTER 4

Slovakia and Poland – 2013

———✦———

Burghausen

Ivor's new SatNav has a gentle, yet strangely irritating voice which one can soon learn to detest. However, it found an alternative route around München which saved us some time. We stopped for lunch at a service station advertising itself as the *erstes FengShui Rasthaus Europas*.

Burghausen consists of two parts: the upper town with the castle and the lower, Renaissance-plus town which has all the attractive painted buildings. Our hotel, the Bayerischer Hof, is right in the centre of the Lower Town, and one of my bedroom windows looked straight out across the square and to the bridge over the Salzach river and into Austria. The hotel dates from the 17th/18th centuries. In the *Innvierteler Bauernkrieg* of 1705 it served as the headquarters of the rebel leader. This uprising, from early November 1705 to mid-January 1706, occurred during the War of the Spanish Succession. After the Elector Max Emanuel had been driven out of Bavaria, it was occupied by troops of Joseph I, the Holy Roman Emperor. The Bavarians rose up in revolt against the imperial occupation. Not that it did them any good.

The hotel is one of those typical South German (and Bohemian) inns with a not very broad façade but which stretches back through a series of courtyards. Frau Höcketstaller, the lady who checked us in, told us that the German side of the Salzach had been safe in the recent flooding (water up to 30 cm below the parapet), whereas the Austrian side had suffered quite badly. We had been slightly concerned: Passau, not far away, had had its worst flooding for something like 400 years. We dumped our bags, after parking the car in the inner courtyard, and decided to go for a walk before supper down towards the river. However, it started raining so hard we had to stand in a bus shelter for about 20 minutes before darting back into the hotel: Wiener Schnitzel for me; Zwiebelrostbraten for Ivor. By the time we had finished it had stopped raining, so time for another walk. This time though the Grüben – a street of fame with metal plaques set into the paving showing different jazz musicians who had visited the town for its festival. One or two of the names I actually recognised.

A morning's walk on Monday across the square, down to the river and then through the Grüben again before heading up to the new town and the castle.

The castle advertises itself as the world's longest castle (*die weltlängste Burg*) at 1051 m. This is both true and misleading. It certainly is very long, but you go through what are in effect five outer courtyards – the first totally indefensible – before you hit the castle proper. Its heyday was in the 15th century under the last three dukes of Lower Bavaria (Heinrich der Reiche 1393–1450, Ludwig der Reiche 1450–1479 and Georg der Reiche 1479–1503; the nicknames are a clue). It then lost its residence function in 1503/05 following the Landshut War of Succession.

Since Georg and his wife Jadwiga of Poland had no male heirs he designated his daughter Elisabeth and any sons she might have as his heirs. This infringed the Wittelsbach family pact whereby in the event of one male line dying out its possessions would fall to the other male line [cf. the succession in Luxembourg in 1890]. Albrecht IV, Duke of Bayern-München, refused to accept this breach of the agreement. Georg died on 1 December 1503 having named his son-in-law, Rupprecht Count Palatine, as his regent. On 13 July the first major battle between Albrecht and Rupprecht took place at Altdorf near Landau. During the course of the battle – a point of interest to students of *Germanistik* – Götz von Berlichingen (fighting on Albrecht's side) lost his hand in the fighting. Albrecht was victorious, Rupprecht withdrew to Landshut and died shortly afterwards. The war ended on 30 July 1504 following arbitration by the emperor Maximilian: Georg's two grandsons received minor, fragmented territories while Albrecht pocketed the rest.

From this point onwards Burghausen ceased to have any political significance, being merely the residence of any spare princes who had nothing to do. In the eighteenth century it was Vaubanised, although in 1809 Napoleon declared it obsolete as a fortresss.

The 6th courtyard – the first one a visitor reaches from the car park – has a well with a clock tower, a plunge bath for horses and the usual domestic offices. The 5th courtyard has the *Hedwigskapelle* (Hedwig as in Jadwiga?) which, unfortunately, we were unable to visit. The 4th courtyard has the customary witches tower and torture tower; the 3rd courtyard the master of ordinance's tower) the second courtyard a café and covered well and then we hit the 1st (= last) *Hof*, which is the castle itself. Some of the exhibitions were closed (probably just as well; they sounded rather tedious), but we tramped round the several floors of the *Palas (Fürstenbau)* examining Romanesque and later art, including some pretty enormous battle scenes showing the Bavarians defeating King Ottokar of Bohemia at Mühldorf.

Ottokar was immortalised in Grillparzer's play *König Ottokars Glück und Ende* and in the painting 'Přemysl Otakar II: The Union of Slavic Dynasties', part of Mucha's Slav Epic (in the castle at Moravský Krumlov). When he wasn't fighting, Ottokar built a number of castles, including Zvikov, Křivoklát, Bezděz (all three visited at one time or another with Ivor) and the Hofburg in Vienna.

Bratislava

Over the Danube and into Bratislava, Ivor having discovered to his annoyance that his Satnav won't work in Slovakia (or Poland). We had booked into the 4-star Hotel Tatra on Namestie 1. mája (1st May Square), a main street with cars tearing past. But we found the hotel garage with no problem and checked in to our 'elegant rooms' (true), the bathrooms equipped with V&B fittings, and with a view out the back to... well, another building plus a few trees. After a rest we headed out and into town, wandering around the rather small Altstadt until we ended up in a restaurant with a German football theme, where I played safe and had trout. Ivor shyly informed me of his 'knicker shortage': he has discovered that he has not packed enough underpants, which has caused his daughters some mirth.

> 'The dull town, though pleasantly situated on the Danube, has neither fine buildings nor objects of art and antiquity to attract a stranger. It is even destitute of prominent national peculiarities in its aspect, or that of its inhabitants, to distinguish it from an Austrian town, but it retains some of its mediaeval gateways'[22].

Slovakia looks a little artificial: it failed to exist before 1918 – perhaps not really until the Velvet Divorce from the Czechs in 1993 – and had to make do with another country's history, and its nominal capital had a majority of non-Slovak inhabitants until the early Twenties.

Because of time constraints we had no interest in seeing much beyond the cathedral of St Martin ('a fine ancient Gothic structure, 1274, but sadly modernized' [Murray]). The kings of Hungary were crowned here from 1563 to 1830, and the cathedral has a photo of Karl, last king of Hungary (and last Habsburg emperor), whom the devout, the deranged and the historically illiterate are trying to have canonised. In his *Phoenix Land* Miklos Bánffy is very disparaging about Karl's comeback attempts. His 'first *putsch*... turned out to be an adventure fit only as a subject for operettas'.

---

[22] Murray's Handbook for Travellers in South Germany and Austria, 14th ed., 1879.

The second occasion was not remotely funny, resulting in the loss of several dozen lives, and Bánffy describes Karl as 'a man weak in every respect who was not fitted to rule and who could not even have managed a medium-sized farm'[23]).

A coffee in a beautiful Jugendstil café on the main square (Hlavné Námestie) then a raid on H&M to solve Ivor's underwear problem rounded off our tour of Slovakia's vibrant capital. Then we drove out along the Danube and through the suburbs to Devín (known as Theben in German). We parked and walked up to the castle. By now it had become very hot.

Glorious Devín

Devín stands on a massive rock above the confluence of the Danube and the Morava. It dates back to Roman times, when it was part of the Limes Romanus, a strategic outpost of the XIV and XV legions in Carnuntum. In the 9th century the splendidly named Prince Rastislav, ruler of Great Moravia, chose it as his stronghold which, according to the Fulda Annals, was known as 'Dowina'. The southern gate, protected by a pair of semicircular bastions, was built in the 15th century on an older Great Moravian rampart. In the first half of the 15th century (after 1419) the Paladin Mikuláš Garai built the middle castle and fortifications. On Mikuláš's death Matthias Corvinus granted the castle to the Counts of Svätý Jur and Pezinok who built further fortifications. *[During the night of 26–27 October I had a bizarre dream in which a group of people were trying to reach either Pezinok or a lighthouse.]* When they died out the Báthorys became owners in 1527, at a time when the castle was already being caught up in the Ottoman advance on Vienna. Revolting peasants captured the castle in 1616 and in 1635 it was granted in perpetuity to Pavol Pálffy and his fairly ubiquitous descendants.

The castle was continuously occupied until 1809 when Napoleonic troops blew it up. After this event, as the guidebook

---

[23] *Phoenix Land* (2011, pp. 194 and 288).

says, 'the Pálffys lost interest in the castle' (not surprising, really. Who wants a duff castle?). A cave in the rock contains an exhibition on the history of the castle, with rather more information than one might wish about the period of the Great Moravian Empire. You can see an iron mouldboard (an attachment to a plough) and whorls (a weaver's tool, apparently). The guidebook has a good ground plan – the castle looks a bit like a cat with its arms stretched out in front, quite possibly yawning – the site is impressive but the disappointing thing is that large parts – notably the 13th century donjon and courtyard – are out of bounds to visitors. This is the first, but not the last, occasion on which we encountered a certain cautiousness on the part of the authorities concerning health and safety.

There is a well, 55 metres deep and, as ill-luck would have it, a legend attached to it. This is best left to Daniel Kollár (Cultural Heritage of Slovakia: Castles Most Beautiful Ruins' (2007)):

> 'The lord of the Castle chose the strongest of his serves and promised them freedom if they dig a well… Actually they dug a well and also found a lump of gold… the lord of the Castle listened to the devil disguised in joker's clothes telling him that perhaps there was more gold. The diggers… were shut in the Castle dungeon and eventually hurled down in the Danube. Before the poor serves died, they cursed the Castle lord and his joker who accidentally fell down of the same place in the Danube a year and a day after.'

Back on the road and specifically the E75 motorway to Trenčin where we are to spend two nights. We decided to throw in a castle on the way, the obvious choices being either Čachtice, to the west, south of Nové Mesto (new town) or Beckov off to the right. We decided against the former on the grounds that it was the home of Elizabeth Báthory, allegedly one of the most prolific serial killers ever. She is supposed to have murdered young women to drink their blood in an attempt to stay young[24]. Refreshingly interesting, of course, but the risk was that it would be a naff sort of theme park, so we opted for Beckov.

Beckov

The little guidebook says the castle of Beckov was *'mentioned in the Chronicle of Anonymus* [sic] *written in the early 13th century AC'*. Perched on a 70 metre rock above the townlet, it is an imposing structure even today (having been destroyed by fire in 1729 and never rebuilt) despite *'the relentless ravages of time'* and it withstood the Tartar invasion of 1241 and the Turkish invasion of the seventeenth century. It's easy to see why: it would be difficult to position siege weapons anywhere near it. Originally it belonged to the kings of Hungary but Matuš Čák seized it in 1296 and used it as a residence until his death in 1321. In 1388 Sigismund of Luxembourg granted it to Stibor of Stiboricz. *'He got generously rebuilt the castle in the Gothic style into his family seat'*. In 1437, the day before his death (rather suspicious, don't you think?), Sigismund granted Beckov to Pavol Bánffy (see above: Devin). A later Pavol Bánffy was killed fighting the Turks in 1599. *'As a result of his death was extinction of the Bannfy family in the male tail'*. (Sounds like Longfellow's Hiawatha: 'verses wrote he front to back').

The castle is built of light grey-white stone and, although parts of it are out of bounds to visitors, there is still a lot to see, climb over and enter plus, thankfully, a small café in the Western Palas where we knocked back some fizzy water to keep us alive. The most impressive part is the upper castle with its great rectangular tower.

This čáp Čák (ca. 1260/65–1321) was a Hungarian oligarch who was *de facto* independent ruler of the north-western counties of the kingdom (today roughly the western half of present-day Slovakia and parts of Northern Hungary).

---

[24] You can try this at home.

Trenčin

From Beckov we followed the ordinary road for 14 km to Trenčianska Turná where we turna'ed left through several kilometres' worth of industrial estates until we hit Trenčin itself with its slightly confusing one-way system. We ended up in the car park of the Grand Hotel, then crossed the street in the blazing sun, dodging the tumbleweed and expecting to be gunned down at any moment, to the hotel itself and found our rooms. As the hotel's own promotional literature says: *'The Grand Hotel Trenčin offers you a morable stay which was also experienced by some of the famous sport celebrities'*. Sounds good...

Trenčin has a population of about 60,000 and is described by Michael Muller as *quicklebendig*. Er... OK... it is a pleasant – *very* pleasant – but rather sleepy town, although it probably comes alive during term time. It is home to the Alexander Dubček University with 7,140 students and a College of Management with 1,275 students. The town was first mentioned under the Greek name *Leukaristos* (Λεθκαριστοσ), depicted on the Ptolemy world map around 150 AD. During the course of the Marcommanic Wars (look it up) between the Roman Empire and the Germanic Quadi, the Romans carved an inscription on the rock under the present-day castle in 179 AD and the place was mentioned as *Laugaricio* – which is not remotely like Trenčin. It is the northernmost known presence of the Romans in Central Europe. Trenčin is the ninth largest municipality in the country, for what it's worth.

All this is fascinating, of course, but we were hungry. We decided not to eat in our hotel (always a sign of lack of imagination), but went up a short passage to Mierová (peace) square, then left as we were curious to locate the Tatra – *altehrwürdiges Jugendstilhotel aus dem Jahr* 1901 (Müller) – where we had tried to book last year. It is now the Elizabeth, named after Franz Josef's wife. It looked pretty good, but we decided to give the rest of the town a chance and walked back up Mierová, under the tower at the end and along Hviezdoslavova (named after Pavol Országh Hviezdoslav

(1849–1921) – dramatist, translator and for a short time member of the Czechoslovak parliament). Then right down a side street to the Café Da Vinci where we sat outside and had a couple of long-overdue beers. Back via Šturovo square (named after Ľudovít Štúr (1815–1856), leader of the Slovak national revival in the 19th century and another impressive all-rounder), then past the synagogue and eventually to the Elizabeth where we had a meal in the posh and excellent restaurant, for a mere EUR57.90.

After a rather sketchy breakfast on the 13th (in this hotel, at least, guests seem to rise early and grab most of the food), a walk up Marka Aurelia, then a slightly more strenuous walk up to the castle where the *pokladňa* offered two tours, one fairly lengthy. We found that only the short one was available, but no matter. We trudged up through various baileys and through the 'Pre-Gate (Propugnaculum)' where we waited in the sun, surrounded by dozens and dozens of schoolchildren, even though most of them seemed to have signed up for a tour involving witches and ghosts. A lady kindly explained that we would have to wait then burst out laughing and said 'you have no idea what I've been saying, have you?' and laughed again when I said I had understood every word.

In 1241, when the Tartars were moving from Moravia into Slovakia, Trenčin was one of the castles they were unable to capture.

> Král says of Trenčin: *'It was particularly famous at the time when Matúš Čák Trenčiansky resided here, who in 1301–1318 seized and ruled over the whole Považie and part of Moravia (The Slovakian King«)'* (p. 205). This was our second encounter with Matuš Čák. He fortified the castle *'appropriately'* (just as well in the Middle Ages) and it became his *'major seat'*. Later owners included Ján Hunyady and his son Mathias Corvinus. During the latter's reign the Zápolya family emerged as pre-eminent amongst the Hungarian nobility. However, they surrendered to the king in 1528 after a siege lasting several weeks. For about 200 years (from 1594 to a disastrous fire in

1790) it belonged to the Illésházy family who sold it to a
Baron Sina whose family ultimately gave it to the town.

As the guidebook says, '*Mostly painters and sculptors find a mighty
source of inspiration in the impressive panorama of the castle*'. Indeed
from the town it looks like a Hollywood version of a Dracula castle.
The schoolchildren in whose company we were obliged to make the
guided tour, obviously didn't find it a 'mighty source of
inspiration', but they can hardly be blamed. Despite its size, there's
not a great deal to see. We started in the Rotunda which houses the
remains of an eleventh century chapel '*a witness of which are the
finding places of graves*'. After that it was upstairs to a mind-
numbing ethnographical museum with glass cases showing what
Bronze or Stone Age man got up to (nothing gossipworthy, alas),
then back outside and up Ľudovít's Tower which has '*the exposition
Weapons from 14–15th centuries*' (mildly interesting) and '*the
exposition Present Slovak Heraldic Production*'.

It is, unfortunately, a feature of so many castles in the Czech and
Slovak Republics: a room, totally bare, but with coats of arms of
previous owners dotted round the room, everyone entitled 'Erb
[shield] plus the owner's name'. But since the owner's name is
necessarily in the genitive, and the genitive ending of most men's
names is '-a', the unwary might wonder why so many of the owners
were women; 'erb Petra' etc. By this time the guide and the teacher
had abandoned any attempt at calming the brats down who were
excitedly running up and down stairs, bumping into the elderly
(Ivor and me) and generally behaving, not surprisingly, like bored
children. Then suddenly the tour was over and we were released
back into the community wondering 'is that it, then?'

Strečno

Kollár has some helpful advice on visiting Strečno: '*Naturally, it can
be... visited after a five hour trip, if you go from, say the mountains
Martinské hole*' (not quite sure what that means, the little tease).

'But the majority of visitors, drivers above all, prefer to start from the parking lot...' Well, there's a surprise, Daniel. So we drove out of Žilina, past the reservoir to the confusingly signposted car park, then a not terribly strenuous hike uphill for about half an hour (with an enforced break during which we and an elderly British couple – the man smoking a pipe and speaking flawless but accented English – waited while workmen carried out blasting). Then to the castle.

The lady at the *pokladňa* asked where we were from, so we said we were British. She beamed and waved us on up to the main entrance for a guided tour where another lady seemed pleased that we were British... and obliged us to join a group of monoglot Hungarians. The guide described each room in Slovak, a Hungarian interpreted and Ivor and I were none the wiser.

> The castle dates from the 14th century when it was erected to levy tolls on merchants using the Váh river. It was later turned into a residence and the fortress had the reputation of being impregnable, although it was taken by opponents of the Habsburgs. One Mikuláš Kostka decided, for no obvious reason, to wage a war lasting a quarter of a century with his neighbours, the Pongrácz family. In the early 17th century the estate passed by marriage to Štefan Wesselény. His son, František, married a lady called Žofia Bosniaková. While he was away in the wars she was left in charge of the castle where she died aged 35 in April 1644. Forty-five years later (not long before Emperor Leopold I had the fortifications slighted in 1698) her body was found almost intact in the crypt of the chapel. A painted stone effigy of the lady can be seen today. The Hungarians seemed quite interested and impressed.

The castle consists of what must once have been massive square towers with a magnificent view over the valley. The tour takes you higher and higher and then back down to the chapel and the shaft down to the crypt with Žofia's effigy.

We made our way back to the car park and returned to Trenčin without further incident. After another couple of refreshing beers we went back to the Elizabeth and again dined in style. *'Sehr gutes Restaurant'*, as Muller says, and worthy of inclusion in a good food guide. Fish for me, a steak for Ivor and loads to drink.'

Bojnice

The zámok – *das wohl schönste und meist besuchte Schloss der Slowakei* (Müller) – stands in extensive grounds on an elevation beyond the end of gracious Hurbanovo square which, like most squares in these parts, is not at all square but a straight, tree-lined road. We found the car park with no difficulty then set out slowly (it's *very* warm) up to the château: a beautiful, blazing hot day, with the parkland swarming suspiciously with small people.

> A wooden castle was erected here in 1113. Matúš Čák (him again) seized it in 1299. He was followed by the Zapolyas and Thurzos. In 1637 the king gave the castle to the Pálffy family. In the late nineteenth century Count Johann Pálffy (1829–1908) emulated Ludwig II of Bavaria and had the place entirely remodelled, starting in 1889, in fairy-tale French neo-Gothic style to the designs of Jozef Hubert, an architect from Budapest. There are other parallels with Neuschwanstein: Johann's heirs contested Pálffy's will and tried to have it declared invalid on the grounds that he was insane. The dispute dragged on until after the end of the First World War. Most of the furniture and fittings were auctioned off in the 1920s and in 1938 the Czech shoe manufacturer Baťa bought' it'. You can spend a long time on a guided tour through the refurnished state rooms.

However, as the handout from the tourist office says: *'Numerous attractive events are held in the fairy-tale castle. During the Valentines weekend love stories and promises of loyalty take place…'.* We had the great misfortune of arriving on a day when hordes of children and their bored parents had been lured there by one such attractive event. The girl at the cash desk said pityingly: 'You won't like it. This week is castle home to Brothers Grimm theme exhibition. Each room is reflecting one of tales. Only for children.'

We wandered round the outside of the moat gloomily, wondering which one of us to blame for this fiasco.

Banská Bystrica

We had booked into the Hotel Kuria, just off the main square. We drove round and round trying to beat the one-way system until we ended up, about a hundred yards away, round the corner in Kollárova street and walked to the hotel. A very pleasant member of staff drew on a map how to get to the hotel from Kollárova, which involved driving about a mile north then a mile back again along Bakossová road – lined with rather neglected villas which must have looked quite attractive in the twenties or thirties. He was waiting for us and helped us in with our luggage and up in the lift which, he said, the manageress objected to people using. A very pleasant man in his late forties or early fifties, with a tic that made him blink, and a desire to practise his quite good English. He found out where we came from and said he had taken his young son to Brussels and Luxembourg shortly after the collapse of communism to show him 'the nerve centres of the new Europe'.

The hotel is really two buildings joined together, the one nearer the town having originally fulfilled several functions including public library and salt depository.

Banská Bystrica is a very attractive place of some 85,000 inhabitants regarded by the young as the *heimliche Sommerhauptstadt der Slowakei* (Müller). The long, elongated main square – the Námestie SNP (I'll come to that later; nothing to do with Scottish nationalists) is traffic-free, lined with beautiful renaissance buildings, with open-air cafés – and hordes of young women displaying their tanned legs – on permanent decking covering most of the square before it narrows to Dolná street (also traffic-free). We had the by now customary two beers before wandering around trying to decide where to eat.

One difference between the Czech Republic and Slovakia is that in the former, which is so obviously centralised and Prague-focused, there's not a great deal to do in the provinces after about 6 p.m. By contrast, Bratislava is fairly small and right on the edge of Slovakia (a bit further to the left and it would be in the river), so the provincial centres are full of life.

We ended up at the *Fishmen* [sic] on the south-eastern side of the square and ate inside, which meant the cellar. We were the only people eating inside and were served by a woman – I imagine the owner, one Helena Hodová – who regarded us with a mixture of amusement and pity. As the restaurant's name suggests, it specialises in fish, many of which could be seen swimming unsuspectingly in the aquarium in the corner of the room. We paid EUR 31,20 for the two of us, a meal including a starter described esperantishly as 'krabí kokteil' and salmon.

Banská Štiavnica

Saturday, 15 June was another beautiful day, with two castles in mind in Banská Štiavnica (Schemnitz, according to Müller and 'the Silver Town' according to its own publicity handout). About 46 km due south: back down to Zvolen, then west for a bit to Hronska Breznica, then due south along a winding, tree-lined road with plenty of sharp bends to whiten one's knuckles. Banská Štiavnica is one of those places that irritatingly straddle two pages of the road atlas, but we (or, to be honest, just me) would have messed up our entry into town in any case. We seemed to miss any sign that might point towards the centre and found ourselves heading due south before we decided to go back north and parked on waste land off Akademická street, from where we walked down to the attractive centre then up to the Starý zámok, or old castle, stopping off first to inspect, briefly, the Protestant church (the town has been predominantly protestant for about 200 years). It is ellipsoid in shape, with galleries.

Back to the Starý (old) zámok: it dates from the 13th century when it was a church which was subsequently fortified to withstand Turkish incursions. It is reminiscent of the *Kirchenburgen* in Transylvania. The castle is five-sided, with twin towers at the entrance and an originally Romanesque church of the Virgin Mary occupying much of the area within the walls. The church itself is of little interest, although it has a few exhibition rooms with various sculptures and bits of stone on display. Just inside the entrance to the castle, on the right up some stairs, are a number of other exhibition rooms displaying clocks, tobacco pipes, butts for archery and rifle practice and various other *objets*.

The castle is quite well-preserved, the outer walls pierced with numerous loopholes and with turrets at the angles which were used as an early warning system in the event of a Turkish army appearing, an ever-present possibility during the 15th–17th centuries when the castle was built. Shady trees in the courtyard make the whole site a pleasant place to be.

From here we walked down to Námestie Sv. Trojice (Holy Trinity Square) – 'today offering free Wi-Fi', according to the handout – where some sort of fête was going on, with stall holders, including one selling second-hand books. A young man invited us to go into the building behind him – the former Berggericht, now with a mining museum and 75 meter adit. Ivor inspected the adit, I looked at the bookshop and managed to find a guide to Spiš and a gazetteer of castles, châteaux and manor houses. The young female assistant was almost literally falling over herself to help me find books on castles.

Back to the car and up to the Nový (new) zámok, which had the advantage of being on a hillock with a tall tower from which a lookout could sound the alarm if he saw the Turks approaching. It was built as an adjunct to the Starý zámok in 1564–1571 and is like a tall fat cube with an integral round tower at every corner rising most of the way to the roof. The zámok is on several floors with permanent exhibitions on the Ottomans, including some of the weapons and letters written by approaching Turkish generals to the municipal authorities, along the lines of 'Town X refused to surrender so we pillaged the place and massacred its inhabitants. So, if you don't surrender, don't come complaining when you lot get massacred'. The castellan was showing round a party of bemused Slovaks, giving a guided tour in dreadful English.

Hronsek

We drove back towards Banská Bystrica but left the main road at Sliač to head to the village of Hronsek where there is a famous 18th century so-called *Artikularkirche* (wooden church) which has been on the UNESCO list since 2008. We parked in the main (and only) street and walked closer, only to discover the church surrounded by cars and a wedding just having taken place. They had reached the stage where an interminable series of photos would be taken.

In the late 16th century about 90% of the population of Upper Hungary were protestants, although they were persecuted during the Counter-Reformation. In 1681 Count Thököly of Kezmarok persuaded the Emperor Leopold to make some concessions to the Protestants. They were allowed to build a maximum of two churches in each administrative district. However, the churches had to satisfy certain conditions: they had to be outside town; made entirely of wood with no nails; have no tower; have no direct access from the road; and they had to be built within a year. Hronsek church was consecrated on 31 October 1726. It can seat 1,000 worshippers.

We walked back, slightly disconsolately, to the car, pausing to look at two other interesting buildings: firstly, a Baroque château (the Soósovsko-Géczyovský kaštiel', built in 1775) – two storeys, rectangular with integral round corner towers and some Rococo stucco work. It is in a rather poor condition – plaster in need of repair, rainwater stains on the façade, although the windows seemed to be in good nick. It stands in its own little park area, devoid of everything except grass and a few trees. I can find no indication of how the château was used from after the war until the fall of Communism, but as it is not a total ruin, or anywhere like it, it is quite likely to have been used as municipal offices or a children's home[25] (there is an appropriate note of melancholy about it).

A little further away is a moated castle, or *vodný hrad* in Slovak, dating from the fifteenth century and given a makeover in 1576. It is being impressively restored, but there are plenty of barriers to keep the nosey out.

Back in Banská Bystrica I visited the Museum SNP (Slovenské národné povstanie: Slovak national uprising) which started on 29 August 1944 and was effectively over on 27 October when the 'capital' Banská Bystrica was captured. It is estimated that about 20,000 Slovaks were killed and another 15,000 ended up in German captivity. Historians now think that the premature launch of the uprising was the work of Soviet partisans, Stalin having no interest in the Slovaks liberating themselves. The museum building is impressive from the outside (with, in the courtyard, memorials to Jewish and Roma victims of fascism) – it was built in 1965 to a design by Dušan Kuzma (1927–2008) – but the interior is slightly disappointing, most of it consisting of cases full of uniforms and medals. There are several permanent-loop archive films, but consisting mainly of scenes of soldiers on parade or politicians looking shifty. But not bad for 70 cents.

Back to the Kuria then out into the main square for a couple of life-saving beers. Weddings were in full swing here, too. Then for a meal. Ivor's turn to choose: the Olivio – a bad choice. Hopelessly disorganised service, the waitress bringing him his main course (tagliatelli with spinach) only a few minutes after giving him his starter (mozzarella caprese which seemed to take forever to prepare. My tomato soup should have taken longer). My main was penne quattro formaggi. We went back to the hotel. I discovered that my room had not been made up so complained to the

---

[25] *Burgen und Schlösser Slowakei* by Eva Križanová and Blanka Puškárová (1990) confirms it is a Kindergarten.

manageress, an Ute Lemper semi-lookalike, who immediately fetched clean towels. Thus mollified we had a drink in the bar, with a noisy wedding party going on in the restaurant and making it impossible to sleep. I was still awake at 2, Ivor at 3.

Orava

On the morning of the 16th, a Sunday, we drove up north again, this time to find Orava, rising on a precipitous limestone cliff 611m in height.

The first written records of Orava (German Arwa) date from 1267 when only the ground floor was built of stone, while the upper floors were made of wood. A multi-story tower, shaped like a triangular pyramid, was built here in the 14th century, probably on older foundations, as a donjon. As the glossy guidebook: says: *'Political and economical situation of Hungary got more complicated at the beginning of the 15th century. Threat of Turkish invasion and religious situation weakened power of the king and strengthened Hungarian oligarchs'.*

> In the period 1539–1543, prompted by the Turkish threat, Ján of Dubovec built a five-story *Palas* in the empty space between the tower and the stone wall of the Upper Castle. In 1556 František Thurzo became the new owner. Born in 1512, he had studied in Padua and had become bishop of Nitra in 1539. He resigned as bishop in 1555 on the death, childless, of his only brother, converted to Protestantism and in 1561 married Katarina Zrinská by whom he had five children.

In 1626 the Orava Compossessorate [SK komposesorát][26] was created, administered by a director elected from the descendants of Juraj Thurzo.

There was a devastating fire in 1800 which destroyed all the

---

[26] I think this is the equivalent of the German *Ganerbenburg*, usually translated (on the rare occasions when the need arises) as 'coparcenary castle' – 'coparcenary' referring to joint heirship.

woodwork and melted the bells in the chapel. Edmund Zičí became director in 1862 and he set about restoring the castle, as far as limited financial resources would allow. He also appointed as head forester one William Rowland, son of an Englishman with business interests in the textile industry.

Some exciting statistics for American readers: the Orava estate included more than 30,000 hectares of forest. In a period of almost twenty years (1864–83) Rowland renewed forests in an area of almost 9,500 hectares which involved planting thirty million trees and using 32,000 kg of seed.

Zičí died in 1894, Pavol Esterházy became interim director and was succeeded in 1896 by the last director, Jozef Pálffy who died in 1919 when the post was abolished.

We parked in a car park a couple of hundred yards away, walked down into a dip then, pre-empting the guidebook, *'up the picturesque access road and knock on the knocker'*, in time for a short wait before the guided tour. Scheduled to last about 45 minutes it took a good two hours and was well worth it. The castle seems to go up and up. Every now and again parents of small children would throw in the towel and watch, enviously, as the rest of us strode on ahead up steps and along walkways. The tour includes interiors – with slightly dodgy English captions – and, of course, an ethnographical museum although, thank God, this part was mercifully short. Ice Age man still hadn't invented leisure.

In the Lower Castle there is a drawbridge at the second gate (with Ján of Dubovec's coat of arms), followed by a tunnel under the 'Grand Terrace', then the third gate (with the arms of Juray Thurzo and his wife Alžbeta Czobor)) and on to the 'Grand Terrace' itself with the top of the castle still a very long way to climb. Then into the Thurzo Palace: polished wooden floors with minimal carpeting and lots and lots of eighteenth and nineteenth century furniture, a rather inadequate-looking armoury and the Wild-West-sounding 'Hunters' saloon', with heads of dead deer and a bear rug on the floor.

This takes us to the Middle Castle, with a bewildering array of wooden walkways and battlements leading to the Corvinus palace. The interiors are now almost all made of wood, with a portrait gallery of past owners dressed in the fur-trimmed outfits of Hungarian magnates. On to the second gallery, much older and homelier, again with wooden floors and panelling but also with floral-patterned wall paintings and a table and collapsible wooden chairs in the 'Knights' Hall' which also has an impressive tiled stove. The armorial hall is a more genteel affair with rather spindly wooden chairs bearing coats of arms. The clock winds back again to the sixteenth century in the Ján of Dubovec *palas* – heavy wooden furniture, some *sgraffiti*, and a dining room for mercenary soldiers. This part of the castle houses the natural history museum – rather good displays of stuffed animals – bears, boars, deer and otters – and the ethnographical museum: carvings, embroidery, leather shoes, filigree silver buttons and so on.

Then out into the open air again for the last leg: the *Horný hrad* (which is not as vulgar as you hope; it simply means the Upper Castle). Apart from the rather exhausting home straight up flights of steps, there is not much to see inside this part of the castle, although it is clearly the oldest part. There is a museum-type exhibition room with very few *objets* on display, although you can look down into the freshwater cistern.

Back in the Lower Castle we had paid to see the Kaplnka Sv. Michala, or St Michael's Chapel, a stunningly beautiful interior with both Renaissance and Baroque features, although the latter predominate. The main altar is as far over the top that one can go without reaching parody, with statues of St Anne and St Joachim and the Coronation of the Madonna. Around the walls are the Renaissance epitaph of Juraj Thurzo, with unnaturally happy-looking putti and (probably) maidservants, a baptismal font, the crypt of the Henkel family (now mentioned, oddly, for the first time) and a beautifully carved and painted choir loft. The sacristy has an exhibition of various vestments (which look quite modern) and a statue of St. Michael beating the Devil with a rather odd sort of sword.

We drove a relatively simple stretch to Spišska Sobota, or rather to Poprad of which it is a suburb. The motorway passes very close to a large reservoir, the Liptovská Mara, then the towns or villages of Liptovský Mikuláš, Liptovský Ján, Liptovský Peter and Liptovský Hrádok – sorry, this is getting repetitive – and through the foothills of the Tatras to Poprad.

Spišska Sobota and royalty

Spišska Sobota – or rather, the *'City Memorial Reservation Spišska Sobota, whose historical centre is one of the best-preserved urban units of Slovakia'* is part of the commune of Poprad, on its eastern side. After the motorway it's easy to miss the turning to Spišska Sobota (Georgenberg in German, but who on earth was Georg?) and we, unwittingly, took the easy option. Several times in fact – my mistake, I'm afraid – before locating where we should be heading.

Safely in the *Penzion u alžbertky* and the usual time-consuming checking-in procedure and locating the rooms – massive, of course – before we descended to the cellar bar for a couple of restorative beers with the charming young manageress, Dominika. Then out into the village to wander round in search of one of the three eateries she had recommended.

The village square is the usual elongated affair with a raised grass reservation lined with trees in the middle. It doesn't look as though much has happened here since the Turkish threat ebbed away several hundred years ago. Attractive white church, attractive trees, attractive *Bürgerhäuser*. All in all, very attractive. We located one of the places – the Atrium, a 16th century Renaissance building – which Dominika had recommended and I had grilled trout while sitting on an unstable metal chair in the garden which sloped slightly from the building.

After our meal we wandered round again and found an interesting plaque:

V tomto dome byvala
Zuzana Anna Hönschová
1747–1826
Manželka
Mórica Augusta Beňovského
1746–1786
Kralá Madagaskaru

[Literally: In this house lived Zuzana Anna Hönschová, wife of Moric August Beňovský, king of Madagascar]

A royal connection! Later I found out who Beňovský (Hungarian: Benyovszky Móric) was: an explorer, writer and officer in the French, Polish, Austrian and revolutionary American armies. In his memoirs he described himself on several occasions as a 'Hungarian and Polish nobleman'. His career began as an officer of the Habsburg army in the Seven Years' War during the reign of Empress Maria Theresa. In 1768 he joined the Confederation of Bar, a Polish national movement against Russian intervention. He was captured by the Russians, interned in Kazan, and later exiled to Kamchatka. He escaped and returned to Europe via Macau and Madagascar. In 1772 Beňovský arrived in Paris where he met Louis XV and was offered the opportunity to act on behalf of France in colonising Madagascar. After establishing the settlement of Louisburg, in 1776 Beňovský was elected by a group of local tribal chiefs as their Ampanjakabe (ruler). In 1779 he went to America, where he tried to obtain support for a proposal to use Madagascar in the American War of Independence. He died in 1786 while fighting with the French on Madagascar.

Spiš

Enough of that, we're off on the motorway again (Monday, 17th), heading east to Spišský hrad. Covering an area of four hectares it is one of the largest castle complexes in Europe and, built of bright white stone, 634 metres above sea level, it is impossible to miss in the blazing sun. In its heyday – the thirteenth to fifteenth centuries – it was home to about 2,000 people. It has five baileys but is much more impressive than Burghausen. It is also very exhausting to walk up to the *pokladňa* in the great heat – and we set off at a fast trot to get ahead of a coach load of Belgian pensioners who pulled into the car park just before us.

King Král has this to say of what he calls the Spiššky zámok (N.B.: not 'hrad'): *'It is composed of three parts, securely encircled by ramparts, the whiteness of which give the ruin a particular charm. There are a total of 5 courtyards and 135 apartments, only a small part of which are preserved today... Spacious view.'* (p. 228).

Building started towards the end of the eleventh century, with a huge circular residential tower 22.5 metres high, with walls 4 metres thick. Nothing remains of this, however, as the foundations collapsed in the late 12th/early 13th centuries as a result of tectonic disturbances. So, how do we know the height of the tower, mmh?

The earliest written records date from 1214 when it belonged to the Arpád and Anjou families. The castle withstood the Tartar invasion of Greater Hungary in 1241 and an attempt by Matuš Čák to seize it in 1312. More extensive building work took place in the fourteenth century with the great new bailey.

Spiš was caught up in the seemingly interminable wars of succession. It was held by the Zápolya family from 1464–1528, then by the Thurzos from 1531 to 1636 (who had previously held the castle for ten years in the middle of the previous century pending repayment of a loan by the king). They were originally from Levoča and had been 'in trade', their wealth derived from mining. They were also hereditary counts of Spiš and had close links with the Fuggers of Augsburg. Krištof Thurzo was born a protestant, converted to Catholicism in 1604 (his wife was a Catholic) and invited Jesuits to the castle. However, in 1613 he converted back to Lutheranism and died the following year after convening the Synod of Spišské Podhradie, which reorganised the Lutheran Church in eastern Slovakia.

Various unlikely legends are associated with the Thurzos, and the facts are further muddied by the activities of a robber baron. The last owners (until 1949) were the Csáky family, although the castle lost any military significance after a disastrous fire in 1780.

From the entrance a very steep path leads up past the middle ward to the Romanesque outer bailey, then back up to the inner bailey and the thirteenth century keep. Large parts of the upper castle (for example, the interesting-looking Romanesque *Palas*) are annoyingly inaccessible to visitors because of repairs or consolidation work, although we were able to wander around the museum area: a torture chamber, an exhibition of armour and weapons, a bedchamber and the Zápolya family chapel (Gothic, fifteenth century). Dripping with perspiration we bought water (and guidebooks) from the gift shop in the old barbican and explored the lower ward – a perfectly preserved high wall enclosing an enormous area which presumably could have been used to contain any army lucky enough to get that far; or it was used as a place for accommodating farm animals from the surrounding area in the event of a Turkish incursion.

Spišská kapitula

From the castle it is a short distance to Spišská kapitula where in 1198 German settlers built *'eine kirchliche Miniaturstadt'* (Müller) which for centuries was the spiritual centre of the Germans in the Zips region. We wanted to visit the early Romanesque cathedral of St Martin (1245–1273). We parked outside – rather warily, as there was a group of children begging rather insistently – and walked the few yards to the ticket office, arriving only a minute or two before the young guide. She gave us a thorough tour of the church in English.

The little guidebook has an odd typo: *'The present-day Spišská kapitula is closely linked with the foundation of the Spiš provosts hip...'* During the Reformation the town was an island of Catholicism in a sea of Protestantism. The Jesuits founded a grammar school here in 1646 and *'In 1776 Maria Theresia and Pope Pius VI promoted the Spiš provostship'* (it's been mended now) *'to the Spiš bishopric'*. In 1951, after the communist takeover and a show trial, the bishop, Ján Vojtaššák, was sentenced to 24 years' imprisonment (although released under an amnesty in 1963), the seminary was abolished and used as a military academy. In November 2001 the Slovak President was criticised for supporting Vojtaššák's beatification. Jewish leaders pointed out that he could have saved some of the 80,000 Slovak Jews who died in Nazi extermination camps; he had served on the war-time state council and knew of the decision to deport the Jews but had failed either to warn them or make any public protest.

Between 1462 and 1478 the Romanesque church was rebuilt in the Gothic style. In 1465 the Palatine Imrich Zápol'ský became the owner of Spiš castle. He wanted a burial chapel to reflect his wealth, so he built one in the cathedral between 1493 and 1499. The oldest part of the cathedral interior is the stone white lion by the side entrance door. He looks friendly enough, but his task is to guard the altars. The church used to have 13 Gothic wing altars, although only four have (partly) survived. (Gothic became Baroque which was then replaced by Neo-Gothic, with various forms of damage being inflicted on the way). The altar of the three kings, the altar of the death of the Virgin Mary and the altar of the Coronation of the Virgin Mary are all outstandingly good. It is possible that they were carved by a sculptor who had trained under Veit Stoss. Most impressive, however, is the altar of St Michael the Archangel – a copy of the work by the Flemish painter Rogier van der Weyden. The cathedral also boasts a wall-painting of 1317 showing the coronation of Charles Robert of Anjou as king of Hungary.

We asked if, despite the signs, we might be allowed to take photos. The guide reluctantly agreed, but so reluctantly that we decided not to take up the offer.

Levoča

Back down the motorway for a stop in Levoča (Leutschau) which still retains most of its mediaeval walls. *'A beautiful, old-fashioned town, founded in the XIIIth Century, with numerous architectural memorabilia, for which it is also known as the "Nuremberg of Slovakia"; it has had a glorious past and was once famous for its schools'*. (Král, p. 227)

> It was founded to replace Slav settlements following the Tartar invasion of 1242. Stephen V proclaimed it the capital of the province of the Zips Saxons in 1271. It was handily situated on a major trading route and became a powerful trading centre. Merchants were obliged to offer their goods for sale in Levoča for a period of 15 days before being allowed to move on. *'The development of the town was impeded in the 16-th to 18-th centuries as a result of the aristocratic uprisings and the Turkish expansion'*. It fell into total decline after the construction of the railway which bizarrely failed to include a station in the town.

The main sight is the church of St James, with a gothic altar by one Master Paul von Leutschau; at 18.6 metres it is the highest winged altarpiece in the world. Unfortunately, access was by guided tour only, we would have had to wait some time in the oppressive heat and we were thirsty, so we gave it a miss. We did, however, see workmen on the roof with no obvious sign of safety equipment. After a refreshing, shaded drink at *'the former town pub'*, we staggered down Košická street to the Košická brána (gate) and walked along the remains of the walls, past a grassy area strewn with discarded coke cans and condoms – obviously the town's youth club – before calling it a day, heaving ourselves back into the Saab and enjoying its air-conditioning as we popped back to Poprad.

After refreshing beers back at the penzion we walked back into Spišska Sobota where we found a delightful gourmet restaurant – the Fortuna – where we sat in the garden (under cover; it started to rain) and afterwards chatted to the owner who had excellent English. In addition to the restaurant, on the other side of the square he has a penzion also called Fortuna. It looks very attractive. The place has been going for several years and he was confident that it would continue to prosper. We felt it deserved inclusion in a restaurant guide.

Kežmarok

Our last day in Slovakia (the 18th), starting with a gentle 15 km drive up the Poprad (German *Popper*) river to Kežmarok (German *Käsmark*), a pleasant town of some 17,000 inhabitants (German *Einwohner*). We (German *wir*) had come partly to look at the *zámok* but, more importantly, to examine the wooden Protestant church, close to which we were able to park (only realising afterwards that we should have paid at a hidden meter). The church is plastered on the exterior and Král (p. 225) describes it as *'the most beautiful and most valuable wooden building in Slovakia.'* It is so valuable that you can only see it with a guided tour, although in practice this meant hanging around expectantly outside until an elderly lady appeared with a key and let us in, after which she was content to sit at a table spread with guidebooks and do her knitting, wearing a woolly hat, while we wandered round on our own.

The guidebook says that *'During almost 750-year existence of the town Kežmarok total 13 wars dragged the bounds of the town'*, but the dragging does not appear to have affected the church. A predecessor was erected in 1687–1688 but the present building dates from 1717. *'Swedish and Danish kings contributed for this purpose with whip rounds in their countries. It is commonly known about Swedish seamen that they helped to build the church: the church ceiling reminds of an upside-down foreship and windows are of round shape'*. The architect was one Juraj Müttermann from Poprad, the carvings – in particular the altar and the pulpit – are the work of Ján Lerch and the paintings by Gottlieb Kramer and his son Jonas from Levoča. The organ was built in the period 1717 to 1720 by Vavrinec Čajkovský (Lawrence Tchaikowsky), also from Levoča. The interior of the church is staggeringly beautiful with its wonderful polychrome woodwork.

We strolled from the church down the main street, past the *Rathaus* square, to the *zámok* and in through the main gates but decided to give the castle itself a miss. The last owner, Imre Thököly, was the leader of one of the major anti-Habsburg revolts and was forced to flee into exile in Turkey where he died in 1705. Since then the castle has belonged to the town, the burghers having bought it in 1720. There are two legends associated with the castle – a white lady and a black lady – neither of which is remotely interesting. The castle is in the shape of a softly rounded triangle and the north-eastern tract is used as a museum. There are various collections including 'The Association of Doctors and Chemists of the Spiš region' and 'The Kežmarok Shooting Circle'. Full of regrets, we decided to get on our way.

We drove up to Spišská Belá, then north-west straight towards the Tatras and on to a place called Podspády where, thanks to my inept navigating, we stuck to the main road instead of turning right along the Javornika river. Never mind. A few kms later we turned, retraced our steps, or wheels, and took the correct turning up the valley and over the unmanned border and into the soft underbelly of Poland for another 20–25 km to Nowy Targ, which I think must mean Newmarket, and which in 1927 had *'Longues rues, bordéees de curieuses maisons en bois'* (Orłowicz; Guide Illustré de Pologne), then roughly the same distance again to a town called Myślenice.

We stopped here because we wanted to find a cash machine to get hold of some zlotys. We decided to have lunch, too. The one-way system confused both of us but eventually we found somewhere to park and walk to the centre *mit typisch deutschem rechteckigem Ringplatz* (Baedeker's *Generalgouvernenent* (1943), hugging the walls of buildings as we went to avoid the rather vicious sun. We found a cash machine, and a rather uninspiring café/restaurant called the 'Eden' operated by a slovenly young woman where we had some fake Italian food.

From Myślenice we drove the remaining distance, another 20 odd km, to Kraków.

Kraków

We arrived at what should have been just before the rush hour, but wasn't. We passed a series of dull suburbs and then realised, to our relief, that we were on Konopnickiej road (and hence heading in the right direction). We turned right and crossed the Wisła or Vistula. Then what looked like a fairly straightforward drive along Dietla road followed. But Dietla was almost at a standstill and there were roadworks everywhere; we couldn't turn left where we wanted to; but suddenly, there we were, unexpectedly in Wielopole street. And there we found our eponymous hotel, but with no obvious spot for pulling up and checking in. A very attractive young woman on reception, looking a bit like the actress Emily Watson, in a blouse several sizes too small phoned the Holiday Inn across the road to see if we could use their car park. Regrettably no, but the Wielopole has a number of allocated spaces in the next road off the inner ring. So that's what we did.

Murray reported in 1879 that the city had

> '60,000 inhab., of which 25,000 are Jews... The city itself has somewhat of an Eastern appearance... though on the outskirts of the town many of the buildings are deserted and going to ruin, yet the number and rich architecture of churches, palaces and convents still remaining, are striking memorials of former greatness'.

Unlike Warsaw, Cracow was not destroyed during the war, the local Polish commander having sensibly decided that resistance was suicidal and the city surrendered to the Germans on 5 September 1939, *kampflos* as Baedeker's *Generalgouvernement* points out, only four days after the outbreak of hostilities. The Nazis hoped in the long term to convert occupied Poland into a vast colony where only ethnic Germans would be allowed to live.

Whatever the facts may be, it is a beautiful city. We walked across the inner ring road and through the *Planty* (gardens, which Orłowicz says are *ornés de plusieurs statues d'illustres Polonais*, although I can't say I was aware of them. Possibly removed by the Nazis?) to the Mały (small) Rynek. A *rynek* is a square, and it is tempting to link it etymologically with the German name for the Old Town Square in Prague: *altstädter Ring*. From here it is a short step to the Główny (main; cf. Czech *hlavný*) Rynek – a huge, almost perfect square (200 x 200m apparently), with the centre occupied by the old cloth hall (Sukiennice). King Kazimierz Wiełki (the Great, *not* the Whelk) had the original built in 1358 but it fell victim to a fire in 1555. It was rebuilt in the next three years to the plans of an Italian architect. Today it is full of cafés and souvenir shops but worth a look all the same. We wandered round, no need to hurry, looking at the horse-drawn carriages luring tourists to their financial doom (another parallel with Prague), then put our heads round the door of the Kościół (cf. Czech *kostel*) Mariacki, or Marienkirche, but decided to save it for some time tomorrow. Given the heat, it made sense – far more sense – to sit outside, have a drink or two or more and watch the world go by. We sat and watched until it started half-heartedly to spot with rain.

Before leaving the hotel we had armed ourselves with a free copy of 'Kraków in your pocket' (*my* pocket, in fact) and, feeling hungry, headed off the Rynek along Sławkowska to no. 13 (the former Tarnowsky palace), to the Czerwone Korale (or 'red coral', I think) listed in the 'Polish' section of the guide to restaurants. The guidebook maintains *'it may have the disadvantage of being discreet from the street'* – in what way is this a disadvantage? – yet *'the simple, but charming folk décor favours colour over clutter'*. Yes, very pleasant indeed, although we saw no sign of the *'photos of dancing highlanders'* (a Scottish connection, perhaps?) or *'peasant maidens frolicking in folk costumes'*. Decent peasant fare, coming to PLN128 (about EUR30) – the most expensive item (appearing appropriately in capitals on the bill as WINO) costing PLN44.00.

Then back to the Główny Rynek (after passing a French restaurant, la Fontaine, accepting a leaflet from the bored girl in the doorway, and apologising for having already eaten), for a final wander round, including a look through the windows of a bookshop (still open at this time of night), before another drink on the square and then strolling back to the hotel.

Wawel

Wednesday: breakfast in the cellar, the usual self-service affair, dodging a group of half a dozen large, loud and cheerfully ugly Dutch people. Then off for a spot of culture, a ten-minute or so walk along the *Planty* then up the *Droga do Zamku* (road to the castle) and the castle complex, or Wawel. There is a handy, central ticket office in a building containing the museum shop, restaurant and café a few hundred yards across the grassy-gravelly square from the cathedral and royal castle where you can book tours of the latter. We booked a mid-morning tour of the royal apartments, and a slightly later tour of the private apartments.

The original Gothic castle was destroyed by fire in 1499. It was restored and expanded by the Jagiellon kings in the period 1504–1535, under Alexander and Sigismund the Elder, who introduced Renaissance Italian art to monumental architecture in Poland. Orłowicz says: *'Après le démembrement de la Pologne, le château fut complètement ruiné par les Autrichiens qui le convertirent en caserne et transportèrent toutes les pièces qui présentait quelque valeur architectonique.'* During the war it was the seat of the *Generalgouverneur*.

The two separate tours (there's no reason why they can't be combined, although keeping them separate is a clever move to get visitors to pay twice) lead you from one breathtaking room to another, with much geometrical floor tiling, *Kassettendecken* and tapestries and decorated stoves in evidence. On the first tour we were allowed, once we had been let in, to wander round on our own and it was while we were in, I think, the Zodiac room that Ivor received a text message from his daughter who had been rather apprehensive about her maths exam. The msg sd: 'Math went good' which prompted Ivor to bellow with rage 'Shame about the fucking English' – which turned a few heads, I can tell you.

In the visitors' centre, in between tours, we had a coffee and raided the well-stocked bookshop, and very decent loos. Then back to the castle for the guided tour of the private apartments: a case of more or less of the same, although our dumpy guide tried to inject a touch of humour into the proceedings, for example by asking us to guess the purpose of various items or rooms. Some of our guesses, inevitably, bordered on the scurrilous. In the inner courtyard of the castle we were entertained, while waiting for one of the tours to start, by a couple being ordered about by a professional photographer as they modelled wedding outfits.

Our trip to the Wawel was rounded off with a visit to the cathedral, or *Katedrala Wawelska.* The first cathedral was built around 1025, the second ca. 1190–1142. It burned down in 1305 and in 1320 Bishop Nanker (careful with the spelling) began to build a new Gothic church. No need for a guided tour; you can wander about on your own, although the attendants are quite keen that you should tick off various points of interest. And so, for example, we climbed with a group of raucous, bored German teenagers up an almost endless series of wooden steps to see the Sigismund Bell, which must be one of the most disappointing sights of *Mitteleuropa*. If you ever feel like doing it, take my advice: don't.

Back in the main part of the cathedral we passed a box in which visitors can post their very own prayers. In my neatest handwriting I wrote: *'Pray for the Pope's conversion to Christianity'* and placed it carefully in the box. I don't know what effect it will have. Apart from this, I have to say that the cathedral has little of great interest beyond tombs of various kings, composers (e.g. Chopin), statesmen, marshals etc.

Murray was fairly unimpressed 134 years ago:

> '... the Polish Westminster Abbey... possesses externally neither splendour nor regularity of architecture; while within the numerous chapels surround it destroy all harmony of proportion.'

We walked out of the complex through the Brama Herbowa and then decided to split up: I was keen to see the Jewish quarter; Ivor had other plans.

Kazimierz: the Jewish quarter

I walked south-east along Starowiśna. It looked a very long distance on the map, but by keeping to the shady side of the street I managed to turn this into a pleasant stroll. This quarter is known as Kazimierz, *die 1335 durch König Kasimir vor den Toren Krakaus angelegt wurde und Krakau überflügeln sollte... später jedoch z.T. Wohnsitz der jüdischen Bevölkerung Krakaus wurde (jetzt judenfrei).* Baedeker's guidebook was written in 1943, *nota bene*.

I turned right into Miodowa, then – after failing utterly to locate the ritual bath – left past Aron Weinberg's boarded-up shop (*towary galanteryjne* – luggage and leather goods) and into Szeroka, a pleasant square (not square of course). J had eaten somewhere in this square on her visit to Krakau – at the Klezmer Hois, I believe, but I had forgotten this at the time so I went into the Hamsa resto bar owned by, or at least inspired by, Yotam Ottolenghi. I mentioned this to Ivor later. His response was: 'Oh, him. Have you read his recipes in the Guardian? They always require at least 30 ingredients, 20 of which can't be found in any known shop'.

I had a delicious fattoush, which I hoped would not make me fattish [joke], washed down by a beer. The guide in my pocket, I later found out, says (p. 46) the restaurant is 'located in a district where dining establishments still treat Jewishness as a faded sepia part of the past'; whereas Hamsa makes 'a bold impression simply by being bright, modern and free of clutter' (that OCD dislike of 'clutter', again). If Hamsa produces Jewish cuisine, why is it listed in the guide as 'Israeli' (there is no 'Jewish' section)?

Then on to the serious stuff. I started with the Remuh synagogue (a little way down Szeroka and on the right) and its cemetery. It is described in the pocket guide as 'The smallest but most active synagogue' in Kazimierz, and is still used for Sabbath services. I asked if there was a discount for the aged but was told by a young man with a beard and sarcastic sneer: 'You're not the first to try that'.

> The building dates from 1553, but was fully restored in 1829, and can easily be visited despite the restoration work currently being carried out. It was the second synagogue to be built in Krakow and so was known originally as the New Synagogue. During the occupation it was used by the *Treuhandstelle* – to store sacks for corpses in the main room and firefighting equipment in the women's prayer room.
>
> [This and much other information on Kazimierz is taken from Eugeniusz Duda: *Jewish Cracow* (2010)].

The synagogue has a beautifully decorated ceiling, a Baroque (?) fireplace and a wall panel listing the names of, I imagine, prominent members of the congregation at the time of what I take to be restoration work in the period 1919–28. Of the 36 names almost all are of German, rather than Polish, origin.

There is also a plaque in Hebrew, Polish and English:

> In memory of the Jewish martyrs of Cracow who were annihilated by the Nazi Germans in the terrible period 1939–1945
> Earth Do Not Cover Their Blood

A party of American Jewish tourists were being shown round the cemetery, which includes the tomb of Rabbi Mojżesz Isserle (known as the Remuh, from the Hebrew acronym of his name) and his wife, Golda Auerbach. The synagogue's name in Polish is *Bożnica* (= temple; >house of God?) *Remuh*.

In 1994–95 a new restaurant was opened next to the synagogue. Duda is unimpressed: 'Unfortunately, it does not at all suit the historical character of Ul. Szeroka… with the whole effect serving only to demonstrate the investor's bad taste and conceit' (p. 55).

At the end of Szeroka is the old synagogue, the Synagoga Stara. It dates from the turn of the 15th and 16th centuries. Before the Nazi invasion this was the centre of religious and social life in Kazimierz. It is now a museum dedicated to the Jews of Krakow. It is just that – a museum – but full of interest. As Mr Pocket says: 'The English explanations assume no great depth of knowledge on the reader's part and are therefore a perfect primer on the subject'. Quite so. The collection includes a *bimah* (the platform bearing the table from which the torah is read) enclosed in an elaborate, wrought iron balustrade. The Austrian Archduke Rudolf and his wife visited the synagogue in 1887.

From here I made my way to the Izaak synagogue (named after its founder, Izaak Jakubowicz), completed in 1644, because I had discovered that there is a klezmer concert there every evening at 6 p.m. and I wanted to reserve a ticket.

Then at the end of the street I turned left, crossed the road past the Jewish Community Centre and next door into the Temple Synagogue. This is a relative newcomer dating from 1862 and intended as a *deutsche Schul* (German synagogue). During the Nazi occupation it was used as a warehouse and for stables. Regular services apparently stopped in 1978, although it still hosts concerts.

It is the home of the Progressive (Reform) Jews, with services conducted according to principles established by German rabbis in the 1840s – in formal terms closer to Christian services than those in traditional synagogues. Originally weekly sermons were given alternately in Polish and German. There was choral singing accompanied by an organ, and women sang in the choir in the interwar period. Today it is the traditional venue for the opening concert of the annual Festival of Jewish Culture. The interior is very reminiscent, albeit on a much smaller scale, of the great synagogue in Budapest, with an impressive ceiling painted in a very obviously nineteenth century style. As I was leaving a female attendant kindly pointed out that my ticket would allow me to go up to the gallery, and so I did.

There – apart from a stunning overview of the interior of the synagogue – I found one of the oddest signs I have ever seen:

Warning!
You are **NOT allowed** to dance and jump in tenement house. Human presence on the floor **over 150** people **strictly prohibited!**

After some more rather aimless, time-killing wandering about, I returned to the Izaak synagogue. I needn't have bothered to reserve: there were only about a dozen people there, perhaps tripling by the time the concert started. The fate of the building during the war is unknown, but in December 1939 an SS man shot Maksymilian Redlich, an official of the Jewish community, in the synagogue because he refused an order to burn it down. In the ten minutes remaining before the start of the concert I admired the *bimah* (reconstructed), the cradle vault, which Duda tells me has stucco work similar to St Mark's, and the women's gallery: 'The loggia is the most splendid in Kraków and has features in common with renaissance galleries'.

The concert itself, lasting about an hour, was given by a four-man group called Tempero (violin, accordion, double bass and percussion), exceedingly lively and joking musically with each other, the stars being the accordionist in his leather hat, the obvious leader, and the percussionist. The rather sparse audience made up for numbers by applauding wildly and the band seemed genuinely rather astonished at the warm response. About two-thirds of the way through a large, broad-backed man with a *kippah* came and sat immediately in front of me and opened a book while the band were playing. It was a religious text of some sort with two columns of text: Hebrew and Russian. He nodded his head vigorously while reading, then after a few minutes closed the book loudly, kissed it several times and walked out, apparently pleased with the music.

I bought the CD, of course, and hastened back to the hotel to tell Ivor. 'It was great; you would have hated it.'

We walked back through the centre and up Floriańska to the Brama Floriańska, the main gate of the former fortifications (built 1300) which survived when the walls were demolished and replaced with the *Planty*, and the barbican (erected 1498). Too late to go in, but we admired them from the outside. Then along Piiarska and past the Piarist [the spell checker helpfully suggests 'pianist'] monastery, turning left into Slawkowska, heading for La Fontaine whose leaflet we had picked up last night.

Mr Pocket is spot on: 'Here delicious French food is served by a well-trained staff who actually appear to enjoy what they do' – absolutely true; they could not have been nicer or more obliging. In the area where we were sitting – *not* the courtyard terrace which Pocket reckons is the 'pick of places to eat at La Fontaine' – the clientele seemed to be without exception Anglophone. Sitting behind us, most of their way through their meal, were two Scottish couples of about our age, the women swooning at the heavily chocolate-themed desserts, the men rolling their eyes at us, then off to the leftish two middle-aged women, both Irish, one of whom was giving the other a detailed account in real time of some trivial incident or other. Later two more British couples (also *d'un certain age*) arrived, sat down, studied the menus then after a few minutes got up and walked out. They don't know what they were missing. We had an absolute blow-out. Starters. Mains, desserts, with wine, port and liqueurs all for PLN403,80 (about EUR96 – very, very reasonable). We chatted to the helpful waiter; he said that although the serving staff were all locals the chef was a genuine Frenchman from, I seem to remember, Bordeaux.

CHAPTER 5

A Habsburg tour
– May 2012

———◆———

Vienna

Wednesday 9 May

I took a taxi from Wien Westbahnhof (where I bought the Guardian) to the hotel. The taxi driver asked where I was from. When I told him he said 'Omigod, I thought you were German – don't mean to offend, squire'. The Erzherzog Rainer is one of the Schick hotels – 'Wiens charmante Privathotels' as they call themselves. My room, on the 4th floor, reminds me very much of the room I had in the 'designer hotel' in Budapest a couple of years ago.

The receptionist sold me a 72-hour Wien-Karte: unlimited use of public transport, free of charge, and discounts on museum entries. It cost €19.90 so I need to make 10 trips to break even. In three days this should not be difficult.

Having dumped my luggage in my room I caught the no. 62 tram – a nice old-fashioned affair with wooden fittings, looking vaguely like a train from a Western – as far as the Ringstrasse, by the Oper. I walked down Kärntnerstrasse as far as the Stephansdom, looking for untouristy restos in side streets. Plenty of them but all full. Back to the hotel where I sat on their roadside wooden terrace, served by a jokey young head waiter. 'Gibt's noch was zu essen?' – 'Nein – nur trockenes Brot' (laughter).

I had a Wiener Schnitzel plus a couple of beers. It's getting extremely hot.

Thursday 10 May

To work. Ten museums in Vienna are having or have had or will be having exhibitions focusing on Gustav Klimt (anagram of 'vast milk gut') to celebrate the 150th anniversary of his birth. Some are on now or will be when I return in ten days. Today will be devoted to three: the Albertina, the Oberes Belvedere and the Leopold Museum.

Start with a decent breakfast then back on the No. 62 tram which this morning had tables between the seats like a commuter train.

The Albertina's exhibition is called 'Die Zeichnungen' – an entirely accurate description. The museum owns hundreds of Klimt's drawings and on display were sketches for other pictures (portrait paintings, some of which were also on display) and very many drawings in their own right. The exhibition was pleasingly underpopulated. There are few things more irritating than finding visitors – usually the elderly and short-sighted – standing very close to the pictures so that you have to dodge about trying to look over their shoulders as they sway about. Everything is here, from Klimt's early days until right up to the last year of his life, reflecting a style that seemed to have crystallised almost overnight and remained unchanging for about 35 years, while still managing to look cutting edge.

As with most commentators, the museum made light of the more erotic drawings of women, in particular those where they are masturbating or obviously recovering from a girl-on-girl experience. Were these activities staged for his benefit? You can imagine the girls giggling as he handed over a banknote or two, then undressing each other and having a jolly good time. He certainly seemed to have some sort of power over them. The rich were happy to have him execute vanity portraits, the working glass girls quite shamelessly earning a bob or two on the side. We have a book of his *Zeichnungen* at home. It would be inaccurate to say that it falls open at the dirty bits since, if that were the case, it would have disintegrated long ago. In any case, where would you start?

'Fischblut' was on display – that sensuous picture of sirens floating in a stream, their long hair extending behind them and the current barely covering their pubic mounds.

It would be interesting to know the precise relationship between Klimt and Emilie Flöge (coincidentally his sister-in-law). Was it purely platonic? It's possible, but his paintings of her and her photos show she was quite a stunner (even when clad in her rather voluminous *Reformkleider*).

Entrance normally costs €11, but if you are a Senior it's only €9. The same ticket allows you to see any of the other exhibitions in the Albertina. I therefore went to the permanent exhibition, next floor up, called 'Monnet bis Picasso'. Also present: Toulouse-Lautrec, Cézanne, Modigliani et al.

Off now to the Oberes Belvedere. At the ticket office I asked about a concessionary rate with the Wien-Karte and the charming lady, roughly my age, said 'Es ist billiger, wenn Sie alt sind'. Yes, over 60s pay next to nothing. The only compensation I have so far discovered for ageing.

I had a light meal on the ground floor in the 'Café-Bistro Menagerie', which was full of elderly sweating English tourists.

I returned to the hotel for a couple of beers and a Käseplatte before setting forth for the Leopold Museum.

It has a hugely impressive staircase which I mounted, after picking my way through an enormous throng of young people.

The exhibition I had come to see was called *Klimt Persönlich*. The title is an accurate description: dozens and dozens of letters and postcards, for example, from Klimt to Emilie Flöge whom he clearly missed terribly when he was on his travels. It is interesting to note that although they were lovers they lived separately; for most of his adult life Klimt lived with his mother.

Afterwards I ate at the Augustinerkeller before heading back to the hotel. There was an Australian couple sitting nearby: my age but knocking on together quite well, giving the impression of years of mildly amusing in-jokes.

Friday 11 May

I took the tram to Karlsplatz and the Karlskirche – the Karl being Charles Borromeo. After the last major plague epidemic in 1713 the emperor Karl VI (the Pragmatic Sanction man and father of Maria Theresa) promised to build a church in honour of his namesake, Carlo Borromeo, who had a reputation as a plague saint. Following an architectural competition, Johann Bernhard Fischer von Erlach was commissioned to build the church and the foundation stone was laid in 1716. After his death in 1723, Fischer's son Joseph Emanuel completed the church by 1737.

The most striking external feature of the church are the two tall columns, with spiralling reliefs from the life of Borromeo, which are supposed to look like Trajan's columns but to me seem to give the whole building the appearance of an Indian temple. Inside it is standard Baroque, but interestingly the side chapels – like English parish churches, but very unusually in German-speaking countries – contain memorials to various first world war regiments. In one side chapel there was a note in English to visiting Australians and New Zealanders to say that there had been a commemorative service on Anzac day.

From here I walked in the powerful sun to the Secession – a beautiful building, of course, but disappointing inside with only the Beethovenfries. It was better displayed when we saw it in Balingen in Baden Württemberg last year where you could stand back and have a good look. Here, it was in a fairly small room – presumably the original dimensions – and visitors could walk up onto a viewing platform. But the frieze is now so close that it's difficult to get an overview. The frieze was originally created for the 14th exhibition in 1902. The Republic of Austria bought it from its previous owner (from whom it had been expropriated by the Nazis in 1939) in 1973 for 15 million Schilling. It was restored between 1974 and 1985.

The Secession shows exhibitions of other artists' works. Some rather dubious. Degenerate or what?

Off now to the Dom, passing Loos' loo which I used and photographed. Adolf Loos, pioneer of modern architecture, was renowned for designing buildings free of any ornamentation whatsoever. Franz Josef – in other respects a supporter of modern art (he awarded a prize to Klimt early in the latter's career) – found Loos' buildings rather offensive. In 1928 Loos was given four months prison for sexually abusing underage girls.

I went into the Dom. If you want to walk up and down the nave and the southern aisle you have to pay an extortionate sum of money to the catholic church which is already wallowing in unearned, undeserved riches. In any case, the Dom is far more impressive from the outside because of the coloured geometrical pattern of tiles on the roof, than on the rather gloomy inside.

I set off in search of the Beisl Reinthaler in Dorotheengasse, just off the Graben, but the pavement tables were already full and I didn't fancy sitting inside in this heat, so I had a wander around, calling off at the Kapuzinerkirche and paying a bob or two – €4, concessionary rate – still a bit steep for a load of old tombs – to go down into the Kapuzinergruft. It is, of course, *full* of tombs, but you can spend a pleasant twenty minutes or so ticking off emperors and empresses – Maria Theresia, for example – and also-rans: there is a plaque to commemorate Franz Ferdinand and his wife, but they are buried elsewhere. However, Franz Josef is there – a massive affair – and Karl, the last emperor: attempts are being made to have him canonised because of his efforts to stop the first world war.

Otto the Palindrome and his wife Regina of Saxony who predeceased him are also there. Otto has a better claim to being a decent cove than his father.

Back then to Dorotheengasse where I found an empty table outside the Reinthaler and enjoyed a decent Schnitzel and a couple of beers which set me back a not unreasonable €16.60. At the next table was a man slightly older than me who kept looking anxiously at his watch until a woman in her early fifties appeared.

A Beisl, by the way, is Austrian for *Kneipe* – a pub with food. It might come from the Czech 'pajzl' (pub) – a diminutive of 'hampejz' which has various meanings including (1) kennel, (2) bowling alley and (3) brothel. Take your pick. Or it could come from the Yiddish *bajiss* (= house). Who knows? Who gives a toss? The Schnitzel was excellent.

On the other side of the narrow street was a hotel bearing a plaque saying that Kafka and Brod had stayed there. By a bizarre coincidence I am writing this on 25 May, the morning after a visit to the Philharmonie in Luxembourg to see the silent film *'Die Frau, nach der man sich sehnt'* which is based on a novel by Brod (Czech for 'ford'). The programme notes refer to Brod's refusal to carry out Kafka's instructions and burn the latter's manuscripts. Apparently someone – clearly not a fan – said to Brod: 'Max, why don't you burn your own manuscripts?'

I ventured out later to the Mozart house in Domgasse, an area behind the cathedral that looks strikingly like parts of Prague. Mozart lived here for two and a half years from 1784 to 1787 and it is where he composed *The Marriage of Figaro*. The house is an attractive old building, but as the guide materials say, no-one has the slightest idea about the actual disposition of the rooms. Presumably bedrooms were higher up, but apart from that one can only speculate. Rather disappointing and, of course, the audio guide (which the attendant insisted on giving me) distracts from what there is. You are left standing rather hunched listening to an act-or-ly voice describing, at several removes, the courtly and theatrical worlds of eighteenth century Vienna, with various sticks of furniture, paintings and artefacts (none of which were part of the original furnishings) to set the scene. However, it was pleasant enough, and the resemblance to Prague quite uncanny. There is also a good museum shop which I raided.

Saturday 12 May

Taxi from the hotel to the Westbahnhof, the taxi driver very interested in my destination and urging me to go to the central market in Budapest. At the station in plenty of time to buy the English papers and stroll onto the platform – which even now looks only one remove from the Wild West (*da fängt der Orient schon an* as Metternich is alleged to have said) – and board the train to Budapest. This is the comfy way to travel inter-city.

Budapest

The train arrived about 5 minutes late at *Keleti pu* where I fought off taxi drivers, bought a ticket – no-one in Hungary with any contact with tourists, except those in restaurants seems to speak much of any language other than Hungarian – and took the metro three stops to *Déak ter*, changed and one stop to *Arany Janos utca*. I had already phoned the agent, another Janos, to say I was on my way. He replied that he might be a few minutes late and I strolled (inasmuch as a stroll was possible with my absurd amount of luggage) to the address on *Deszewffy Utca*.

> Arisztid Deszewffy (1802–49), a general in the Hungarian Army, was executed for his part in the Hungarian Revolution of 1848, and is considered one of the 13 Martyrs (all generals) of Arad (which is now in Romania). He commanded 100,000 men against Russian troops and surrendered because of the massive size of the encroaching Russian army. He was executed around 4 a.m. by firing squad, along with three others. The Prince of Liechtenstein intervened at the last minute to spare them from hanging, which was considered public humiliation.

The building is rather unprepossessing from the outside: stonework stained by years of pollution and, if you look up, pockmarked walls. Whether this is the legacy of the 1956 uprising I don't know. No answer to the bell. In fact, no idea which bell to ring, so I called Janos again and in a couple of minutes he and a bearded fellow, his friend Jozsef, arrived on bikes. Janos asked if I needed help carrying the luggage up 62 steps and when I said 'yes' replied 'sorry, I can't help; my back hurts'. Jozsef was no help either. We are on the third floor, on a walkway surrounding the inner courtyard and with a view onto the street.

Janos and Jozsef kindly explained how the keys work – rather on the lines of turn one way to lock, turn the other way to unlock. Seems easy to grasp… I handed over 30 quid but there was no explanation of why it had to be sterling. They also took a €100 deposit which Jonathan had not warned me about. However, the flat is very attractive and very large with two bedrooms (I grabbed the better one), two bathrooms, a kitchen – with (full) jam jars everywhere – and a large and pleasant sitting room.

Janos and Jozsef also recommended which of the public baths to visit.

Jonathan arrived in due course. We walked into town. It was getting nippy and windy. So we had Kaffee und Kuchen (blueberry & poppy seed) at Gerbeaud on *Vörösmarty tér* (founded 1858; according to Lonely Planet 'a visit is mandatory'. It did not disappoint). It was now getting bitterly cold so we walked virtually next door to the Onyx bar where one of the waitresses said she had lived in Hammersmith. Later we had a meal at the Casablanca resto.

Sunday 13 May

I woke up late to discover Jonathan had slipped out to get rolls and butter. Good man; he knows his place. We cracked open one of the 50 or 60 jars of jam then walked to the Metro and bought two three-day travel cards. We took the metro to *Kallman* square. It was beginning to turn cool, with the wind blowing and trees shaking. With help from an elderly lady we took the bus to the castle district.

We walked from one end – the Vienna gate (Bécsi kapu) – to the other, the other being the Royal Palace. The walk took in Táncsics Mihály utca, a street full of little houses painted in bright colours, and '21 magyar vendéglő' with *some wonderfully innovative modern takes on traditional Hungarian'* cuisine (Lonely Planet). We took a take each. The Royal Palace contains the Hungarian National Gallery, the Budapest History Museum and the National Széchenyi Library, none of which we bothered to visit. We did visit the Matthias Church (where Matthias Corvinus marred his queen, Beatrice in 1474), although it is a rather fraudulent neo-Gothic creation (1896). Liszt's Hungarian Coronation Mass was first performed here in 1867 for the coronation of Franz Joseph.

Later, after more non-specific sight-seeing we stopped for a drink and a snack at the Auguszt Cukrászda (as recommended by my friend Hélène).

Monday 14 May

A walk up to Nyugati (nougat?) station near the flat and to a shopping mall (rhymes with 'pal', not 'pall') with a Match supermarket. We bought cheese, salami and bananas and took them back to the flat for a pre-dormy feast.

Having eaten our fill – Oh yes, we have no more bananas – we walked along pedestrianised neighbouring streets, across one called O Utca (vocative?) to the Opera to check the times of guided tours. Then via a devious route past tarted-up apartment blocks in the old Jewish quarter to the Great Synagogue or Nagy zsinagóga. It can seat about 3,000 and is apparently the largest synagogue in the word outside New York.

It was built in 1859 to the design of Ludwig Förster, a Viennese architect. Although not Jewish he seems to have specialised in designing synagogues, and churches. Perhaps as a result some features of the building recall Christian churches. For example, there is a central rose window and the synagogue is sometimes referred to as the 'Jewish cathedral'. The building was renovated in the 1990s largely with private donations, including $5 million from Estée Lauder.

In an annex to the synagogue there is the Hungarian Jewish Museum which we duly inspected. There's a plaque on the outside wall saying that Theodor Herzl, founder of modern Zionism was born there in 1860.

Off for refreshments at another of Hélène's recommendation: the Lukács Cukrászda, described by the Lonely Planet as *'dressed up in the finest of decadence'*, so just right for two provincial lads from Gloucestershire.

Tuesday 15 May

A walk down Váci Utca, the main shopping street, but I failed to find the bespoke shoe maker that J and I had spotted a few years ago. And then on to the central Market which is a market, of course, but lively and absolutely rammed full of colour.

Then, full of anticipatory excitement, we took the metro from Kalvin to Kossuth for a guided tour of Parliament, but discovered it wouldn't be open until tomorrow. We cut our losses by walking via Freedom Square and the American embassy to St Stephen's basilica. Described by Lonely Planet as a *'gem of neoclassical architecture'* it is not terribly interesting or gem-like. Building work started in 1851 but was not completed until 1905. It contains the right hand of St Stephen, but we dexterously avoided this, took a few duty photos and released ourselves back into the community.

Another walk, this time to the Hungarian State Opera House – *'small but perfectly formed'* as Lonely Planet puts it or *'a magnificent neo-Renaissance pile'* according to the Rough Guide. We had a guided tour. It was worth the money if only to see a plaque dedicated to Miklos Banffy, briefly Foreign Minister of Hungary (1921–22) and director of the opera house. The building itself is attractive and very reminiscent of the Opéra Garnier in Paris.

Evening: the Bazilika restaurant near – wait for it – the basilica.

Wednesday 16 May

Another attempt to have a guided tour at 10 of the Parliament. We walked there and arrived at 9.20 and joined the queue. By 10.10 we were no closer to the box office so we gave up in disgust and instead walked to the nearby Museum of Ethnography. In addition to its permanent exhibition, e.g. re-creations of peasant houses, it had a temporary exhibition on rug making in Hungary and places that used to belong to the kingdom of Hungary. We both thought it very good. The English captions to the exhibits were good on the whole with some words oddly separated, e.g. 'a tan' instead of 'at an'.

Health-conscious as always, we walked across the Margaret Bridge and made our way to the Lukacs baths – *'popular with keen spa aficionados'*, as L. Planet says; so, just right for Jonathan; *'a bathing suit is required'*. Well, I can't manage a suit, but are trunks OK? We must have been here for about an hour: a very pleasant experience.

In the afternoon we went to the Museum of Applied Arts which *'owns a king's ransom, of Hungarian furniture dating from the 18th and 19th centuries'* (L. Planet) and is well worth a visit. A long walk back to the centre and another visit to Gerbeaud.

In the evening we walked to the Marquis de salade which serves Azerbaijan, Russian and Hungarian dishes. Apart from the absurd name I couldn't recommend the restaurant, I had steamed lamb (or 'steeds jamboree' thanks to predictive spelling on my i-phone), which was bloody tough, I can tell you.

Thursday 17 May

We settled up with the rather odd agents who returned our deposit.

A rather crowded railcar train to Győr then a shortish walk to our hotel, the Klastrom occupying the eighteenth-century priory behind the Carmelite church. Quite an attractive place, despite the lack of a lift. If you imagine central Győr as a sloppy square, our hotel is in the bottom left-hand corner. The city itself is pleasant enough, but it was hard to fill the day with sights. We had lunch at the Palffy.

We dutifully inspected the Carmelite church and the surviving bastions of the castle. Then up Chapter Hill (Káptalandomb) to visit the cathedral. A traipse around the Xantus János museum full of artefacts relating to local history. We ended up at the Péter Váczy collection: 15th–18th century Hungarian and European sculpture, paintings and furniture.

To make up for this rather dull day we dined at the Dinne in Kreszta Ház which Mr Rough correctly describes as having *'wholesome and generous portions of stock Hungarian dishes, in convivial surrounds'*. Or 'surroundings' as we say in English.

Friday 18 May

We walked to the hotel Famulus to pick up our hire car. No problem with language as the owner is a Scot.

A short drive of 20 plus kilometres took us to Pannonhalma abbey. Prince Géza invited the Benedictines to establish an abbey here in 996. It is basically Gothic(ish). You have to have a guided tour. There were just four of us: Jonathan and I and a Hungarian couple. The guide handed us a sheet in English and said 'You can ask me anything you like'. Unfortunately, they were the only seven words of English that he knew. You get to see a film then go along a modern walkway to the abbey. I have to say it was profoundly disappointing- with the exception of the magnificent library.

We came across another guided tour, this time a party of Israelis. This may seem odd, but in 1944 Abbot Krizosztom managed to secure immunity under the International Red Cross which enabled him to save refugees and Jews. He was subsequently, and rightly, honoured by Yad Vashem with the posthumous title of Righteous Among the Nations.

There is a herb garden attached to the abbey.

Slightly miffed, we headed west towards Fertőd. The sole reason for going there – and, indeed, our reason – was to visit the

Esterházy palace. It is built on originally malarial swampland which was drained by hundreds of serfs. Then in 1720 Count Joseph Esterházy ordered work to start on the palace. The architect, Erhard Martinelli, had contracted to build a hunting lodge of 22 rooms (just a 'lodge', eh?) in 23 months. Whether he succeeded I don't know, but Joseph's son Miklos (or Nikolaus) 'the Ostentatious' built something better and building continued until his death in1790. Miklos built a village – Esterháza – for the staff and craftsmen, stables for 110 horses and quarters for his personal army of 150 grenadiers. However, after Miklos his successors shifted their main residence to Eisenstadt on the Neusiedlersee (not very far away; then in Hungary, now part of the Burgenland in Austria). The palace was occupied again at the beginning of the twentieth century but the furnishings and fittings were looted in the last weeks of the war. Proper restoration did not start until 1958.

The guided tour covers 23 of the 126 rooms in the palace. Tours are in Hungarian only, but leaflets are available in other languages. I picked up one in German. As Mr Rough says, the highlights on the ground floor are the Sala Terrena and several blue-and-white chinoiserie salons. Upstairs there is the banqueting hall where Mildorfer's *'superb fresco... is so contrived that Apollo's chariot seems to be careering towards you across the sky whatever angle you view it from'*. There is also, not surprisingly a Haydn exhibition.

I came here *en famile* when the children were quite young and we had been staying on the Neusiedlersee. We crossed the border one day, parked and discovered several other cars from Luxembourg.

The palace is full of portraits of various members of the Esterházy family, views of their landed possessions and gardens and pretty much anything else that you would expect to find in a beautiful eighteenth-century *Schloss*.

As an antidote to all this culture we crossed the main road from the palace for a coffee in the former guardhouse, recommended by my colleague Nigel, before continuing our journey to Sopron (Ödenburg in German).

Sopron has a population of 62,000 but feels comfortably small – or at least the old town does. It is centred on Fertő ter (Neusiedlersee square). We still had time to take in the sights and so we did: the triple-aisled Goat Church, a Franciscan establishment with a ridiculous founding myth. The construction was allegedly financed by a goatherd whose flock unearthed a cache of valuables, in gratitude for which an angel embraces a goat on a pillar. In most countries this is illegal.

Then the Firewatch Tower (erected after a disastrous fire in 1676) and the Gate of Loyalty, built-in honour of the locals' refusal to accept the offer of Austrian citizenship in 1921 following a 'controversial' (dixit Wikipedia) plebiscite (German-speakers still account for 6% of the population).

What else? Well, we took in the town walls and Uj utca, an attractive street with cobblestone pavements with a tiny medieval synagogue at no. 22 diagonally opposite a slightly newer one at no. 11.

In the evening we dined at the 'Erhardt et Vinum Étterem Borpince', an attractive modem resto in a Baroque house with a wine bar in the courtyard; traditional Hungarian dishes. My notes say that it was the 'best meal of the trip'.

CHAPTER 6

Moravia and a bit of Austria – May 2014

We had a largely uneventful and sunlit trip until Regensburg. The SatNav proved exceptionally useful in negotiating the back streets of greater Regensburg and avoiding the crowds flocking to the *Dult*, the annual fun fair and, in fact, trade fair. It is held twice a year. Quite soon we reached our hotel, the Sorat, in Müllerstrasse on the Jahninsel near the *steinerne Brücke*. I had a lucky upgrade to an executive suite, an absurdly large affair. Presumably because there was only one upgrade available and the booking was in my name. I had an enormous sitting room with a balcony overlooking, indeed overhanging, the Regen, a large bedroom, a bathroom and a separate loo. Ivor, however, had to make do with a poky garret.

After restorative drinks from our minibars we set off on an initial wander round town. What does Murray have to say? He's not very encouraging. He lists and comments on some of the inns – '*Kronprinz*, then points out *dirty; Nürnberger Hof; Weisser Hahn, for bachelors*'[27] then points out that the 31,000 inhabitants include 6,500 Protestants and 300 Jews and finishes with quite a downer: '*In its present state it has an air of dullnes*'. Well, we shall see whether we agree. By contrast, Baedeker is neutral about the city but

---

[27] Murray quotes in this chapter from are from the *Handbook for Travellers in South Germany and Austria* (14th edition, 1879).

suggests the Grüner Kranz (*'second-class, well spoken of'*) and the Post (*'unpretending'*)[28].

We crossed the *steinerne Brücke* which is undergoing refurbishment and up through the narrow streets to the Kohlenmarkt and Rathausplatz, the two running into one, then on and up the Untere and Obere Bachgassen to locate the Schloss for tomorrow, before heading back down to the Ratskeller for a Wiener Schnitzel for me and a Zwiebelrostbraten for Ivor. Oddly enough, the Ratskeller has only been a restaurant for a relatively short period of time (since 1910), but a succession of olde worlde rooms and covered courtyards, where we sat, is deceiving.

Regensburg (or 'Ratisbon' as both Murray and Baedeker insist on calling it) is very beautiful – this was my first visit – and we were both quite captivated by it. The centre is full of mediaeval tower houses slightly reminiscent of San Gimigniano, and in one small square – the Heideplatz – there is a statue of Don John of Austria (1547–1578), an illegitimate son of local girl Barbara Blumberger and the emperor Karl V (who stayed in the Goldenes Kreuz in 1546, possibly enjoying the *table d'hôte*, which Murray says was good). His – John's – great claim to fame is that he was the commander-in-chief of the Holy League's fleet which destroyed the Turkish navy at the battle of Lepanto in 1571. The Turks had the numerical superiority (300 ships to Don Juan's 213), but their fleet was annihilated. Despite losing some 13,000 men, the Holy League was able to liberate about 10,000 Christians. The Holy League's victory meant that the Ottomans' attempt to expand further into the Mediterranean was thwarted.

First stop today (the 26th): the St. Emmeransschloss, formerly an abbey but converted in 1809 into the palace of the Thurn und Taxis family – *'an extensive but not a handsome modern edifice'*, which is all that Murray has to say apart from *'It is hardly worth the trouble to enter it'*. I think this is a slightly, but only slightly unfair judgement. It is rather disappointing. Baedeker, by the way, is

---

[28] Baedeker quotes in this chapter are from *Southern Germany and Austria including Hungary and Transylvania* (5th edition, 1883).

silent on the Schloss. It is, of course, an excellent marketing success for the dowager Fürstin (Mariae Gloria geb. Gräfin und Herrin von Schönburg-Glauchau[29], to give the lady her full name) but you soon realise there's not a great deal to see. What is interesting, however, is that the family were originally from northern Italy and their name was Tasso (Italian for 'badger' which features in their coat of arms), Germanified as Taxis.

What the visitor sees of the Schloss is the result of restoration work in the nineteenth century. From the *cour d'honneur* you go up the marble staircase which, the guidebook helpfully tells you, is made of marble, and into the large dining room and then we get a bit of history.

> In 1490 Francesco Tasso was commissioned by the emperor Maximilian to organise a permanent postal service between the imperial courts in Innsbruck and Brussels. By using staging posts at regular intervals, with a permanent supply of fresh horses and riders, Francesco cut the travelling time from about four weeks to about four days. As a result Maximilian raised him to the nobility as a 'von'. Further honours were bestowed on the family in the course of the seventeenth century: Freiherr (1608), Graf (1624) and finally Fürst (1695). The family were granted management of the postal services in perpetuity.

Back to the guided tour, with the winter garden and then the throne room: three generations of Fürsten were imperial commissioners at the Permanent Reichstag in Regensburg between 1748 and 1806. We saw the other standard representative rooms – ballroom (transferred here from Frankfurt in 1890 and fitted out with electric lighting), the balcony room (with a portrait of Sisi), rooms of varying colour (Silver, Yellow and Green) – before being released back into the community. Everything bears the stamp of

---

[29] We have come across this family before; see Červena lhota.

Fürstin Gloria, once the idol of the gossip columns because she was only 20 when she married Fürst Johannes, 34 years her senior. Their son Albert is nominally the Fürst, but the Fürst seems to be the last: Gloria appears to run the show.

We had a look at the church next door (St Emmeran), a Benedictine basilica and the work of the Asam brothers (1731–1733). It is everything one might expect of a baroque church. I seized the opportunity to take a photo of a statue commemorating a man called Bozo.

In the afternoon we went to the Dom (St Peter's), famous for its mediaeval stained glass and a group of statues representing the Annunciation, including a laughing angel.

After this we split up. Ivor wanted to explore more bookshops, while I wanted to see the Ludwig der Bayer exhibition. It was scattered over the Domfriedhof (uninteresting; seemed to be mainly tombstones) a church next door (St Ulrich's with quite a lively film, but not terribly revealing: modern man in mediaeval dress walking the audience through the history of the city) and the Stadtmuseum (excellent).

> Ludwig (1282–1347) was the younger son of Ludwig II, Duke of Bavaria. He contested the succession with his elder brother Rudolf (whom he defeated), was elected Holy Roman Emperor in 1314 and inflicted a resounding defeat on the Habsburgs at the battle of Mühldorf in 1322. Ludwig's election as Emperor was disputed and there was a *Doppelwahl*, with Friedrich the Fair, Duke of Austria supported by almost half the electors, although in the end Ludwig prevailed. He had the support of the Luxembourg mafia (Blind King John of Bohemia, Archbishop Balduin of Trier and Peter of Aspelt, Archbishop of Mainz) plus the Duke of Saxony and the Margrave of Brandenburg.

The Stadtmuseum's exhibition was spread over several false floors inside a decommissioned church. There were few other people to disturb me, and I had ample time to linger over the exhibits.

In the evening we had a drink in the hotel bar then, as far as we were able, dodged the thunderstorm that had been impending all day and made our way gingerly through the rain to the Regensburger Weissbräuhaus, an old brewery-cum-restaurant – wooden floors, *sehr gemütlich*, with huge shining brass vats – where we sat at a table near three Americans: parents plus daughter who appears to be studying here. The parents were bearable, but the daughter had an unbearably whiney/chainsaw voice.

To Olomouc

Today, the 27th of May, we drove from Regensburg via the Prague ring road to Olomouc, a distance of about 550 km, almost all motorway. The road from Prague south to Brno seems to consist of alternating stretches of 5 kms of motorway, then 5 kms of road works with narrow lanes, and I must admit I slept most of the way.

Our hotel – the Prachárna (the meaning of which will become apparent later on) – is in the north-western suburb of Křelov and *just* far enough out of town to discourage us from walking, so after checking in we drove into town, ending up parking in Opletalová street more or less opposite a gym, silently shaking its head at our lack of exercise.

> Olmütz (Holomauc)... one of the strongest fortresses in the Austrian dominions, situated on the March, or Marawa; it has 15,000 Inhab. and a garrison of 10,000 men with 80 field-guns. In case of attack, Olmütz can be flooded to a depth of 5 ft. for a distance of 3 m. on each side of the fortress. (Murray)

The fortifications were dismantled in 1888.

We walked around town: up to the Horní náměstí (upper square) with its massive *radnice* (town hall with astronomical clock) and statue of the Holy Trinity, then the Dolní náměstí (lower square) with a shop window with the sign 'grunt', so we did, to show willing, and up to the left past a second-hand bookshop that was just closing, sod's law. On past Sv. Michal's church and Sv. Sarkander. Jan Sarkander, (1576–1620) was a Catholic priest – and graduate of Olomouc university – executed by the (Protestant) Moravian Estates for refusing to divulge what was said in the confessional. He was canonised in 1995.

Then to Denisová, which is essentially the main street leading past the church of P. Marie Snežná (Our Lady of the Snow) and ever onward (the road now having turned into 1. maje) until we turned left along Domská to the quite pleasant Václavské náměstí (Wenceslaus square) with, of course, the cathedral and the archdiocesan museum. I remember visiting the cathedral with Jonathan. It is not terribly interesting. The door was open, so we went in and confirmed the lack of interest. It's a nineteenth century retread. We can give the museum a miss, too: pleasant, but dull, although I seem to remember having had a coffee there once.

So, back down Domská, across the main road and up Wurmová (a strange name, perhaps recalling a German burgomaster) which has, on the left-hand side, a series of eighteenth-century buildings – formerly the grand residences of various canons – and culminating in the archbishop's palace. *'The Bishop of Olmütz* [says Murray] *is the only Austrian prelate who has the right of electing his own dean and chapter'*. Then off to the right past various university buildings and back past the church of P. Marie Snežná and through a short arcade where someone – the tourist authority, perhaps – had left a chained piano which any passing musician was invited to play. And someone was playing just then.

In 1848 the imperial family fled to Olomouc from Vienna and it was here, in the archiepiscopal palace, that the mentally challenged Kaiser Ferdinand abdicated in favour of the 18-year old Franz Joseph (whose father Archduke Franz Karl had wisely waived his right of succession).

Olomouc suffered heavily during the Thirty Years War, thanks in part to an occupation by the Swedes who plundered it and made off with the ancient library. In 1618 the city had a population of about 30,000. When the Swedes left it had fallen to 1,675 – and a further 500 or so were later wiped out in a plague epidemic. Today the city has a population of just over 100,000. In 1930 the population was 66,440 (of whom 22.6% were Germans) and in the 1935 general election Henlein's Sudetendeutsche Partei picked up 14.9% of the votes. In other words, if my arithmetic is correct, and assuming the inhabitabnts voted on ethnic lines, two-thirds of the German inhabitants voted for the Nazis.[30]

Olomouc is described in the modern Baedeker[31] as a 'lebendige… Grossstadt', which is on the optimistic side.

We walked back to the car and then drove back to the hotel where we had a good meal served by a pert red-headed waitress: starters, then a steak for Ivor and trout for me. If you are not terribly keen on poultry or pork – staple items of diet in peasant countries – and you find steak rather boring, you have a hobsonian choice of food in the Czech Republic. Trout, salmon and pike seem to be the only options.

Bouzov

Our first major *sortie*. Ms Satnav (she's female and a bit of a dominatrix) took us out through Křelov, past signs to a *pevnost* (fortress) and on to the motorway as far as Litovel where we drove cross country – beautiful country – through soulless villages, including one called Starý Pivovar (old brewery) to Bouzov (Busau in German), one of the most touristy castles in the Czech Republic.

It dates from the turn of the 13th/14th centuries – so it is a fairly late build – and the first owner of the (wooden) castle

---

[30] Statistics from Bahlcke et al: 'Böhmen und Màhren' (Handbuch der historischen Stätten), 1998.

[31] *Tschechien*, 6th edition, 2014.

was, inevitably, one Búz of Búzov (hence the brewery?). In the late 14th century it passed to the Moravian margrave Jošt, nephew of Karel IV, then to the Lords of Kunštát (who seem to have been very important in this region) and the Lords of Poděbrady. It may have been the birthplace of the last native Bohemian king, George of Poděbrady. Later it was owned for two periods by the Podstatský family, and the guidebook tells us that the castle *'did not enjoy nothing but enhancements'*. What? Oh, I see: there was a fire, a tower fell down...

In 1696 the last Podstatský sold the castle to the Teutonic Knights who retained it until the Order was abolished by the Nazis in 1939 who seized their assets. The Golden Age of Bouzov came under Grand Master Archduke Eugen (Evžen in Czech) who commissioned a Munich professor of Architecture, Georg Joseph von Hauberisser, to refurbish it in the historicist style. The work lasted from 1896 to 1910 and the Archduke invested 20 million sovereigns of his own money in the venture. In 1912 the castle was opened to visitors.

We had a guided tour, the guide being a young woman who reminded me very much of our friend Raffa, although Raffa hasn't dyed her hair bright blue as far as I know. The tour takes you over a stone bridge with the inevitable statue of St John Nepomuk, then through the Elizabeth palace, the oldest part of the castle and named after the Archduke's mother. Upstairs we saw three rooms: two bedrooms and a study, all furnished beautifully, the individual items having ivory and tortoiseshell inlay and intricate carvings. On the wall of the study is a porcelain wash basin which, the guidebook is keen to point out, *'is not the only washbasin in the castle connected to the water mains'*. Very handy, I'm sure.

Then there is the armoury, although the mediaeval weaponry would have been fairly useless in real combat in the late nineteenth/early twentieth century, a 52m deep well and a marble sculpture of St George taken from the Order's house in Venice.

Upstairs again to the guests' quarters: a bathroom and five knights' rooms, the last of which has a wooden barrel-vaulted ceiling brought here from Sterzing castle in South Tyrol. There is also an upright piano, should any guest wish to tickle the ivories after using one of the wash basins.

The topmost floor contains the bodyguards' room, again barrel-vaulted, with a massive fireplace and, finally, the knights' hall. It spans the entire width of the palace, with stained-glass windows and a sun-symbol in the vaulting with rays depicting the sky at night and by day. There are crests of owners of the castle but fortunately, we did not dwell too long on these. The room leads into the chapter hall where meetings of the Order took place, with wooden seats at the sides and a canopied throne for the Grand Master. All very pompous, to give the Archduke the impression that he had a real job to do, even though the Order was reduced by now to a charity. The room has the largest chandelier in the castle with 48 candlesticks: a statistic to rival the depth of the well. The Grand Master's private quarters – huge but not necessarily overbearing or over the top – complete the tour.

Šternberk

We moved on to Šternberk, our journey somewhat impeded by the need to avoid roadworks and follow official detours which didn't lead anywhere and which slightly unnerved Ms Satnav. As the cock crows Bouzov to Šternberk is a straightish line but we had to go via the one and only Uničov and tackle Šternberk from the north, overshooting the signs to the *zamek*, then finding a public car park outside a pub. The castle looks impressive and is largely intact: a compact complex dating from various periods.

It was founded after 1253 by Zdeslav of Šternberk who acquired this area to the North of Olomouc from Přemysl Otakar II in exchange for military assistance. As the English version of the castle's website helpfully says: *'It concerned*

*of courageous defence of Olomouc which was right in
1253 besetted by Hungarians and Kumans. It is pretended that
Zdeslav of Šternberk commanded the defence of the town,
defended Olomouc successfully and as a reward he was allowed
to built a castle here'.*

It was owned by the Liechtenstein family from the end of the 18th
century until 1945 when they were sent into exile. Despite being
ethnic Germans, as citizens of Liechtenstein – and not the German
Reich – I am surprised they were not exempt from the Beneš
decrees. A few years ago there was a scandal when it was revealed
that one of the smaller Czech conservative parties had been
bankrolled by the Liechtenstein family in the hope of facilitating
restitution of their castles and estates. In the period 1886–1910 they
renovated what was in effect a ruin on historicist lines. We bought
tickets from the *pokladna* and then, to kill the twenty minutes before
the guided tour started, had a look at the rather extensive and
interesting exhibition of photos and documents commemorating the
Liechtensteins and their recent(ish) visit.

We had signed up for the Liechtenstein collections tour which
in effect gave us the chapel, the knights' hall and Renaissance
arcades. The youngish guide knew that we were not Czechs so
issued us with an English text which we read while she provided
explanations in Czech and we nodded as if we had understood. To
her (and my) surprise I was able to ask an intelligent question, in
Czech, in the chapel: why is the statue of the Madonna wearing a
cloak lined in red and not blue? She replied that both were
possible, but this one happened to be red. Fair enough; it's what I
would have said in her shoes. The knights' hall was large, the
Renaissance arcades spacious, light and airy. There is not much
else to be said: it was charming and interesting enough for 45
minutes or so. We thanked the guide and walked down into the
little town.

On 4 March 1919 the Czechoslovak army put down an attempt
in Šternberk to proclaim an independent province of Sudetenland.

Just over 11,000 of the pre-war population of 12,000 were ethnic Germans.

Back to Olomouc for our evening meal at a cheapish sort of place near the Moravska where Jonathan and I had eaten on our previous visit. In fact, we sat in exactly the same seats. It was *U červeného volka* (the red bull): this time I had salmon, while Ivor had the trout, before heading back to the hotel for a drink.

Sovinec

It is Thursday 29 May. We set off north again, past Šternberk and out into the wilds to the tiny settlement of Sovinec where, just short of the castle, we found a car park. Sovinec was founded in the 1330s by two brothers, Pavel and Vok. Picture the scene:

> Traveller: Where's the castle?
> Peasant: Vok knows.

The castle is built on a rocky outcrop (of the Jeseniky mountains) and originally it had a cylindrical tower on an octagonal plinth. Vok's descendants expanded the castle, improving the fortifications and generally making it much larger. During the Hussite wars the owners hedged their bets by supporting first the Hussites and then the Emperor.

> The castle passed peacefully from one family to another until Jan Kobylka, a Lutheran, fought on the wrong side at the battle of the White Mountain in 1620, was pardoned by the Emperor in 1621 but was obliged to sell the castle to Archduke Karl as a home (another one) for the Teutonic Knights. The Swedes besieged Sovinec which capitulated in October 1643. The Swedes stayed until 1650 when the castle reverted to the Order. During the Second World War the castle was used as a POW camp for French officers. *'A special group of SS had its seat in Sovinec, and hermetically sealed the castle from the outside.*

Thus the activities of the castle in those last years of the occupation are covered by an impenetrable veil of secrecy and speculation' (Wikipedia). In early May 1945 there was a huge fire and the state started reconstruction work in 1951. From 1950-1960 the Moravian Philharmonic of Olomouc was in residence.

Again we had a young woman as guide with rather extravagant hair. Again, I was reminded of Raffa. We were let loose for a quarter of an hour or so before the guided tour could begin. We used the opportunity to go up the main tower – towers act as a magnet for Ivor. Then the tour started in the main courtyard.

No chance of 'representative rooms' of course; it's a ruin. Instead we had a rather long introductory lecture (the guide providing us with a (very) brief summary and asking me to confirm that a boundary stone is indeed called 'a boundary stone' in English). Then it was up the wooden staircase to inspect the interior. Some of the rooms have been populated with shop-window dummies wearing historical costume, and a fireplace has been made up, should they wish to spring to life and warm up a bit. Otherwise it was a pleasant way of spending a morning and we ended up by traipsing through the museum with collections from the time when the castle was used as a seminary and later as a forestry school. The others on the guided tour seemed fairly bemused by this, and then we were back at the ticket office buying guidebooks and I managed to chat to the guide and a bearded male colleague in very bad Czech which, of course, they thought was absolutely marvellous.

Outside, walking the short distance back to the car, we passed a memorial to one of the French POWs:

VINCENT GILBERT
Kpt. Franc. Armády
* 10.9.1882 v Montlucon (Alier)
× 17.1.1941 v Sovinci jako
Valečný zajatec zdejším hradě

(Vincent Gilbert, captain in the French army, b. Montluçon, d. in Sovinec as a prisoner of war in this castle).

I have Vincent and Gilbert relatives. What did he die of? This is where the *impenetrable veil of secrecy and speculation* comes in. He was only 58 so it was probably malnutrition.

Helfštyn

And now for a pleasant cross-country motoring in Ivor's sleek automobile, down past Olomouc, onto the motorway and off east towards Ostrava and the Urals beyond. In fact, we turned off at Lipník nad Bečvou, then drove on to Týn nad Bečvou and up a rather unpromising track until we reached the car park below Helfštejn: a huge, ruined castle – 'a dilapidated château' as Baedeker calls it, but one of the largest in the Czech Republic – with **no guided tour**. Whoopee!

> It was founded shortly after 1306 by a robber knight called Friduš who didn't survive a punitive expedition by Blind King John. Then it was owned by the Kramař (literally 'grocer') family off and on until the mid-fifteenth century after which it seemed to change owner roughly once every 15 years until it passed into the possession of the Dietrichsteins (see Mikulov below). They and their heirs (first the Hatzfeldt-Wildenburgs, then the Althans; see Vranov, below) held it until 1922 when the state confiscated it and then bizarrely restored it to the Althans in 1930 who owned it until 1945.

The castle is long, expanding gradually from the entrance complex then suddenly, after a moat, swinging left to form a massive fortress-cum-residence. Helfštejn has five gates and four courtyards. The palace cellars (in the main castle) house permanent exhibitions about the art of the blacksmith and the operation of the mint. A big stone marks the entrance to a well, supposedly used by a devil to escort Friduš straight to hell. Every year Helfštejn hosts *Hefaiston*, a gathering of master blacksmiths from various countries. The cellars – OK, OK, but what about the rest of the building? Well, most of it is totally inaccessible to visitors. You can walk up to it, touch it, but you can't get in, which rather defeats the object of a visit to what my children used to call a scrambly castle.

One part which you can enter, however, is the so-called 'Hussite tower' although, as the guidebook coldly says *'věz nemá s husity nic společně'* (the tower has nothing to do with the Hussites). Nevertheless, you can climb up a series of wooden stairways from gallery to gallery until you reach the top (fifth) gallery which gives an excellent panoramic view over the countryside.

We drove down and back to Lipník which has some of its original walls still standing, and a disproportionately large town square. The little town housed a Piarist Gymnasium (one of whose alumni was Gregor Mendl, the 'father of modern genetics'), while the municipal school was divided in 1873 into a Czech, a German and a Jewish section. Apart from this we saw little to detain us – as Murray says: *'picturesque externally, with old watch-towers around it, but dull and dirty within.'* Perhaps he is being a little unfair, as he goes on to say that it has *'one of the finest cemeteries in the Austrian dominions, which contains a remarkable echo.'* Had we known, we could have spent a fun-filled hour or so there shouting rude words and hearing the sound rebound. I took some money from a cash machine outside the Money Bank[32].

Boskovice revisited

It was Friday the 30th. Just before Hrochov a young deer crossed the road slowly and oblivious of Ivor's reputation.

We entered Boskovice from the east, trailing through rather drab suburbs until we reached the main square when I realised – slowly

---

[32] Cf. 'bread bakery', 'meat butcher's' etc.

– that I had been to the town before, a realisation which became apparent when we drove up past the château to the castle.

Again there was, thankfully, no guided tour of the thirteenth-century Gothic castle as it is largely a ruin, but with a pleasingly clueless translation of the text for visitors. Large parts of the castle are still standing, and the various areas are clearly labelled, but the tiny museum has an unnecessary emphasis on the founding legend. This involved a man called Velen. One day he found a lost aristocrat in the woods – not an unusual occurrence in those days – gave him food and drink then made a bath for him. The aristo was then lashed with birch twigs – a spot of S&M. Velen obligingly dried his guest (frottage?) and *combed out his long hair with the wooden comb*. The grateful aristo returned to Brno and ennobled Velen. This, apparently, is the origin of the original coat of arms: a seven-toothed comb on a red background. What a load of nonsense...

When we came to leave a workman stopped to chat and, having ascertained that it was our car parked outside the entrance, said the police would get us.

- Why? Because we're foreign?
- No.
- For being the wrong colour?
- No.
- For being badly parked?
- No, for driving up a 'local traffic only' track.

We laughed scornfully at this nonsensical idea, drove back, swerved sharply to avoid a group of schoolchildren, and parked outside the château which Jonathan and I had visited.

The château has its origins in a Dominican monastery (founded in 1684). In 1819 the Dietrichstein family started work on converting it into a château: a *'fierce reconstruction'*, according to the slim guidebook. In 1856 the château and estates passed from the Dietrichsteins to the Counts of Mensdorff-Pouilly. Interestingly, after the war – although the estate had been expropriated by the

Communists – the Graf and Gräfin were allowed to stay on, albeit in only three rooms, until their deaths in the early 70's. Graf Alphonse was a cousin of both Victoria and Albert. Graf Alexander was Austrian Foreign Minister from 1864 to 1866. In September 2022 another Alphonse was given a six-month suspended sentence for money laundering.

As the guidebook says, *'If you allow yourself to be drawn in by the austere yet cozy [sic] exactness of Empire architecture, Chateau Boskovice will be the source of many pleasing experiences for the eye and soul'*. This is pretty much true, at least as far as the eye is concerned. Although undoubtedly elegant it also appears to have been a properly lived-in family home with, for example, a rococo children's theatre – a present from Queen Victoria – and miniature children's furniture.

Next door there is a pleasingly elegant hotel – originally the *'Rezidence'*, used by the family until the château was converted – obviously owned by the family.

According to the pre-war censuses the population was overwhelmingly Czech but it was once home to the largest Jewish community in Moravia. Before 1938 it had almost 400 Jewish citizens, of whom only 10 returned in 1945. Today there is a Jewish trail around the town.

In the evening we took taxis to and from the town centre to the Moravska restaurace. Modern Baedeker refers to the 'rustikale Einrichting mit viel Majolikakeramik' while the Rough Guide says it has 'wait-staff [*sic!*] in folksy costumes'. The wait-staff – who on earth uses this weird expression? – were rather pushy, trying to offload unbidden starters on us before we had had a chance to study the menu (or prices). However, the food was good – yes, starters, then veal for me and goose for Ivor followed by puds (unusual for me), beer, wine and mineral water; all for CZK1,800, including a tip (roughly EUR65).

The experience was enriched by two men at the next table: one Czech, the other Dutch, a visiting academic who, at one point announced: 'I am hated by banana taxonomists.

Hukvaldy

Out east again today, the 31st. First stop: Hukvaldy. This involved heading out on the R48 (aka E462) and leaving at the Fryčovicve/Rychaltice exit, then driving about 4 km south, through the village to the castle car park. From there we walked past stalls selling various local produce – a festival was about to start – and then up through parkland for about a mile until we reached the castle.

Hukvaldy – basically long and narrow – underwent a number of changes in its 700-year history, from early Gothic castle to baroque fortress. As the English leaflet explains: *'Building phases are marked off colourfully and tonality is import with the same coloured text in the signature'* – so, no risk of getting lost.

The building dates from 1260–1270, the work of one Frank of Příbor, son of Arnold of Huckeswald (hence Hukvaldy). The bishops of Olomouc bought it in about 1347, building work was suspended for almost a century, it was captured by the Hussites in 1428 then bought by George of Poděbrady (see above; Bouzov) in 1465 who in turn sold it to Bishop Tas of Olomouc in 1469. The castle's fortifications were strengthened after 1526 in the light of the threat of permanent war with the Turks.

In 1555 Bishop Mark Khuene *'let there be built a new renaissance palace with big sunny rooms'*. Later *'there was established in Hukvaldy the prince's prison for prince's and followers of church reformation'*. Then an embarrassing admission: *'1566–1568 was established a deer park, but in a different place than we can find it now'*. How on earth can you lose a deer park? Mmmh? Hukvaldy was not spared by the Thirty Years War. *'For the whole year of 1626 Pribor's'* (we're running out of diacritics) *'bourgeoisie escaped to the castle in front of the Danish… The castle got a reputation of the miracle fortress'*. Later there were various minor incidents (*'1730 the deer park was moved next to the castle'* [even harder to lose it, I would have thought], *'1738 the well was destroyed by mistake and that was the beginning of the castle's demise'*; in 1742 and 1758 inept Prussians failed to capture the place; after 1775 *'Castle become a ruin'*).

There is quite a lot to see in the castle, and lots of stairs have been repaired so that young families were able to run up and down the towers, or watch the various mediaeval-type activities taking place in what the leaflet calls the *'Big square'* (large bailey?), where children were being encouraged to try their hand at archery; *'there used to be a slithery according to the old tradition'*. No idea what that might be, but it has now slithered away and next to it is the chapel of Sv. Ondřej (St Andrew), pleasant but dull. The *'front fortification'* or *Kulatina* – from 'kulaty' meaning round or circular? – (dating from the 1480s) is vaguely circular with a wall walk about fifteen feet up enclosing an area of seating, presumably for some sort of mediaeval spectacular.

We walked back down the hill using a short cut which was certainly shorter, but dangerously steep in places. Hukvaldy's other claim to fame is that it was the birthplace of Janáček, and there is a statue in the grounds of the Cunning Little Vixen.

Jičin to go

We headed off to Novy Jičin (German Neutitschein: the population was overwhelmingly German before the war). In Murray's day the town belonged to the Theresianum in Vienna. Baedeker called it *'charmingly situated'* while Modern Baedeker optimistically claims it is a *'lebendige Industriestadt'*.

As we entered the town we had the feeling – common in these parts – that there had been a massive transfer of population shortly before our arrival. Either that or all the inhabitants were knocking back a copious lunch at home, certainly not in the restaurants. The town square is supposed to be one of the wonders of Moravia. It certainly lives up to its reputation: with its arcades, Renaissance and later buildings, all unspoilt, on all four sides of the square and with some interesting gables. I recorded a short video film. We saw five people: three youths outside a (closed) ice-cream parlour and a woman pushing a baby in a pram. No-one else. And this at about 1 o'clock on a Saturday (but the shops had closed at 11).

We wandered as far as the church (locked, although it was possible to peek in) then towards the *zámek* which now houses the city museum. We decided to give the special exhibition of hats a miss (created in 1949 on the 150th anniversary of the first hat factory here). Instead, because it was sodding hat – sorry! 'hot' – we sat inside the Hotel Praha drinking coffee and mineral water. One waiter took our order then vanished and a totally different man brought the drinks.

Novy Jičin looked the sort of town that might, under other circumstances, have been quite lively; if something lively were happening, for example. In the 1930s almost 14,000 people worked in the tobacco factory here.

No matter. We drove on to Starý Jičin (Alttitschein, as Baedeker confirms) where we parked in the village and walked, wheezing and sweating, up to the Starojický kopec ('hill', like the German 'Kopf') and the ruined castle past the posters tacked to trees advertising

Strašidelný
hrad

tomorrow and on Sunday from 7 in the evening. A 'Strašidelný hrad' is a spooky castle, featuring in this case a *kat* (hangman), *čert* (devil), *vodnik* (water sprite), *upir* (vampire) and, of course the usual *bilá paní* (white lady). Thank God it's Friday...

The castle forms a rather corpulent ellipse and is owned by the local council which clearly does not have enough money to spend on repairs or even consolidation. It was built about 1240 by Arnold of Huckeswald (see Hukvaldy above). It belonged to the Žerotín family from 1500–1622 who built the Renaissance 'palác'. The emperor confiscated it in 1622 and gave it to the Dietrichsteins. It was occupied by the Danes in 1626–1627 and garrisoned by Swedes in 1643. By 1780 it had become a ruin.

We wandered about. There are magnificent views from the castle, but most of the inner bailey is overgrown with trees and vegetation and there are no signs indicating which bit is which. Some young people appeared to be hacking away some of the undergrowth, no doubt in time for the spookfest tomorrow. In the one tower that was still intact there was an exhibition of artists' impressions of what ruined castles in Moravia might have looked like had they not been ruined.

There was a wedding in full swing back at the hotel so we sat in the temporary bar set up in the reception area to have a drink or two. Every few minutes one or other of the guests (large, ruddy men; a variety of women with a marked correlation between age (older) and length of dress (shorter)) staggered past to get to the loos. We watched them in between eating soup and a beef dish.

Buchlov...

Sunday 01.06: We left the Prachárna after breakfast, the dining area being full of wrecked-looking couples and horribly bright-eyed children from last night while, out in the concourse, a large group of women was forming, and knocking back coffee. All very elegantly dressed – very high heels, very short dresses, loads of makeup (so only air-kissing), hovering around the entrance to the seminar room and treating total strangers as long-lost friends. It seems odd to have a seminar on a Sunday. Ivor's suggestion – that they are trainee Avon ladies – seemed entirely plausible. As I was packing I saw a cuckoo fly low from right to left over the car park.

I asked the receptionist about the name of the hotel. I had discovered that 'prach' means powder but had failed to make the obvious connection: he explained that the hotel was built on the site of a former gunpowder magazine which used to service some of the forts originally surrounding Olomouc.

We drove southwest down the E 462/R 46 to Rousínov, then off onto the 50 (also *E* 50, to be absolutely clear) south eastward past Slavkov (Austerlitz; we visited the gloomy château about ten years ago), then off due east through small villages and open fields until we turned more south-easterly after Střilky and drove through about five miles' worth of very attractive forest until turning off up to the left to Buchlov.

We arrived with only about 20 minutes to kill and asked at the pokladna for an 'anglický text'. The lady said the guide would issue foreign-language texts at the entrance to the tower.

> The castle – originally owned by the crown – is described by the guidebook as belonging to the transition period of the Romanesque Gothic. The oldest feature is the late Romanesque arch (ca. 1240s), the work of stonemasons also working on Prague castle. An Early Gothic chapel was built (1259–1266), modelled on the Sainte Chapelle in Paris. The castle was besieged by Matthias Corvinus in 1468. It acted as the administrative centre of the royal forests. In 1511 it passed from royal to private ownership: initially the lords of Žerotin, then (1544–1644) the near unpronounceable lords of Zástřizly, who transformed it into a renaissance castle. The representative and residential parts were concentrated in the 'upper castle' and the fortifications were modernised. The Swedes captured it in 1644 during the Thirty Years War. Later it passed to the Petřvald family. In 1698 work started on Buchlovice palace (see below). The last owners (from 1763 until 1945) were the Counts Berchthold of Uherčice (which sounds a lot less pleasant in German: Ungarschitz), originally from the Tyrol, who settled in Moravia after the Battle of the White Mountain.

Our guided tour started inauspiciously. I asked for the promised 'anglický text' and was told by the girl that she didn't have any. We then had to walk up a flight of about 60 steps in the blazing sun for a lecture at the top of the gate tower on the castle's history. Below the terrace is the 'Linden of Innocence'. According to legend, it was planted with its roots upwards and the crown in the ground as proof of the innocence of a soldier sentenced to death for poaching. Enough of this nonsense.

We entered the courtyard of the 'Upper Castle' and were shown into the kitchens. At this point, a lady who had realised we were Brits (from the way we were grumbling at the lack of an English text) came up and, abandoning her husband and teenage children, kindly volunteered to interpret for us. She proved very useful and good (it turned out that she was a teacher of English from Slovakia).

We had a very thorough tour, via the armoury, baroque library (where like so many châteaux in these parts you can play the Where's Wally game, trying to spot any volume in Czech), the hall with the Buchlov Madonna (early 14th century), and all the residential apartments. These are quite interesting in that Zikmund I, Count Berchthold of Uherčice (1799–1869) played an active part in the anti-Habsburg uprising of 1848–1849 in Hungary. He was sentenced to death, but his life was spared following pleading by his wife Ludmila Vratislavová of Mitrovice and he spent the rest of his life under house arrest. He devoted this time to the family's collections (some decidedly odd such as a – genuine – mummy in a fake Egyptian tomb) which he opened to the public in 1856. Another Count was a co-founder of the collections in what is now the National Museum in Prague. His half-brother had turned the palace of Buchlovice into a hospital following the battle of Austerlitz in 1805 – a noble gesture which backfired in his case: he caught typhus and died.

...and Buchlovice

We thanked our interpreter profusely as we walked back to the car park to drive the last couple of miles down into Buchlovice town to see the eponymous zámek. We had half an hour or so to wait for a guided tour. The 'town' has only about 2,500 inhabitants but in 1805 Franz I granted it civic status and the right to hold four annual fairs; perhaps in recognition of the gesture of allowing the château to be used as a hospital after Austerlitz.

The zámek was built in the first third of the 18th century by Jan Dětřich of Petřvald whose architect was the Italian Domenico Martinelli. It consists of two buildings, both stylised horseshoes – the lower building for the nobility; the upper, for the servants – separated by a large open area with a fountain where we waited until the guide unlocked the gates of the lower building and ushered us inside. A young man in his thirties, uncharacteristically for these parts wearing a jacket, he started well, but soon lost the interest of most of his listeners. There are the usual state rooms, library and bedrooms and, in the first corner we come to, a room of some genuine historical interest.

Count Leopold II Berchtold (1863–1942), the owner before the First World War, was active in the diplomatic service of Austria-Hungary as ambassador in London, Paris and Saint Petersburg. On 16 September 1908 he arranged a secret meeting in this room of the foreign ministers of Tsarist Russia and Austria-Hungary which led to a division of spheres of political influence in the Balkans and the annexation of Bosnia and Herzegovina by the Austrians. Leopold was appointed last Austro-Hungarian Foreign Minister but one in 1914.

Although interesting the guide spoiled it by giving us an interminable lecture on how the First World War started. Children became fractious; grown men wept with boredom; their womenfolk angrily hissed 'We could have been on the beach', until we were allowed to move on. We were glad to escape, but it was a beautiful building with beautiful parkland and a pleasantly cool café. The building is on a slope so the café is underneath, off the tunnel through which carriages must have passed to dump their noble occupants.

We went back the way we had come, skirting Brno and heading due south on the R52/E461 then southwest on the 53 until we reached Znojmo and found the hotel quite easily on Pražská, the road out to the west.

Znojmo

Baedeker says: *'The environs are picturesque and fertile. Cucumbers and other vegetables are extensively cultivated here'*, so it was with some pent-up excitement that we walked into town. It has a population of about 34,000, but I don't think we saw more than about five of them that evening. And no cucumbers.

We spent the morning of the second of June exploring Znojmo, which in practice meant wandering through town down through Masarykovo náměsti to the climbable tower – where we had to ask the lady at the *vinoteca* on the ground floor for the key. She ushered us up a flight of metal steps and then we climbed on our own to the top of the tower; magnificent view, including the old town walls and, less magnificently, an obtrusive modern building at the opposite end of Masarykovo náměsti; so hideous it could only be the Palace of Culture. We wandered along part of the old walls, dodging a party of schoolchildren as we went, then headed back up through town to a branch of Kanzelsberger where I bought an updated road atlas, my old one failing to mark the exits (and hence the distances) on the bits of motorway in Moravia.

We had a look in the *Kostel Sv. Mikuláše*, a Gothic building of 1338 replacing an earlier 12th century Romanesque church. Amongst the other items of interest I picked up was a leaflet offering *Duchovní obnova za uzdravení* (spiritual renewal for healing), a three-day affair to be held next week – 6 to 8 June – at the exhibition centre in Brno, and led by a Catholic priest from India called Father James Manjackal. An irresistible name but we think, on reflection, we will give it a miss. We wandered past the old brewery and down to the *hrad* which, of course, was shut for repairs or quite simply because it was Monday.

The town is proud of the famous[33] people associated with it, including Prokop Diviš, a priest and wildly eccentric man, by the sound of it. His achievements, according to a hand-out at the tourist information office, included inventing a musical box instrument *'which gave out the sound of harp, lute, piano, French horn. It had deep voice and even human voice'*. Not only this, but he is *'deservedly ranked to electropathy pioneers'* although – wait for it – *'The peak of his scientific work is the invention of lightning rod'*. Quite a character. Then there was Jan Vlk (John Wolf) who composed patriotic songs and *'initiated founding of the first Czech banking institution in Znojmo'*, so in fact nowhere near as interesting as Renaissance man Prokop.

A much bigger catch was Alfons Mucha, although his links with the town are tenuous, to say the least. However, his enormous Slav Epic paintings can be found in the château at Moravský Krumlov, a mere 40 odd kilometres away, so why not claim him as a native? Then there was lady novelist Růžena Svobodová who *'devoted all her life to literature'* and *'managed to get deep into human mind'*, her works being *'based on elaborate description of outside world atmosphere and impressive inner world depiction'*. She was only 51 when she died *'in the middle of vigorous work'*. We can only speculate…

Cornštejn

Back to the hotel to collect the car and off to Cornštejn, virtually the only castle or château we could pinpoint in the region which, *mirabile dictu*, was open on a Monday. Out on road no. 38 then to the left along the 408 to Citonice and on through Miličovice and Lesná where the local museum (classic motor vehicles) was advertising a novel way of raising money by flogging off the exhibits. The 308

---

[33] Or at least famous in Moravia.

took us down to Vranov nad Dyji where, after a particularly lucky bend, we saw in front of us the château standing proud across the little valley. We shall return tomorrow when it's open. In the meantime, on to Lančov where, after 2 km, my brand-new road atlas shows the red-marked road turning first buff, then white then into a dotted line which, despite our fears, dropped us off at the little car park near the castle which Modern Baedeker fails to mention: an unpardonable omission.

Because the Dyje (the German *Thaya*) was damned at Vranov (the work lasting from 1930 to 1933), Cornštejn is surrounded on two sides by the river. The maintenance engineers were spared, at first at least, from the Beneš Decres: they were all ethnic Germans and had to be kept on until they had trained up the Czechs.

> The castle was built on royal demesne land which was granted as a fief in 1308 to the Lichtenburgs (N.B.: '-burg', not '-stein'). In the 1320s Raimund of Lichtenburg, favourite of King Wenceslaus II, decided to strengthen the defences of Bítov castle and the land connecting it with Vranov by building a fort: Cornštejn, the first written record of which dates from 1343. Originally a small Gothic noble residence with a courtyard, enclosing wall (enceinte) and *Palas*, it gradually developed into a large medieval fortress.
>
> In 1422 the castle was besieged by the Hussites, which prompted the owners to fortify the strategic hill south of Cornštejn with a detached outwork. We can skip a century. After the Lichtenburgs died out in 1576, the new owners – the Streuns of Schwarzenau – abandoned the castle and may well have had all the roofs removed (a tax avoidance dodge). In 1945, thanks to the Beneš decrees, the last owners – the Haases (owners of Bitov; see below) – were expropriated.

The guidebook is clear that Cornštejn is a *pevnost* (fortress), rather than being built in the first instance for residential or representative purposes. Its ground plan resembles a stubby boot kicking upwards at the end of a rather broad trouser leg. The castle proper is where the shin ought to be. It has the huge advantage of having signposts in Czech with decent translations into English and German, the only oddity being the seventh gate where the Czech *zřícená* (ruined) is rendered as 'downfallen'. Large parts of the castle are in good repair – about two-thirds of it having been consolidated, or even rebuilt, in the 1970s by the South Moravian Museum of Znojmo.

Apart from us there were two women cyclists and a young couple, none of whom disturbed our pleasure in any way. After we had thoroughly 'done' Cornštejn we stopped at the *pokladna* (second gate of the eastern forework, since you ask) to stock up on guidebooks and postcards, served by a rather shy young woman. Seated nearby were an older man with a beer belly and a young man with long hair. The two young people were obviously employees of the South Moravian Museum. Old beer gut had the franchise on the refreshments. We ordered two coffees, which turned out to be instant. We chatted. He wondered if we had anywhere to stay; we replied that we had, but he gave us his card for the next time – a little *penzion* nearby. The young people joined us as we sat at the trestle table.

After a bit the older man asked if we would like to try some of his home-made liquor. It was light red, looked like red wine, but tasted of something infinitely stronger. God only knows what it was, but it was exceptionally good. They were in no hurry to boot us out and we were in no hurry to move on so the older man offered us a cup of *bezinkový čaj*. A moment of puzzlement: *'benzinový čaj* (petrol tea)'? Surely not... Hearty thigh-slapping laughter all round at the English milord's fabulously funny joke. The older man waved out of the ruined window at the branches of a nearby tree and exclaimed 'Bezinka!' Ahha, elderflower. Yes, why not? The young man took a handful of elderflowers and heated up a saucepan of water, then threw in the flowers and left it to stand. We both assumed it would be disgusting, but in fact it was delicious.

The older man explained that it was good for the heart, the liver, the kidneys, and in fact just about any organ you can think of.

Reluctantly, we left and headed back to the hotel for a couple of steaks. OK, I think steak is rather naff but the Prestige has obviously got a very good cook.

Vranov

Tuesday, third of June. We headed back out on the road we had taken yesterday until we reached the car park for Vranov and had to walk for about 20 minutes through the woods and up to the zámek, with about 10 minutes to wait until the tour started. We wandered over to the lookout point and took photos. There was a reasonably large party of elderly Czech tourists and a young woman with a rather severe look standing on her own and holding a clipboard. I assumed she was the guide. In fact, she wasn't. She must have been a trainee guide following the real guide round to see what she had to do.

> Vranov was first mentioned in 1100. Little seems to have happened until about the 16th century when it changed hands quite frequently. A man with the unlikely name of Arkleb of Boskovice held it in 1516. The Althann family, originally from Bavaria, held the castle in the last quarter of the 16th century. They were created hereditary Reichsgrafen in 1610 and from 1714 were Erbschenken of the Holy Roman Empire. This was an honorary post; the sole responsibility appears to have been giving the people free wine when the Holy Roman Emperor was crowned in Frankfurt. Nevertheless, the castle was confiscated because Wolf Dietrich von Althann took part in the Moravian Estates' rebellion of 1619. In about 1620 the estate was purchased by Wallenstein's favourite, General Johann Ernst von Scherfenberg. The town of Vranov was looted by the Swedes in 1645 and the castle was besieged (unsuccessfully).

The new Baroque château was started by Michael Johann II of Althan (1672–1722) who had managed to recover Vranov in 1680. He was fortunate in acquiring the services of Fischer von Erlach who created (after 1687) the stunning 'ancestors' hall', an oval room with an enormous cupola with a breathtaking grand allegorical mythological fresco, the work of Johann Michael Rottmayer. The Viennese sculptor Tobias Kracker[34] put sculptures of prominent members of the family in niches around the room.

Once you have seen this majestic room everything else is a gentle anticlimax. Fischer von Erlach also created the chapel of the Holy Trinity with the Althan family vault in the basement. Our guide ushered us on: a pleasant, well-preserved lady in her fifties wearing stylish jeans. She issued Ivor and me with the requisite *anglický text*, so we were quite happy.

Michael Johann's son, Michael Hermann, continued his father's work, as did (after 1722) his wife Marie Anne Pignatelli, a cultivated lady who was the 'favourite' (= mistress) of the emperor Karl VI. She arranged for a number of – let's be frank – quite tedious sculptures of classical figures to be installed on the staircase leading up from the courtyard: Hercules fighting Antaeus and Aenaes saving his father Anchises from burning Troy, Justice defeating Hope – that sort of thing. Very edifying, of course, but there's a limit to how much pleasure you can derive from it.

The last Althann – Michael Joseph – concentrated on decorating the interior *'oscillating between Late Baroque and Romantic style, under a strong influence of the emerging Classicism'*. Well, make your mind up, son. Unfortunately, he went bankrupt and the estate was acquired in 1793 by Joseph Hilgartner of Lilieborn. In the 19th century it passed first to the Polish family Mniszek then, from 1876, to the related Stadnicky family. One of the Mniszeks (Stanislaw) was responsible for wall paintings inspired by a sort of cod freemasonry.

Despite this regrettable hobby, in 1816 Stanislaw purchased

---

[34] Inventor of the famous savoury biscuit.

what was a rather insignificant earthenware factory which he turned round. In 1828 he obtained exclusive right to produce new types of Wedgwood pottery (pronounced something like Vetchvld). The factory was forced to close in 1882 in the face of competition from cheaper products, despite attempts to export to Turkey. The last Stadnicky was dispossessed by the Nazis in 1938 and the château given to a German, Baron Gebhard von der Wense-Mörse who, of course, was ejected by the Czechs after the war.

A Bítov what you fancy...

We drove on (having decided not to visit the chapel) via Cornštejn and across the bridge, up to the town of Bítov and past rather odd holiday accommodation to the car park where we had to walk the mile or so down to the castle, which seemed almost deserted. There was a young woman at the *pokladna* just inside the first gate, then no sign of life save for a couple of museum-cum-shop assistants/attendants chatting quietly on a bench in the shade of attractive elms. You wander up past the gate tower, then along a narrow defile (the zámek up on your right, and embankment on your left) under a footbridge and turn left, past the church and left again to the starting point of the tour (the castle door at the other side of the footbridge).

> After the collapse of Greater Moravia in the early 11th century the area around Bítov was a refuge for Slav tribes fleeing from the German colonisers. It was first mentioned between 1061 and 1067 when it was a wooden structure with earthen embankments. The first known castellan (1222–1228) was a man called Ben. His predecessor may have been Bill. The castle was owned by the Lichtenburg family (see Cornštejn, above) in the 14th and 15th centuries, succeeded at the time of the Thirty Years War by the Vlašim family who (after Swedish incursions) redesigned the castle as it appears today.

After an inheritance dispute in the 18th century which required the intervention of Maria Theresa, Bítov passed to the Counts Daun. They died out in 1904 (daun and aut) and after an interlude in which two Polish families (including the Radziwills[35]) owned the castle it was sold in 1912 to a recently ennobled Austrian industrialist, Georg (known as Karl, for no particular reason) Baron Haas von Hasenfelss. He was succeeded two years later by his son, another Georg (or Julius, as he was inexplicably known), an officer in the Uhlans.

Other aristocratic families tended to avoid Georg or Julius because of his comparatively humble birth, but this does not seem to have bothered him since he was particularly interested in animals, building up what amounted to the largest private zoo in the new Czechoslovak republic. His pet lion Mitzi-Mausi used to have lunch with him. Apart from animals, he took a keen interest in girls from the neighbouring villages.

In May 1945, although an anti-fascist, he was forced out of Bítov by partisans. Unable to bear the loss of the castle and/or the animals and/or the village girls, he shot himself on 11 May.

The only other people taking part in the guided tour (through what the Rough Guide calls, rather meanly, 'the contrived neo-Gothic décor and soulless, unlived-in rooms') were a couple in their 50s or 60s from Leipzig. We managed to make it clear to the guide – a pretty young girl – that as long as we had the English or German texts there was no need for her to do anything apart from opening and closing a succession of doors. Starting with the *sala terrena* (which has chandeliers made of painted sheet metal) there is a series of rooms done in Victorian neo-Gothic style – not without charm – but the tour ends in a temple of naffnesss, a series of rooms containing stuffed animals that used to belong to the zooman, climaxing in a whole room full of stuffed dogs – the largest collection of its sort, apparently. I was (slightly) interested to note that a mastiff is an *anglická doga*, but on the whole I

---

[35] Distantly related to the Kennedys.

found it rather revolting and was relieved to get out into the fresh air.

We looked through the door of the chapel then zapped the shop and exhibition rooms. There were two exhibitions: one of fairly horrible paintings by an untalented unknown; the other, a collection of old toys and games.

We drove back to Znojmo through a series of villages including one called Chvalatice (not far from Bítov) with a First World War memorial with the inscription *'Wir starben, um Euch zu schützen'*, so clearly this was a German-speaking area until the end of the Second World War. There is a story that Hitler wanted to create in Prague a 'Museum of an Extinct Race' – the Jewish people. He failed in this, of course, but unwittingly turned the Sudetenland into a 'Museum of an Extinct Race' – Hitler's puppet Henlein and Edvard Beneš having in effect ensured the near total obliteration of the Sudeten Germans as an ethnic component of the Czech Republic.

Mikulov

It is Wednesday, 4 June and we are off East(ish) today to and through former Liechtenstein territory. Our initial goal was Mikulov. To get there we had to drive half a dozen sides of a triangle. We passed Pohořelice, the German Pohrlitz, near which the more than 800 victims of the 'Brno death march' (following the expulsion of the Sudeten Germans) were buried.

From there we headed east-south-east past a series of very attractive lakes then about a mile on a causeway separating the reservoirs of Nové Mlýny [new mills] I and Nové Mlýny II. The road then straightens itself out again – we're getting close to Austria and we want to make a good impression – past hills to the left, with the ruins of two castles: Nový hrad – New Castle, not very original – and, on another hill (can't read the map; the print's too small – ah! found the magnifying glass) *Sirotčí hradek*, or Waisenstein, thanks to its founder, one Siegfried Waise.

And at last we turned off the main road and into Mikulov where we parked on Komenského, left the car in the baking sun and strolled up the Stězka svobody ('path of peace') along Naměsti (square) and into the real square which has, at its lower (right, to us) end the *hrobka* (crypt of the Dietrichsteins; they will appear soon), whereas immediately round the corner to the left was a pleasant old inn – *U rytířů (zum Ritter)*, built after a devastating fire in 1561, with sgraffito showing biblical scenes (the Flood, the baptism of Christ etc.) and worldly scenes: hunters, musicians and dancers, for example. It had a wooden terrace out on the square where we sat and drank coffee, and had to stuff our fingers in our ears because, on the dot of 12, the piercing sound of the nuclear warning siren brought all life to a standstill for several minutes.

When it died down we went to the tourist office immediately opposite, picked up the usual leaflets and went up the alley to the side of the inn which took us very soon to the imposing zámek.

In its mediaeval heyday Mikulov guarded the border between Moravia and Austria. The original wooden structure was replaced by a stone castle in the mid-13th century on the orders of Přemysl Otakar I. In 1249 he granted it to Jindřich (Heinrich) of Liechtenstein whose family owned it until 1560 when it passed to the Dietrichsteins in 1575. The best-known member of this family was Cardinal Franz (1570–1636). At the age of 29 he became bishop of Olomouc (being a friend of Pope Clement VIII may have helped). He turned Mikulov into an aristocratic Renaissance palace and transferred the entire chancellery of the bishopric and his court from Olomouc. He was also president of Emperor Rudolf II's privy council and Governor of Moravia from 1621–1628 and was responsible for pushing through the Counter-Reformation in these parts. He seems to have fallen out, briefly, with the Emperor, but he was restored to glory and appointed Cardinal-Protector of the Holy Roman Empire.

The château then led a quiet existence – and was the site of a preliminary peace treaty between Prussia and Austria following the battle of Königgrätz in 1866 – until right at the end of the last war when there was a great fire on 22 April 1945. It now houses the regional museum *'and you can find many interesting exhibits here'*. We decided not to.

> Until the Nazi occupation there had been a thriving Jewish community in Mikulov. In 1421, the Jews were expelled from Vienna and Lower Austria by Duke Albert II. The refugees settled in Mikulov (at the time 'Nikolsburg') under the protection of the Liechtensteins, and more settlers were brought after Ladislaus the Posthumous expelled the Jews from the Moravian royal boroughs after 1454. For three centuries until 1851 it had been the seat of the Chief Rabbi of Moravia. The Jewish population declined, from a peak of about 3,500 in the first half of the nineteenth century – presumably (over) half of the population – after freedom of residence was granted in 1848, but in 1904, there were still 749 Jewish inhabitants of Mikulov, out of a total population of 8,192 (just over 9%).

About 90 houses of the Jewish ghetto have survived; in the early 19th century there were at least 12 synagogues. The Old Synagogue (dating from about 1550; enlarged 1689; rebuilt 1719–23 after a fire) is still standing. Our walk round the grounds of the zámek took us to a flight of steps leading down to it. We walked in (wearing our hats, as men should) and stood looking down from the gallery into the interior of the building, until a young woman came up to us and politely explained that it was not (yet) open to the public. We had walked past workmen carrying panels for an exhibition, and we left quietly.

At the 1930 census the population of Mikulov was 7,307, of whom 6,409 (87.7%) were ethnic Germans. Two Austrian presidents – Karl Renner and Adolf Schärf – attended the (pre-war)

Piaristengymnasium. Renner (1870–1950) was Chancellor and Minister of Foreign Affairs from 1918–1920 and President from 1945. He was vehemently anti-Semitic and (despite being a Social Democrat) had urged Austrians to vote 'yes' in the *Anschluss* referendum of 1938. Marko Feingold, concentration camp survivor and president of the Salzburg Jewish Community, said in 2013: *'Karl Renner… had long been known in the party as an anti-Semite. He didn't want us concentration campers in Vienna after the war and he also frankly said that Austria would not give anything back to them.'* Adolf Schärf (1890–1965), also a Socialist, was President from 1957–1965. He, too, had previous. Following the *Anschluss* he was arrested and served time as a political prisoner. However, three months later, he 'aryanised' the office of Arnold Eisler, a Jewish lawyer and party colleague who had to leave Austria. He took over Eisler's law firm and it was never restituted. On the other hand, after the 1944 July plot he spent another five weeks in prison. Sounds a bit of an opportunist.

Lednice

We decided to move on. A 20 minute drive took us to Lednice where we parked in the village centre car park, baking in the sun, and walked *'Po stopách Lichtenštejnů'*, as a booklet has it, to the zamek. What do you think this means, gentle reader? Well, 'po' looks like a preposition; in 'stopach' we can see something that looks like 'step'; and 'Lichtenštejnů' is probably an inflected form of Lichtenštejn. Yes, you've guessed! It means 'In the footsteps of the Liechtensteins'. Well done!

We had about half an hour to wait until the next guided tour, so we sauntered through the beautiful and massively extensive gardens (first, formal French grounds, then with well-rehearsed spontaneity an English park), stopping at the lake, which features herons, grebes and storks, and deciding we had just enough time not to try to see the Chinese pavilion. Then we returned to the house.

A few years ago, when I was thinking of including Lednice in the annual CzechRep trip I had a look at the zámek's own website, where a Google Translate version of the name appeared: 'Refrigerator castle' ('lednice' is, literally, a cold store or ice-box – but come on, think!).

> The Liechtensteins arrived (from Styria) in Moravia in the mid-thirteenth century, were granted Lednice (German 'Eisgrub') in 1582 and stayed until they were forcibly ejected after the Second World War. An existing fortress was replaced with a Renaissance château, then in the long seventeenth century by a Baroque palace which was rebuilt in Neo-Gothic style by a Viennese architect, Georg Wingelmüller, in the period 1846–1858: eight wings and four internal courtyards. Immensely wealthy, the Liechtensteins clearly had time and money on their hands. In Murray's day the estate included *'2 market towns, several villages, pretty lakes, pleasure grounds, temples, towers &c., and a building which marks the frontier between Austria and Moravia'*. Taken all together their possessions in Bohemia and Moravia amounted to 1,600 km² – ten times the size of the Principality of Liechtenstein.

The guided tour consisted of us and about half a dozen young Czechs who were only moderately interested in what they saw. The tour starts with the Knights' Hall which is fairly sparse but does have vaulting inspired by English late Gothic; then the summer dining room: panelling, vaulting and a few pictures. The most interesting and most beautiful room is the library which has, in one corner, a magnificent oak spiral staircase, its components held together by pegs and glue, with not a nail in sight. Then there is the Family Hall – the only preserved Baroque room – which contains a copy of a portrait of Aloys II Joseph (responsible for the neogothicisation) who represented the emperor at Queen Victoria's coronation. There are also a few colour-coded rooms, as befits this sort of place: the Turquoise Ceremonial Hall, with a ceiling made of Canadian walnut; the Blue (Dancing) Hall with a fairly low panelled ceiling, and the Red (smoking) hall – long and, well, hall-like. All in all a pleasant tour.

More interesting, in a sense, is the *'vast hothouse'*, a pioneering work in cast iron, 92 metres long. An orangery was established in 1642, but the greenhouse was built in 1843–45. The pillars are made to look as if they are bamboo trunks. Statistic alert! The covering consists of 13,482 handmade glass tiles. The design is based on the work of two French-sounding Englishmen: Desvignes and Loudon whose 'Sketches of Curvilinear Hothouses' (contemporaries used to scrap like prize fighters to get hold of a copy) recommended a semi-cylindrical shape to reduce loss of heat from the sun. It's certainly pretty warm inside the glasshouse: 15–25°C. We wandered past the fig trees, the Norfolk Island pine and date palms, dodged the Giant Spear Lily and admired the Abyssinian banana trees.

At the pokladna I had asked in my best Czech for two OAP tickets. The woman – a parody of an East European lady tractor driver – looked us up and down sneeringly and said (in Rosa Klebbish German): 'Sie Senior; er *(pointing at Ivor)* Erwachsene'.

Exhausted by the heat, we stopped for refreshments at the café near the car park, sitting under trees; it felt very much like provincial Austria. At the next table were four patient, battle-hardened teachers, their teenage pupils dotted around at other tables.

Then back to Znojmo. Feeling rather adventurous we thought we would risk everything and try the only vegetarian restaurant, *Na Věčnosti* (which means 'for ever', although this was not a comment on the service which was prompt, smart and pleasant). It is located in an eighteenth-century building, two windows and a door wide. The room off to the left of the passageway is fitted with a bar, while the main dining area is the room at the back. It has wooden flooring throughout, with bare brick walls and a good range of ridiculously cheap dishes (at lunchtime a *plat de jour* will cost you CZK79 [roughly EUR2.85]) – chickpea burgers, or pancakes stuffed with dried tomatoes and cheese), and decent Dudák beer. As the Rough Guide puts it, in the Czech Republic 'vegetarianism is still a minority sport' so this restaurant – outside the capital, too – was quite a find.

Into Austria

We are now (Thursday, 5th June) leaving Moravia and moving on into Austria, the idea being to look at Hardegg – just on the Austrian side of the Thaya – then continue to Dürnstein.

Back up the 38 then off to the left to Horni Břečkov followed by a gentle 7 km descent via the hamlet of Čižov to the border. Or so we thought. We passed groups of hikers – sixth formers or their equivalent – staring at us oddly but in Čižov there were signs suggesting the road was closed. We laughingly ignored them and drove on down to the river where we discovered the bridge to Hardegg was not suitable for motor vehicles. So near and yet so far... We got there in the end after a 35 km detour: back up to Horni Břečkov then back down via Vranov and on to Šafov where we took a narrowing road through the woods which was clearly going nowhere, but suddenly wasn't, and eventually ended up in the right village.

Hardegg

First mentioned in 1145, it was acquired by the Counts of Plaien in about 1187. Hardegg itself is first documented as a town in 1290. Located on the border with the Kingdom of Bohemia, the area was devastated during the Hussite wars in 1425. In 1483 Hardegg was bequeathed to the Habsburg archdukes of Austria. Emperor Maximilian I granted it to his ministeriales of the Prueschenk family and elevated them to *unmittelbar*, answerable only to him, Counts of Hardegg in 1499. From the Thirty Years' War onwards the castle decayed, until it was acquired by the Khevenhüller dynasty and rebuilt in the late 19th century to the plans of Carl Gangolf Kayser [appointed court architect to Emperor Maximilian of Mexico in 1866].

The castle is perched above the town and the river, together with the rickety bridge, and is largely in ruins with the exception of the *Palas* and chapel. The donjon is still intact and five storeys high, but there is no way of reaching its entrance which is 11 metres up. Gräfin Francesca, a rather bedraggled looking lady in her sixties, sold us our tickets, There were only three other visitors: two Czech women in their twenties, one of whom appeared to be a model, and her small daughter. The other young woman took a series of photos of the model posing (fully clothed, of course) in unlikely spots. The chapel building has little to recommend it, but upstairs there is one of the oddest exhibitions imaginable, devoted to Kaiser Franz Joseph's younger brother Maximilian.

France had invaded Mexico in 1861, with the implicit support and approval of other European powers, following President Juárez's suspension of interest payments to foreign countries on 17 July 1861, which angered Mexico's major creditors: Spain, France and Britain. Seeking to legitimise French rule, Napoleon III invited Maximilian to establish a new Mexican monarchy. With the support of the French army and a group of conservative Mexican monarchists, Maximilian travelled to Mexico where he declared himself Emperor on 10 April 1864. He lasted just three years.

He seems to have been remarkably well-intentioned, not to say anachronistically naïve to the point of stupidity. One of his first acts as Emperor was to restrict working hours and abolish child labour. He cancelled all debts for peasants over 10 pesos, restored communal property and forbade all forms of corporal punishment. He also broke the monopoly of the Hacienda stores and decreed that peons could no longer be bought and sold for the price of their debt. To the dismay of his conservative allies, Maximilian upheld several liberal policies proposed by the Juárez administration – such as land reforms, religious freedom, and extending the right to vote beyond the landholding class. At first, Maximilian offered Juárez an amnesty if he would swear allegiance to the crown, even offering him the post of Prime Minister, which Juárez refused.

With the end of the American Civil War in 1865, the United States began to be able to give more explicit support to Juárez. The Mexican Empire collapsed, and Maximilian was captured and executed in 1867. His wife Charelotte (Carlota) had left for Europe earlier to try to generate support for her husband's regime; she suffered an emotional collapse after his death and was declared insane. There are two or three rooms stuffed full of photos of poor Maximilian[36].

The *Palas* looks as though it acts as a sort of banqueting hall. It also has a number of overlarge paintings, including one showing peasants gathered below the castle and raising their right arms in salute to the castle. Very 30-ish and sinister. We took a short cut back through the cellars (enormous) and back to the *Kasse* where the Gräfin gräciously sold us postcards.

On to Dürnstein

We drove on, through a fairly underpopulated part of Lower Austria until we hit Horn where we had a brief stop, tried to get into the ruined castle – tried to find it, in fact – and walked round the old town walls as far as possible. A pleasant little place with a rather sombre past: it enthusiastically welcomed the Anschluss.

Then south along very pleasant roads with a couple of hairpin bends near the oddly named Plank am Kampa, skirted Krems and then drove upstream on the left bank of the Danube to Dürnstein where, as a birthday treat, we had booked into the Hotel Schloss Dürnstein which is up in the old town but at its western extremity. It is very swish, part of the *Relais et Châteaux* group, and slightly eccentric, in the sense that there were house martins nesting in a chandelier in the reception area and swooping about. The hotel had clearly been a private residence before it became an hotel. The bedrooms are arranged off galleries around the four sides of the

---

[36] For an excellent life of Maximilian see Edward Shawcross: *The Last Emperor of Mexico: A Disaster in the New World* (2021).

inner (covered) courtyard. Our rooms – an odd arrangement: lobby with my bathroom then doors to Ivor's room (with an ensuite) and my room – both have views straight over the Danube, while Ivor's, being on a corner, also has a view up to the rest of the old town.

We settled in. That is to say: I went for a swim in the indoor pool while Ivor read. The indoor pool (there is also an outdoor one, but I'm not stupid; I don't want to be gawped at) is accessible from the ground floor after a rather long walk from the lift then down some steps which are murder to negotiate if you make the mistake of wearing the slippers kindly provided by the hotel. However, I had it to myself and swam up and down lazily for about half an hour in an atmosphere straight from a Hollywood take on opulent Istanbul. Then back upstairs for a change of clothing.

> Dürnstein was first mentioned in 1192 when Richard the Lionheart was imprisoned in the castle by Leopold V, Duke of Austria following a quarrel during the Third Crusade. Richard had angered Leopold (the Virtuous) by throwing down his standard from the walls at the Battle of Acre, and the duke suspected that Richard had ordered the murder of his cousin Conrad of Montferrat. So Leopold – not quite so Virtuous, eh? – imprisoned Richard on his way back to England. According to legend Richard's faithful friend, the troubadour Blondel, found Richard by singing one verse of a song outside the castle and Richard responded by singing the next verse. Leopold, perhaps as a result of this racket, gave custody of his prisoner to Emperor Henry IV, who imprisoned him at Trifels castle, which is not quite such an alluring location. Dürnstein castle was almost completely destroyed by Swedish troops under Lennart Torstenson in 1645.

We went for a walk before supper. Dürnstein is a very attractive little place, full of trippers from river cruises during the day, but relatively empty in the evenings. We strolled from the hotel to the other end of town, then back part of the way, ending up in the

'Sänger Blondel' where, as it was such a pleasant evening, we sat outside in the quite large courtyard/garden where we were served *Tafelspitz* (Ivor) and lamb chops (me) by an elderly gentleman with impeccable manners.

Later we returned to the hotel and had a drink or two in the bar where we were served by a burly young Slovak who had been working as a waiter in Germany and Austria and was keen to practise his English.

It is now (6 June) the most important day of the year: my birthday, and Ivor's too, although I am four years older than him and incomparably more mature, as Rosa Klebb at Lednice seemed to imply. What to do? Well, the obvious thing would be to explore the ruin of Dürnstein castle but given the heat (it's a twenty-minute climb) and the fact that we had both seen it before, albeit a long time ago, we decided to visit Rosenburg in the afternoon, and to 'do' the little town in the morning.

The little town was crawling with groups who had come ashore from the various river cruisers. 'Crawling' almost literally, as most of them seemed to be quite old, but all in good spirits and enjoying the sun as they traipsed round wearing little identification badges and listened to the guides telling them what to see and why.

The obvious thing to buy in Dürnstein is plums. There are little shops all over town, most of them seemed to be owned by Wieser, selling jars of Marillen, Marillen-Marmalade, Zwetschken, Zwetschken-Curry and lots of other plum combinations. We bought some, then did the few sights, essentially the abbey. Stift Dürnstein was established in 1410 by Canons Regular from Třeboň and from 1710 rebuilt in the Baroque style. The Stift was dissolved by order of Emperor Joseph II in 1788 because it served no useful social purpose (it was neither a school nor a hospital). It is a four-winged building and you can wander about looking at various bits of statuary. All very pleasant, particularly as it is cool inside and very hot outside. We then walked back to the hotel, carrying crates of local wine which we had bought following a mini-tasting, and set off for our last castle of the trip.

Rosenburg

Back via the rather confusing Krems bypass and north again to Horn, then off cross-country following Ms Satnav's directions with gritted teeth and white knuckles as we screeched through farmyards and kicked up clouds of dust on D-roads, until we reached Rosenburg's massive car park.

We paid and walked through the 'Turnierhof', a broad stretch of lawn, or as Murray says: *'the Lists for jousts and tournaments, 153 paces long and 60 wide, with double galleries or boxes for spectators, quite perfect'*, with the *Lustgarten* somewhat lower down on the right. Workmen were erecting stands for the *Rosenberger Rosen- und Gartentage* which would be starting the next day. We crossed the moat – full of beautiful flowers – and into the *Vorhof*, inner courtyard in fact, where a wedding reception was taking place and where we inspected the cafeteria and shop while waiting for the guided tour to start at the *Warthaus*.

Rosenburg was first mentioned in 1175, in connection with a certain Gozwin de Rosenberg, whose family owned the castle until the early fourteenth century. The castle has been in the possession of the Hoyos-Sprinzensteins since 1681. It suffered a massive fire in the early nineteenth century and in 1839 was described as a ruin, with only a few habitable rooms. However, in 1859 Graf Ernst decided to restore it to its former glory, which is what Ivor and I saw.

Our guided tour included a party of children – last year of primary school, I imagine – who behaved very well (thanks to their young teachers), taking a keen interest in everything the guide told them and enthusiastically taking part in the little games she invented for each room ('Can you find three objects beginning with 'S'?' – that sort of thing). The only minor complaint I have is that there were so many of them that it was often difficult to take photos of *objets* and sticks of furniture without an 11-year old's head or foot appearing in the picture. The rooms we saw on the tour had either superb wall panelling or magnificent wooden ceilings and floors. The guide unlocked each room in turn, then locked it after we had entered. Early in the tour a young couple dawdling behind the rest of the party found themselves locked out, but the guide was unmoved by their plaintive cries. 'There'll be another tour along later' she said and shrugged.

Of note were the library (originally intended for music and dancing), the *Sitzungssaal*, the armoury, the inevitable Red Room and the chapel which has a gallery surrounding it on three sides so the children were able to wave at each other through the opposite windows. In retrospect my impressions are a little blurred: a succession of panelling, seventeenth century furniture, sixteenth century wood reliefs and carvings, *Kassettendecken*, a piano whose keys were the wrong colour (black for white and vice versa) and the Hoyos rooms, devoted to the history of the owners.

One of them, Joseph Theodor, was one of the last people to have seen Crown Prince Rudolf on the day he committed suicide, which must have left him with some embarrassing explaining to do. To crush any speculation and counter any reproaches on the part of the Imperial Court, he published a private account of the last hours of the Crown Prince's life.

Fertöd – Esterházy palace

An unusual place name …

... and another one

The author (right)

CHAPTER 7

Czech Republic – July/August 2015

Friday 24 July

Freising

I found the Bayerischer Hof without much trouble. The car park is behind the hotel which has a choice of three rear entrances. At the third attempt I struck lucky. The interior of the hotel is pleasingly old-fashioned. I checked in and set off walking to the Dom, having learnt it was a must-see, with about 20 minutes to spare before it shut. It was a steep hike up the Domburg, but when I got there I found the Domplatz taken up entirely with seats for a performance – well under way – of Orff's *Carmina Burana*. I asked an usherette and she told me it was impossible to visit the Dom, so I walked back down through town past the hotel to the end, almost, of the street and found a café where I sat on the terrace, drinking beer, and watching the smartly dressed audience from *Carmina Burana* sauntering orff to their cars.

Still very hot, so back to the hotel to freshen up then out for a meal at La Petite France in the main square, which I had passed earlier. There was no chance of sitting outside so I went upstairs and inside and spent a large proportion of the meal – good in parts – chatting with the owner (a genuine Frenchman) in French. Apéro: Hugo – good. Main course: bouillabaisse – disappointing; not very much of it and certainly not much fish; dessert: cheese –

the best and most copious selection of cheese I have ever had in any restaurant.

Saturday 25 July

It took Jonathan almost half an hour waiting for his luggage to appear, while I clocked up €7 in parking charges. Must remember to charge him. And now, we are off on an adventure. The aim today is to take the motorway, then ordinary roads to the border, then work our way to Holašovice (a UNESCO-listed village) where there is a Volksfest taking place this weekend, which promises to be good.

Freyung

The first leg was the A 92 motorway to Deggendorf then south on the A3 to the next exit and across country via Schönberg and Grafenau to Freyung where we decided to eat. We found a Gasthof – almost inevitably *Zur Post* – at the end of the main street and were able to park free of charge (it was Saturday) and went in for a meal. Plain but good. Then a walk along the main street to the town square. Here there was also a Volksfest going on: all sorts of stands, bandsmen lolling about drinking beer, young women in embarrassing animal costumes about to perform a tacky dance.

Then on to the border and on up road no. 4 as far as Nová Roužna then a series of *routes barrées*, which would have gladdened the heart of a Luxembourgish highways engineer and other roads which would have made Romanian roads look good, prevented us from our cross-country trip to Smědeč – which in turn would have allowed us to snake our way to our destination – and we were forced to change our plans. Apologies: this is getting boring… We gave up after crossing a half-abandoned railway and the 'road' petered out to a rather narrow bridle path. We turned round and did a massive detour to Prachatice (top left instead of bottom right).

Prachatice

Prachatice has its origins in the 11th century, following the beginning of trade on the salt route starting in Passau. The settlement later grew in importance when, in the 13th century, it was granted the right to store the salt that was traded on this route. This privilege made it the only town in Southern Bohemia that could buy the salt that was exported from Passau.

> During the Hussite wars Prachatice was attacked twice and eventually conquered by the Hussites who killed most of the population of the town. The Rožmberks controlled Prachatice until 1601 when Petr Vok, the last member of the family, sold the town to Emperor Rudolf II. It remained firmly under royal control until the Rebellion of the Bohemian Estates when it sided with the rebels. In March 1620 the citizens swore a rather premature oath of loyalty to Friedrich von der Pfalz (who appears on a caption to a painting in the Frans Hals Museum in Haarlem as 'Frederik V from the Palts'), the Winter King, but in September of the same year Imperial troops under Buquoy laid waste to Prachatice and ordered many of its citizens to be slaughtered and a large ransom to be paid to the emperor. Later the creation of an imperial salt monopoly and the transfer of salt imports to Česke Budějovice spelt the end. The town belonged to the Schwarzenbergs (heirs to the Eggenbergs) from 1719 to 1848 and a massive fire caused considerable destruction in 1832. It is interesting how in *Mitteleuropa* towns and villages could 'belong' to an aristo.

Originally a predominantly German town (1900 census: 3,334 Germans and 941 Czechs), the German population declined rapidly until in 1935 Czech parties won a majority on the town council. Under the Nazis, Prachatice was ceded to Bavaria but surrendered to the Americans without firing a shot in May 1945.[37]

---

[37] Bahlcke/Eberhard/Polivka: *Böhmen und Mähren* (1998), pp. 469–470.

I had never been there before and it was absolutely delightful: a main square and a few small roads leading off it, and nothing much else. But enough. We wandered round, taking photos of the lower gate (the Dolní brána) and, near it, the crenellated Heydlův dum (Heydl house) with depictions of men cheerfully clubbing each other to death, the former Latin school which both Hus and Žižka are said to have attended, and the arcaded Rumpal and Bozkovský houses with their weird frescos, inspired apparently by Hans Holbein. On the way back out of town we discovered, in Hus street, believe it or not, the Hus house. *'It is said that Master John Huss [sic] used to stay there during his studies in Prachatice'*, as a bilingual panel says. It now houses the town library.

A leaflet from the town's information office has this to say about the house:

> *The originally gothic one-floor house rebuilt in the renaissance style... until the currently preserved form with high, with volute circumferential attica divided by pilasters... The letter sgraffity is complemented with five out of six fields of atique figural scenes into the Věžní Street ngraved with a thin line in the plaster: ... a man in a long coat with... a cock underarm of his right arm... Above the ground-floor window facing the Husova Street is engraved with a thin line a sigh of Vyšehrad provost...*

I have no idea what this might mean.

We cruised down the 138 until we reached Český Krumlov and out on the ring road (the Objížd'ka) south to Vyšší Brod, and indeed Linz if you're not careful. We checked into the Romantick hotel, found the car park was full (and the zapper provided by the young manager wouldn't work), so he let us have his space at the front. We showered and walked to the zamek.

Český Krumlov

We're out in the suburbs, so had to walk slowly uphill along Plešivecká past 'Skippy', a traveler's [*sic*] hostel, presumably catering to Australians, and 'Milk Wood' (for drunken Welshmen?) to a small square, then down a flight of 80 steps (oh God – I'm thinking of the walk back) to the river again, then past the Schiele centre, along Dlouhá (long street) then over the wooden bridge and up to the castle, which included a 79-step climb, and up the slope of various baileys until we reached the ticket office to check the opening times for tomorrow.

Back down into town, past the Lazebna ('lesbian', according to Jonathan although, sadly a *lazebník* is a barber), over the bridge and we ended up in the Hotel Dvořák which has a pleasant riverside terrace.

Sunday 26 July

We ticked off the zamek then walked back through town to the *Lazebna*, where we had a cooling beer and failed to spot any lesbians, then on to the Schiele Art Centre in Široka (Broad street) which, *mirabile dictu*, has a permanent exhibition about Egon Schiele. 'About', rather than 'of', because the museum owns very few original works by the artist. Nevertheless, it was extremely well done.

There were other exhibitions, too: the Seidels, *père et fils*, who ran a photographic studio in town and were pioneering photographers in the area, specialising in the countryside and people of the Šumava. Then various works by Josef Váchal (1884–1969), of whom I confess I knew nothing. He was a writer, painter and printmaker. His father's cousin was Mikolaš Aleš. Originally influenced by Art Nouveau, he seems to have gone through all the 'schools' available during his long life. There was other stuff, too, but horribly abstract with glaring colours.

At leisure back to the hotel for a meal. Its restaurant has only recently opened and is called the *pivonka* (peony; all the rooms are named after flowers, rather than being numbered; mine was rose). It advertises itself as a *řížková restaurace* (a *řížek* being a Schnitzel, and nothing to do with rice as I had first cluelessly thought). I had 'cold summer soup' (= gazpacho) and a Wiener Schnitzel, but made of minced veal as they hadn't got any real veal (Eh?) plus a salad. Quite adventurous and certainly one of the best meals I have had in the Czech Republic.

Holašovice

A day (the 27th) of minor exertions, starting with our postponed trip to Holašovice where we drove through the village, parked at the other end and wandered about. 'In 1524–1530 the settlement of Holašovice was completed by subjects coming from Bavaria and Austria – altogether 17 homesteads', as a handout celebrating the village's status as a *světova památka UNESCO* (world heritage site) says.

Holašovice consists essentially of a central, elongated village green, raised a few feet above ground level, with a road on each side with buildings, mainly from the mid-nineteenth century, many with the original draw wells outside. A shame, perhaps, that we had missed the festivities although this would have meant, for me – the cautious driver – sipping apple juice while Jonathan got rat-arsed. So, all in all, better to see it in the cold light of day.

Next to where we parked was a *keramika* shop which was open. We had a look inside and I ended up buying two large mugs with floral patterns. There were signs in the shop saying that their products were either (a) suitable or (b) unsuitable for dishwashers and microwaves, but I couldn't work out which. I shall have to write to the owners. Their name is Mürgl, which makes sense in the context of German settlement in the sixteenth century.

Back in Český Krumlov

We walked into town, up to almost the very end looking for a decent restaurant and eventually found it: *Le petit jardin* – genuinely French – in the Latran area of town. We had not booked so we sat outside in the small courtyard for our starters – scallops – then it started to rain and we were moved indoors to a table ready and waiting for us, next to a large party of a dozen or so 60-year old Germans. For our main courses Jonathan had confit de canard while I chose tagliatelle, which we washed down with a fine Czech rosé. Jonathan chose the crème brûlée for dessert, while I had a deliciously large cheese platter. It was easily the best meal of the trip.

Tuesday 28 July

First stop: the tourist office on the main square, Svornosti (harmony), to check the opening times for Vyšši Brod. A pleasant but rather thick young woman was very willing but unable to find the information for us. 'I could tell you the bus times if you like' (voice rising towards the end of the sentence). – 'But we're going by car and want the opening times of the abbey' – 'Oh.' Never mind, we had a rummage through the semi-concealed souvenir shop at the back of the tourist office and I bought a guide in German to the *Schlosstheater*. Slightly dated ('no visitors allowed in for the time being'), but useful.

We walked back via the Synagogue, built to plans of Viktor Kafka (1880-1942; died in Terezin) and opened in 1909 as the excellent little exhibition explains. It was closed down by the Nazis in 1938 and after a chequered career was returned to the local Jewish community in 1997. As we were looking at this a group of Hungarians were being given a guided tour of the synagogue itself: simple and pleasant (the synagogue, not the visitors). As they left, their leader asked if I spoke English, then asked me to return the key to the woman who had let his group in. This we did, then walked back to the hotel to pick up the car.

In the early 1990s, a rich Israeli woman came to Český Krumlov, announcing that she wanted to see the interior of the synagogue, promising to invest some of her capital in repairing it. The Town Hall provided her with the keys, but she never returned them, leaving instead huge holes in the wall as a reminder of her visit. The secret caches she opened probably held Torah, jewels, or religious artefacts, but their actual contents will remain forever a mystery. [From the town's official website: http://www.ckrumlov.info/docs/en/atr117.xml]

Vyšši Brod

Road no 160 to Vyšši Brod and Rožmberg is very attractive, about 35 kilometres following the Vltava valley through the woods. At times the road seemed disturbingly narrow, and the edges fall away abruptly several feet. But the sun was shining and the river was almost crowded with what looked like hundreds of canoeists and rafters. After Rožmberg we had to turn right at the T-junction onto road 163 and shortly afterwards crossed a railway line. For once the lights were flashing in earnest as a goods *vlak* trundled by, but too slowly to pose a *pozor*.

There is a decent car park at Vyšši Brod. Then it's a walk of only a hundred yards or so along a tree-lined path to the *klášter*. We signed up for the next (German) tour which consisted of two German couples (a party) and us. The guide was a demure young woman with wonderfully clear and accurate German – so good that Jonathan could follow her with little difficulty. She gave us an interesting and not too lengthy tour. At one point one of the Germans asked what K + M + B meant (Kaspar, Melchior, Balthasar), chalked over a doorway. It was odd to find a German – even a North German – needing to ask this. Then upstairs to the abbey treasury, most of which is of little interest, and on to the monastery's USP, its magnificent library of over 70,000 volumes which we gawped at in peasant wonder.

Vyšši Brod is a Cistercian abbey. It was formally founded on 1 June 1259 by the Rožmbergs and, because of the family's protection, was spared during the Hussite wars. The oldest parts include the sacristy to the south of the nave and the chapter house next to it. The abbey church was one of the largest in the country at the time although in the Middle Ages there were never more than 25 monks. Except on religious holidays the church was reserved for monks only.

Monasticism seems to have fizzled out in Vyšši Brod in the late eighteenth century, to be revived in the late nineteenth. By the 1930s the number of monks had risen to a record 73. The Nazis dissolved the abbey in 1941. It was revived after the war, only to be dissolved again in 1950 with the monks sent to labour camps. It was revived again in the 1990s.

Rožmberk nad Vltavou

On – or rather back – to Rožmberk. We parked down in the village – there's no alternative – and went up the hill to the castle. Here we had to join a Czech tour – nothing else available, although we armed ourselves with an *anglický* text. It proved an interesting linguistic experience: I read the English first while waiting for the tour to begin then tried to follow the Czech explanations on the basis of this knowledge. This was reasonably successful.

I first visited Rožmberk when we went *en famille* to the Czech Republic. What I remember most about that visit was that we joined a large group of mainly young people who had clearly come up from the nearest campsite and had just as clearly not bothered to wash for several days. They stank. The other thing I remember clearly is the legend of the White Lady which is too tedious to repeat; ever.

The castle was founded by Vok I of Rožmberk and the first written mention dates from 1250, which makes it almost exactly contemporaneous with the founding of Vyšší Brod. Various settlement disputes led to the castle falling into some considerable disrepair, not helped by a disastrous fire in 1522. However, the guide book has this to say:

There was a glimmer of hope for Rožmberk in 1539 when Petr V of Rožmberk yclept Limping became the guardian of the orphaned children of Jošt III of Rožmberk and their mother Anna of Rogendorf. Petr V managed the entrusted property as a good husbandman. ['yclept'!]

When the Rožmberks died out the castle passed to the lords of Švamberk who made the mistake of being on the wrong side at the White Mountain and the castle then passed into the hands of the Buquoy famly who owned it until 1945.

There is plenty to see inside: a Crusaders Gallery, based on a design by Pugin; the great hall with pictures of prominent Rožmberks; a dining room, bedroom, picture gallery and knights' gallery; and, finally, a billiard room. All in all, a pleasant way to spend an afternoon.

Back to the hotel – the hotel's resto was shut – they seemed to be cleaning everything, including the beer pumps – so we rapidly took the decision to go back and *cultiver Le Jardin*. Totally different staff, this time, but we sat outside and had exactly the same as the previous occasion (except this time we both had cheese for dessert).

Wednesday 29 July

Žumberk

A pleasant, roughly 80 km round trip, the roads getting less and less colourful on the map – and off to Žumberk. The microbrewery which services our hotel is located here, but we didn't see it.

The village is built on a knoll overlooking a lake (probably artificial). There seems some confusion as to whether the building is a *hrad* (castle) or *trvz* (manor house). It doesn't matter; I'll call it a castle.

> It was founded in 1250, was acquired by the Rožmberks (Petr Vok) in 1602, but after the Battle of the White Mountain was granted – like Rožmberk and a lot of other places in this region – to Buquoy and, as the German guidebook says, underwent *harte Germanisierung*. The 1921 census showed a population of 629 (of whom 95% were Germans) which had fallen to 28 by the 1991 census – so the Beneš decrees had obviously had a devastating effect on this village. The castle underwent considerable restoration between 1971 and 1973 and is well worth a visit.

Žumberk is a fortified affair with towers and connecting walls, all rendered in white, surrounding the central building. We entered through a cool passageway and then the lady at the *pokladna* told us that there was no English guidebook, but she drew us into the renaissance courtyard and explained – in Czech, *nota bene* – what we were supposed to do. Firstly, in through the door on the left for an exhibition which moves round the building, culminating in displays and a slide show about the fishing industry in this area of lakes and ponds. Then back out of the other door, recross the courtyard, go up the steps, put on a pair of felt slippers, enter the first-floor apartments, follow them around to the opposite door, return the slippers to the pile and report back to the *pokladna*.

The exhibition on the history of the castle is interesting in its own right as is the stuff about the lives of fishermen, but the real attraction of the castle is the enormous, seemingly unending display of richly decorated folk furniture from the eighteenth century onwards. Each room had a list of the items on display explaining where they came from. Although we had been told that photography was not allowed, I took dozens of pictures and a couple of videos. No flash, see? Later, Jonathan was to say that Žumberk was one of the highlights of the trip for him.

Then we drove back across country again – noting, to my surprise, the fact that agriculture seems to have been given a boost in Southern Bohemia; there is extensive arable farming and also one or two quite large herds of cattle – an unusual site only a few years ago.

Zlatá Koruna

And here we are, back at Zlatá Koruna (Goldenkron) with 20 minutes to spare before the first tour of the afternoon at 1 p.m. Once again I took the trouble to read the rather ropey *anglický text*, before listening to, and trying to understand, the guide. Again, no photography was allowed but, again, if no-one's looking you can get away with it, providing you don't use flash. The tour was vastly more interesting than the one Ivor and I did years ago.

> Zlatá Koruna, like Vyšši Brod, was a Cisterican monastery. It was founded in 1263 by Přemysl Otakar II. It is on a headland surrounded on three sides by the Vltava river. The architectural centre of the monastery is a church (a three-aisled basilica with transepts) facing almost north. The oldest preserved building is the single storey chapel of Guardian Angels dated ca. 1370. The chapel is similar in style to the oldest part of the church of Vyšší Brod monastery. One of the masons involved was Michal Parléř (1359). The Gothic buildings of the abbey were renovated in the late 16th/early 17th centuries and later extended to house a brewery. The only room that was preserved unaltered is the abbey chapel (first mentioned in 1387). When the monastery was suppressed by the Emperor Joseph II in 1785, it was bought by the Schwarzenbergs who rented it until 1909 'for unsuitable industrial purposes', as the guidebook says.

That night we ate in the hotel then wandered about in town. It started raining so we stopped off at an Italian pavement café (with massive parasols) called the Monnalisa [*sic*] and sat outside drinking coffee and nibbling cakes. The owner was clearly Italian but the scantily dressed waitress was obviously Czech.

Thursday 30 July

Off to Plzeň today on Part II of our Great Adventure. Stage 1: up the road to Tabor. We drove round (past the Palcát where Ivor and I had stayed) looking for a multi-storey car park, which was full, then luckily found a free space in the non-pedestrianised part of the main drag of the old town. It was a short walk from here, past sgraffitoed buildings, to the main square and the old town hall where there was an exhibition on Jan Hus to commemorate the 600th anniversary of his execution in Konstanz. The exhibition was not very extensive, but very good, despite the hopeless English translations of captions and in the guidebook.

It started badly: 'Jan of Hustinec, a man of the big as well as small history.' Later he becomes 'a speaker of serfs'. 'When young he used to play chess, however, he refused backgammon and other hazardous games'. Quite right; play safe, Jan. I notice from the acknowledgements that it was translated into English by one Eva Vybíralová – not a native speaker (and ignorant of how to punctuate 'however' when it means 'but'. Tut tut). But these are minor quibbles: the exhibition was pretty good and well-worth the detour.

We were getting hungry. We decided to avoid the *Muzeum čokolady a marcipanu* and head for the Hotel Dvořák. We only wanted a snack so we sat on the terrace and ordered club sandwiches and a beer (of course) for my non-driving co-driver and an alcohol-free bottle of monkey's urine for me. The service was appallingly slow, despite there being no customers inside the building and only a small party outside: grandmother, young mother, boy of about five plus dog. As the minutes dragged by and our food failed to appear we watched the others bickering, and the mother giving the small child a mighty slap. Rather cruel, we thought but at least it stopped the little sod whining.

The Dvořák has an overall rating of 8.1 on Booking.com. I couldn't resist reading the reviews left by guests on Booking.com. Take this one from Rosemary, an Australian: 'Breakfast terrible… Room large but orange'.

Then back via an *Antikvariat* I remembered to the car which we recovered a minute or two before the parking ticket expired. It was during the ensuing afternoon that my navigator really proved his worth. We set off on road no. 19 which should have given us a clear run to Plzeň, but not long after leaving Tábor there were worrying road signs about the bridge near Orlik being closed. Jonathan carefully plotted us a route which, at Milevsko, turned more westerly, taking us past the turning to Zvíkov and then across to road no. 4, past lots of villages ending in '-ice' – Jonathan claims there's one called Čokice – then north and at the crossroads west through Mirovice.

On past Rožmital, then on and on and on until we hit the motorway south of Plzeň, crossed it, followed it for a mile then turned left along the very long approach road to Plzeň following the signs and turning left at the T-junction opposite the brewery, along Pražská and, blimey, here we are *U Zvonu* (zur Glocke).

Plzeň

Our first stop was the tourist office on Námesti Republiky, which is dominated by, or rather surrounds on all four sides, the cathedral of St Bartolomej. On my three previous trips to Plzeň I had failed to get into the cathedral, which is why we went to the tourist office to check the opening times. Yes, it will definitely be open tomorrow from 10 a.m. to 5 p.m. Satisfied, we wandered round, window-shopping until hunger got the better of us and, at my suggestion, we went back to the hotel to eat because I remember it had very good food. It did this evening, too, although we appeared to be the only diners.

Friday 31 July

Religious experience

We set off for the cathedral, arriving there a couple of minutes before 10. The cathedral was founded in the late 13th century together with the rest of the town and building work continued for over 200 years. The Rough Guide singles out two particular points of interest: 'the late-Gothic vaulting of the *Šternberská kaple*' and the *'thirteenth-century wooden statue of the Plzen Madonna'*. A flyer from the tourist office says the Madonna is made of marlstone, whatever that may be. Either way, it's clearly worth a visit.

But not easy. You can get as far as a locked grille, but if you want to wander round you have to wait until someone unlocks it. This someone turned out to be an elderly woman who arrived at 10.10, unlocked the grille, went in and locked it behind her. Then nothing for a long time. We could see her in the distance wrestling with a stand of postcards or candles, but after a bit decided we could better use our time by visiting the old synagogue, not far away from the centre and across the inner ring road.

> The synagogue is an attractive late nineteenth century building – officially opened on Thursday, 7 September 1893 to welcome in the Jewish New Year of 5654 which started the following Sunday evening. It is large enough to have seated all the 3,500 or so (according to Mr Rough) pre-war members of Plzeň's Jewish Community but – thanks to the Nazi occupation – far too big for the remaining couple of hundred. 2.605 Jews were deported to Terezin in 1942 and thence, if they hadn't already died, to Auschwitz. Only 204 survived, many of them, not surprisingly, subsequently emigrating to Israel and the United States.

The building was partially restored between 1994 and 1998. It is used as a synagogue, of course, and also as a concert and exhibition hall and you can wander around freely, providing you wear a *kippah* which always feels as though it's about to fall off. There were two fascinating exhibitions of photos by Ladislav Sitenský and Vladislav Vitek of the liberation of the city. I have a photo of Jonathan wearing a *kippah* and looking more than usually implausible.

At length we wandered back to the cathedral, after inspecting a few bookshops on the way. This time it was possible to get past the grille (unlocked) but a funeral was taking place. I had a sneaking suspicion that the tear-stained mourners might have been upset at the sight of an old git in shorts wandering around taking snaps.

Plan B was brought forward an hour or so. This plan consisted of getting out into the country and visiting the châteaux of Kozel and Nebilovy (both unknown to Mr Rough).

Kozel

Out towards Šťáhlavy, then through Šťáhlavice where a small cat suddenly rushed across the road in front of me. Fortunately I was observing the speed limit and slammed on the brakes to avoid it, but the incident left us feeling rather shaken. We parked in the blazing sun and walked the short distance through the field, across the river (the Komaticky, since you ask) then up along the steep path through the attractive grounds to the château of Kozel itself with only twenty minutes to wait for our guided tour.

The *zámek* is an open square, one storey in height, Actually, two storeys, but the top one must have been rather pokey and for servants only. It is in effect a hunting lodge. 'Kozel' means 'goat' in the Tscheckish tongue (it's also the name of a well-known local beer), but I don't suppose people used to hunt goats.

> It was built for Johann Adalbert Czernin of Chudenitz (1746–1816), Master of the Imperial Hunt at the court of Josef II. He had been influenced by Rousseau's idea of a return to nature but of course only the rich could afford to return to it in this way, although the château was probably quite modest by contemporary standards. It was built between 1784 and

1789, most of the interior decoration being the work of Antonín Tuvora (1747–1807) who was influenced by Piranesi. The architect was Ignaz Nepomuk Palliardi (1737–1821). Johann Adalbert Czernin died without heirs, despite having had two wives. Ownership of Šťáhlavy and Kozel passed to his great nephew Christian Vinzenz Count Waldstein-Wartenberg (related to the Wallenstein of Thirty Years War fame) whose descendants remained here until they were expropriated in 1945. One member of this family, Ernst Waldstein-Wartenberg, founded an engineering works which in 1869 was bought by Emil Škoda who turned it into the largest engineering company in the Habsburg Empire.

The interior of the château is bright and airy even though a guided tour of about twenty people seems to take up rather a lot of space. The first three rooms were reserved for the Count's visitors. There are the usual château features: a smoking room with Meissen porcelain, a guest room with Louis XIV furniture, a dressing room, a hunting room recalling the original purpose of the château, billiard room, dining room, the inevitable Blue room and adjoining Green room, music room, bedrooms and library, together with the owner's study. At my age you can predict fairly accurately what you are likely to see on a guided tour through a place of this vintage, but this does not detract from its sheer beauty. The tour ends in the theatre, originally stables for Czernin's favourite horses but converted by the Waldsteins in 1830. It is not big – and not a patch on Český Krumlov – but it has its original furniture and fittings and was intended for *ad hoc* plays starring the host and his guests. And it is quite charming.

Having been charmed we decided it was time for a coffee and some rather repulsively red sausages which oozed moisture when pricked (Jonathan's choice, not mine; obviously). We sat, fortunately in the shade, on the ultra-sunny terrace behind the *pokladna*, served by a charming girl with excellent English who issued us with a fly swat to ward off the predatory wasps.

Nebilovy

From there to Nebilovy it is a 10 km drive back to the main road and out the other side through woods to the little château. It is a baroque affair, built in the period 1706–1719 by Johann .Lukas von Hildebrandt to replace a Renaissance fortress. Hildebrandt had an Italian mother and a German father, studied civil and military engineering in Rome and settled in Vienna where he worked for a number of aristocratic families, including Prince Eugene of Savoy. Jakub Auguston of Plzeň, who had Nebílovy built, must therefore have been very well-connected, and very rich. It's not the sort of place that I would normally put near the top of a 'to do' list, but I cannot repeat often enough how beautiful it is inside.

We asked for a tour with an *anglický text*, but then it emerged that the lady at the *pokladna* could provide a German- or English-speaking human guide, a young fellow who claimed he was better at German but then capitulated to Jonathan's preference for English. We set off. He introduced himself as Oliver. *'We are instructed to tell people our names so that they can complain to the Ministry that they had a rotten tour guide called Oliver'*. In fact, he was very entertaining.

He explained that the château had originally consisted of two parts facing each other across a very large square and joined by lateral wings, which had been demolished by the Communists to make it easier for wagons and carts to enter and dump farm produce and salt. Like Kozel, Nebilovy had been decorated by Antonín Tuvora, as we found when we entered the individual rooms. The tour starts from inside the gateway and goes up a flight of steps to the loggia, hung with late seventeenth century Dutch paintings of flowers and still lifes (lives?) with flowers mounted on pale green wallpaper; the 'Graphic Arts Salon' with Rococo genre prints and more of Tuvora's works; the Green salon (light green, pink and grey are the predominant colours at Nebílovy) with baroque portraits, Rococo furniture exemplifying an aristocratic interior of the late eighteenth century; the bird room – so-called because of the bird motif everywhere; and the chapel of St Anthony of Padua, consecrated in June 2001.

What we had not been prepared for was the fact that each room seemed to house not only furniture and *objets* but quite a few rather horrible dolls. Oliver sighed: *'There's a woman who has a collection of over 2,000. Most of them seem to be here. I don't know why. They're quite creepy'.* But they were not enough to detract from the pleasure of our visit.

We followed the rooms along the main wing, and then turned right; more rooms, more dolls. Then just as we were about to turn right again we stopped in front of a pram full of dolls. We inspected them with horror. 'If you think they're bad, look at THIS!' cried Oliver and produced a really frightening specimen – a boy of about 10 years of age with mad, piercing eyes. We were now in the nursery where the presence of dolls should not have been so surprising. A few educational works were lying around. Oliver picked one up – written before the First World War – with useful advice to parents. Such as? Such as *'don't let the children play with their genitals.'*

Back outside, and across the open space with fountain and peacocks to the opposite building which had been severely wrecked by the Communists and is now being gradually restored. One room in particular – the Taneční sál, or ballroom, with a high ceiling, newly painted, with beautiful parquet flooring – took our breath away. After that a quick look at the chapel then back to Plzeň, but of course too late to get into the cathedral.

Plzeň

We split up. I went first to the Ethnographical Museum on the main square (not mentioned by Mr. Rough; probably because the unassuming entrance is quite easy to miss) which had a temporary exhibition on Plzeň under the Nazi occupation. It was not very extensive but crammed with artefacts and photos and plotting the lives of a fictitious typical Czech family under German rule. Most of the educational material was easy enough to understand. It was during the occupation that the country switched from driving on the left to driving on the right.

Next stop the Museum of Religious Art in the cloisters of the former Franciscan monastery on Františkánská street – 'little visited', according to Mr Rough, which is a shame because it was pretty interesting and it includes a chapel of St Barbara with magnificent rose-coloured frescoes from the 1460s depicting the saint's martyrdom, having fallen out with her father. There's a lesson here for all stroppy girls. The cloisters are, of course, filled with various examples of religious statuary, with captions in Czech and English, including the rather badly phrased 'Relief of the Death of the Virgin Mary'.

I returned to the hotel and, after this exercise, treated myself to a refreshingly large gin and tonic in the bar. Then back up to my room, knocked on Jonathan's door and discovered that he had found what he thought was a veritable gem of a restaurant on Rooseveltova, where we could sit outside in the courtyard. I had been keen on eating in the hotel again, but I mistakenly gave in to his pleading and we set off. I will spare you the grim details, but Jonathan was well-pleased with himself. 'I *told* you it would be good', he beamed. Yes, you did, and I will never forgive you.

Saturday 1 August

Manětín

Out through the northern suburbs of Plzeň then off to the left on the no. 20 through Chotíkov and on past the crossroads at Nová Hospoda. The signs here were pointing to Manětín to the right but Jonathan decided we should go on to Uněšov and turn off there. And at last Manětín.

The château was built by the Lažanský family and subsequently passed by marriage to the Seilern-Aspang family who were expropriated in 1945, although I think the last Gräfin did not leave until 1947. 'The pearl of Barock art in the Pilsen region', it takes up the entire southern side of the former market square. We had only a few minutes to wait for the guided tour, during which time I managed to chat to the ladies in the *pokladna* and make myself understood. They were interested that I was learning Czech but couldn't understand why so I told them the usual story of being interested in castles and châteaux and the Czech Republic being an ideal place to pursue this interest. I asked for an *anglický text* and read it before the tour started so that I could listen to the guide and see how much I understood.

After an impressive staircase – we had to stop half way up while the guide gave us a lecture on the history of the family and pointed out one or two artistic details – we turned right at the top and crowded into a series of rooms. She warned us that it was strictly forbidden to take photos inside the building.

The interiors gave the *zámek* quite a homely feeling, helped by a lot of the original furnishings and indeed photos of the former *gräfliche Familie*, including one poor sod who was called up at the start of the war, fought on the Eastern Front and, as the *anglický text* says 'got lost in Russia'. Easily done, I'm sure; it's a large country. 'Welcome to Russia: Mind the steppes'. He was called Johann Karl, according to Martin's *Almanach českých šlechtickýcch rodú*[38], and was not quite 23 when he died.

The dining room also had an intimate feel and it didn't look as though the table could seat more than half a dozen people. One interesting feature is that at some point in the nineteenth century the Graf had arranged for portraits to be made of all his staff, and here they are hanging in different rooms. It would be interesting to establish whether the master-servant relationship was better than average. Perhaps this is why the last Gräfin was able to stay on until 1947.

On through the great hall which is now used for concerts and wedding receptions (photo), then into the library (video + photos) which is on the small side for a Czech *zámek* – only about 5,000

---

[38] The Czech equivalent of *Debrett*.

volumes, of which apparently a dozen or so are in Czech – then along a covered walkway to cast a glance inside the deanery church, then back through the library and to the stairs again. We had a look outside. The grounds are very beautiful – some flowers, but mainly laid to lawn with gravel paths separating the beds – and so is the château from outside.

Back in to the *pokladna* to see if there was a guide book of any sort. Unfortunately not, but the lady sold me a 'leporello' – a word I had heard before but had forgotten. It means a set of photos done up like a concertina. I don't know why it's called this. Nothing obviously to do with Don Giovanni's servant. There were captions in English, but she included with it a sheet of explanations in Czech, too. 'Well, you said you were learning Czech, so this is good practice'.

Time for lunch. We could have eaten outside but the terrace was fairly full of humans and wasps, so into the cool, dark inside. Just a snack. Once again Jonathan ordered a hideous sausage affair, the mere sight of which made my stomach heave and I settled for the only other dish I recognised and felt I could keep down for an hour or so: the *hermelín* cheese which I had had last night, again standing in a sort of onion sauce. Water, of course, for me and a beer for Jonathan (not driving, see?).